Grant MacEwan: No Ordinary Man

The Honorable J. W. Grant MacEwan, OC, LlD, MS

Grant MacEwan: No Ordinary Man

By R. H. Macdonald

Western Producer Prairie Books
Saskatoon, Saskatchewan

Printed in Canada by
Modern Press
1

Saskatoon, Saskatchewan

Western Producer Prairie Books publications are produced and manufactured in the middle of western Canada by a unique publishing venture owned by a group of prairie farmers who are members of Saskatchewan Wheat Pool. Our first book in 1954 was a reprint of a serial originally carried in *The Western Producer*, a weekly newspaper serving western Canadian farmers since 1923. We continue the tradition of providing enjoyable and informative reading for all Canadians.

Design by Ray Statham

Canadian Cataloguing in Publication Data

Macdonald, R.H., 1915-
Grant MacEwan

ISBN 0-88833-029-4

1. MacEwan, John W. Grant, 1902-
2 Historians - Canada - Biography. 3.
The West, Canadian - Historiography.
FC3675.1.M32M32   971.2'007'20924
F1078.M32M32   C79-091115-9

Dedicated to Doris Macdonald
Constant companion and adviser in all ventures

Contents

Preface   ix

1. New Country—New Family   1
2. Birth and Childhood   13
3. Move to the City   24
4. Move to Saskatchewan   35
5. Melfort, Tractors, Trading   46
6. Willa MacPherson — Catalytic Agent   54
7. A Freshman at OAC   64
8. Final Year at OAC   74
9. Back in Saskatchewan   85
10. Iowa State College   90
11. The Assistant Professor   97
12. Buys First Land   107
13. Matador and the U.K.   114

14. Marriage   120
15. Campus Life, First Book   130
16. 1937, The Worst Year   137
17. The War Years   145
18. Exhibitions, Politics, Piles   150
19. An Offer   159
20. Dean at Manitoba   166
21. Politics Again   177
22. Wandering after Defeat   185
23. To Calgary   189
24. Party Leader   195
25. Civic Politics Again   205
26. To Edmonton   216
27. More MacEwan Parties   231
28. Retirement?   246
    Epilogue   262
    Index   264

Preface

The idea for this work originated in 1974 when, as chairman of Western Producer Prairie Books, I suggested to (the then) Lieutenant-Governor Grant MacEwan in his office at Edmonton that he had written so many books for us it was time for us to publish a book about him. I had a writer in mind, but the idea backfired when Dr. MacEwan said I was the one to do it and that he would give me open access to his person and papers to make it possible. I begged time to consider his proposal.

Despite all limitations and other commitments, it proved to be an intriguing challenge. Grant MacEwan had lived a most interesting life and continued to do so; he had started as a farm boy to rise to great heights; he had risked and lost only to rise up and risk again; he was a man of principle and deep convictions — how deep I could only suspect at the time. In addition he was among the few who seem always to be at the center of events, which he never failed to view with a perceptive eye and an unfailing sense of humor. In short, commitments were cleared and research was begun on this most interesting of Canadians.

It was early decided to carry the story from a point before his birth to the time of his retirement as lieutenant-governor. No sooner was this decision taken than MacEwan, now a private citizen, began accomplishing furiously once again (if he had ever ceased) making an epilogue necessary.

A seemingly minor point, but important none the less, is that at one point Grant, born McEwan, added an "a" and became MacEwan. So as to not confuse the reader (and protect the sanity of the proofreader) I have adopted the latter style and have so applied it to his father and MacEwan relatives throughout the book.

When a work is spread over a number of years, the author is bound to discuss the subject with many people. It would be impossible to acknowledge debts owed to those who contributed one way and another to the writing of the MacEwan biography. Wherever it is possible the source is made known in the text; but it was not always so, and a large number must go unacknowledged by name although I am nevertheless grateful for their help.

The resources and staff of a number of institutions were most helpful, including: the Saskatoon Public Library; the University of Saskatchewan Murray Memorial Library; the Regina Public Library; the Calgary University Library; the Calgary Public Library; the Glenbow-Alberta Institute Library; the University of Alberta Rutherford Library and

Cameron Library; the Government of Alberta Legislative Library; the Mills Wood Campus of the Grant MacEwan Community College, Edmonton; the Alberta Provincial Archives; the Government of Saskatchewan Provincial Archives (Saskatoon and Regina); the University of Saskatchewan Alumni Association records office; the University of Manitoba Information Office and Dafoe Library; the Brandon Public Library and Brandon University John E. Robbins Library; the Government of Manitoba Archives; the Elton (Man.) Municipality Historical Committee; the Daly House Museum, Brandon.

Newspapers were generous with help and permission to quote from their pages, including: *Calgary Albertan* and its editor, Peter Hepher; *Edmonton Journal* and its editor, Andrew Snaddon, and managing editor, Don Smith; *Calgary Herald; Saskatoon Star-Phoenix; Brandon Sun* and its vice-president, Fred McGuinness; *Winnipeg Free Press; Winnipeg Tribune; Regina Leader-Post; Financial Post; Western Producer; Country Guide; Farmers' Advocate; Country Life; Canadian Cattlemen, Ontario Milk Producers.*

Other sources no less important were the special collections at Calgary University (MacEwan papers), University of Saskatchewan (presidential papers, College of Agriculture papers), and a collection of University of Saskatchewan presidents' annual reports loaned by Vice-President J. A. Pringle. Full use was made of the MacEwan personal papers and journal, the latter being more a chronology of events than a diary of thought and opinion, but where such were expressed, the interpretation was checked with contemporaries insofar as it was possible to do. The writer drew on his own experience as a student at the University of Saskatchewan in the late thirties and subsequent association and interest — for a time as an elected member of the Senate — for further interpretations of persons and issues. An unpublished thesis by political scientist Gordon A. Anton (University of Calgary, 1972) provided most useful background on Alberta provincial politics.

Having dealt with MacEwan as chairman of Prairie Books through about ten of his books, some of the unattributed opinion on his relationship as a writer to his editor is that of the author.

The author acknowledges a debt spanning twenty years during which Jean Swanson, as Book Editor and author in her own right, helped guide a fledgling publishing enterprise toward maturity. Lending to the task her considerable talents and respect for the printed word, she established an acceptable house style which she managed to enforce with an understanding and gentle touch. Having worked on all of the MacEwan books published by Grant MacEwan during that time, it was fitting — and comforting — that this work fell under her careful scrutiny.

To all persons, mentioned and unmentioned, and institutions making this work possible, the author acknowledges his indebtedness. Without such generous help it would have been impossible to set down the story of this fascinating personality.

R.H.M.
Saskatoon
September, 1978

Chapter 1

New Country - - New Family

When the tall, lean, white-haired Grant MacEwan, carrying a long aspen staff debarked by his friends the beavers, strode forth to lead sixty citizens ranging from six to eighty-six years of age on a Saturday morning nature walk beyond Calgary's Glenmore Lake in late June 1978, a spectator was heard to say: "There goes our modern Moses; he has the best conscience in today's sick society."

A month later, and twelve days before his seventy-sixth birthday, when the same MacEwan jogged away from Calgary's City Hall to carry the Royal Baton containing the Queen's message on the first leg of the final thrust to the Commonwealth Games in Edmonton, an author friend, John Charyk, watching the scene on television in Hanna, Alberta, said: "I hope he's only going to run a block."

He didn't. MacEwan ran the first mile and passed the baton to an athlete a fraction of his age. He expected no concession on account of age, asked none, for Grant MacEwan is as western as Regina gumbo, as tenacious, and almost as durable.

Grant MacEwan is a true product of the West. He sprang from two waves of people constituting one of the great migrations in history. The first crossed the five-hundred-mile Pre-Cambrian barrier of rock, lake, and forest separating Central Canada from the vast inland plains, to settle in what was to become the first province created by a new nation, Manitoba. The second swept farther westward to settle the provinces of Saskatchewan and Alberta.

MacEwan was born on a pioneer Manitoba farm of the first wave and grew to maturity on a Saskatchewan farmstead of the second. Even on the farms he displayed interests across a broad perspective which he later developed during sojourns in both provinces. However, it was not until he reached Alberta that all his talents seemed to come together in harmony, giving full rein to a highly individual and extraordinary personality.

To understand the man who was to epitomize much of the West, it is best to review briefly the short history of the new land, the family trees of his parents, and the circumstances under which Destiny brought them together to produce such a son.

*   *   *

In the last quarter of the nineteenth century, everything seemed to conspire toward the opening of Canada's vast western settlement. Everything but world economic conditions, that is, and even the long depression that followed on the heels of the panic of 1873 made its contribution, when all is taken into account.

After Confederation, Canada bought the Territories from the Hudson's Bay Company and this was followed by a number of internal measures and external influences which combined to turn the eyes of youth westward. It was the age of steam and iron. Railways had thrust across the United States and plans were afoot to build the Canadian Pacific Railway, binding the new country together and connecting the inland areas to world commercial routes and international markets; treaties had been signed with western Indian tribes, and a mounted police force had been created to maintain the law; the land had been surveyed and a Land Act was passed which made homesteads freely obtainable by the courageous and hard working. Improved agricultural machinery made it possible to attack the tough prairie sod and to handle large tracts of it; new varieties of grain were developed, each shortening the growing period and lessening the threat from early frost, and each increasing the yield.

By 1890 available unclaimed land had virtually disappeared from the United States frontier forcing would-be homesteaders to look elsewhere. So it was that, as the supply of American land dried up, the sons of farmers in the Maritime Provinces and Ontario, where most land had long since been taken, looked to their own western frontier to satisfy their needs — the more so because the new region was very much in the news of the day.

The province of Manitoba had been formed in 1870 and the remainder of the Northwest Territories organized into administrative districts in 1882 under a Territorial Council. Thus all who came were assured they would be able to live under familiar Canadian institutions. Added to such assurance were encouraging stories emanating from the new province. The West in 1876 had shipped its first wheat eastward and word spread rapidly that such a sample had never been seen before. The red spring wheat was hard, but new milling techniques made possible the production of a fine white flour, heavy in gluten, with excellent baking qualities. Grain dealers offered a premium for such wheat; yields on the virgin land were high; it was not necessary to labor for years to cut down trees and uproot stumps to prepare cropland as there were few trees — and

John Walter Grant, Jeannetta and Christie Gray Grant in 50th wedding anniversary photo taken in New Glasgow, N.S. *(Waldren photo, Nelson Collection)*

none over much of the territory. All that was necessary was to arrive, set up camp, unload the plow and start breaking the land for a crop in the next year. By word of mouth and through publicity material published by the government, railway promoters, and real estate agents, the magic term "bonanza farms" was coined to describe the attractive situation. What was more, the land was free.

The offer was heard far and wide, and after the first homestead in the West was taken out on July 1, 1872, settlers began to appear in a trickle, increasing each year and becoming a flood as the railway reached Winnipeg and beyond. A few were immigrants who, out of necessity, came in groups — the Mennonites and Icelanders; a number came from England, Scotland, and elsewhere, but the vast majority came from eastern Canada. Of the latter, by far the largest number were young men fron Ontario, with a scattering from other eastern provinces including the Maritimes.

*   *   *

One of the early arrivals from the Maritimes was a young man from Pictou County, Nova Scotia. The family were prominent millers and merchants who had become relatively prosperous from their operations on the East River at the town of Springville, where they had lived for four generations. The family name was Grant.

However prosperous they had been, their fortunes fluctuated with the economy, and in the 1870s the depression that affected most countries did not spare Canada nor the Maritime Provinces where John Walter Grant

The John Grant home, a Maypole party, in Elton Municipality north of Brandon
(Elton Historical Committee Collection)

operated the business with his brothers. Like them, he experienced difficulty in supporting a family of nine on his share of a seriously reduced income. Some of the family would have to look elsewhere for their future livelihood.

So it was that his nineteen-year-old son, John Gray Grant, set out to make his own way in the world as hundreds of other young Maritimers were forced to do. Normally they traveled to Boston, the eastern seaboard of the United States, or, latterly, to its far western frontier, where they took jobs or land. However, in 1879, when John Grant said good-by to his family — including his eight-year-old sister Bertha and twelve-year-old brother James — he took the newly opened route to western Canada. A railway was being constructed, jobs were to be had, and free land could be taken up almost for the asking.

He worked on the Canadian Pacific Railway that year, saving for the future when he would need to buy homesteading equipment. By the time the railway had reached the capital of the new province, he had saved enough money and, impatient to get on with his plans, he could not wait for further railway construction. Strong as a bull, he packed as much as he could on his back and walked the 150 miles to the gently rolling uplands north of the Assiniboine River Valley.

A quarter section of good rich land about eight miles north of where he knew the railway was to be constructed was selected and John Grant set about establishing his farm. Untouched sod was broken, crops planted. In time he married Martha Cumming, the daughter of a neighbor from Ontario, and they helped build a community that included Zion Presbyterian Church and a schoolhouse. Homesick for the forests of Nova Scotia, he planted hundreds of spruce trees about the farmstead. The first house he built burned to the ground and was replaced with a fine L-shaped one on a much grander scale. As their family grew to seven, it was added to. The large comfortable home surrounded by a veritable forest of trees became known throughout the district as Balsam Place, the scene of many friendly neighborhood gatherings and special events throughout the forty years John and Martha were to dwell there.

When Martha and John were expecting their third child, John wrote to Nova Scotia to invite his sister Bertha to visit Balsam Place and to help out during the lying-in period. Bertha accepted, and in 1894 arrived in the burgeoning city of Brandon. John's little sister had turned into a tall, dark-haired beauty of twenty-three years with flashing eyes, an open face, a ready smile, and the deep-throated, full-bodied "Grant laugh."

It was a joyful reunion, not only with her brother John but with another brother, James Alexander Grant, who had preceded her by three years and had also become a Manitoba farmer. Arriving as he did long after all land in that part of the province had been claimed, James had been lucky enough to win the bid at an auction sale of school land the year before Bertha's arrival — his new half-section farm was only four miles east of his brother John's. It had been fifteen years since the three had been together.

Fortune decreed that Bertha Grant would remain in the West after the original purpose of her visit had been accomplished. Having demonstrated beyond doubt her ability to care for those needing attention, and having won the hearts not only of her relatives and their families, but of others in the community as well, her name came up when Brandon General Hospital was selecting candidates for its nurses' training course. She won a place as a student, became a graduate nurse in 1897 and, following graduation, was taken on staff at the hospital.

* * *

During the years the Grants in Nova Scotia were turning toward the West, a MacEwan boy in Guelph, Ontario, was being drawn by his dreams in the same direction, but with a different purpose. There were some similarities in their backgrounds and some differences.

The Grants and MacEwans had arrived in Canada at widely separated dates but they were both of pure Scottish origin. The Grants had been wrenched from their homes during the Highland Clearances 100 years before and left their lands high up in the shoulder of Scotland, where the renowned Aberdeen Angus cattle were founded, to be transported to Nova Scotia on the ship Hector in 1773.

Alexander Hedley MacEwan's father, George MacEwan, was born in Buchlyvie, Stirlingshire, Scotland, not far from the shire in which the great Clydesdale breed of horses originated. He came to Canada in 1857 when but a boy of twelve years and became a blacksmith, practicing his trade on the York Road out of Guelph before joining a sewing machine company as an engineer — a job he held for forty years. In 1868, he married Agnes Cowan, another Scot, whose family claimed relationship with Sir Walter Scott in their lineage. Two years after their marriage, Alex was born. He was to grow up in an age when there was much romantic adventure in the air.

*George MacEwan, 228
Glasgow Street, Guelph
(MacEwan Collection)*

At every opportunity, Alex MacEwan would be off reading forbidden "western stories," an idle activity frowned upon by his rather strict Presbyterian parents. As a youth his spiritual home was more in the wild American West than anywhere else. Although interested in machines, he showed no disposition to follow in his father's footsteps nor to linger in eastern Canada.

By his eighteenth year he had become a strong, vigorous young man of medium height, of quiet disposition, and of remarkable stamina. If he had any weakness, it tended to be in his eyes, but this was of little importance to him as his leanings toward a future were neither business nor scholarship but rather toward the wide outdoors. He wanted to become a cowboy, riding the range in Idaho or Nevada, the scene of many of the stories he had read.

Since leaving school he had worked on farms adjacent to Guelph, had contributed a share of his earnings to his parents for his keep, but had set some aside toward the day he would turn in the direction of the setting sun. In 1889 that day arrived.

With his small savings safely tucked away and carrying a letter from his last farmer employer testifying that he was honest, reliable, and a good worker, Alex MacEwan set out for the West. Although his destination was the western United States, he chose to travel on the Canadian Pacific Railway, which now reached the Pacific coast. It would take him across the entire country without the necessity of transferring from one rail company to another, and would deposit him just north of his intended destination. He would travel as far as his savings would take him which, with luck, would be Idaho.

The trip from Guelph quickly depleted his modest savings, and by the time he reached Manitoba, Alex MacEwan had spent his last dollar and was faced with the necessity of going to work to make a grubstake for the remainder of the trip. He came to that conclusion on the train as the next stop was announced. That city was called Brandon.

Many parts of western Canada had enjoyed good crops the year before young Alex MacEwan stepped down from the CPR train on to the Brandon station platform and he was hired in short order to work for a farmer in North Brandon, about eight miles out of town. The man's name was Moses Abbey. He was a bachelor, with a bachelor's disdain for the niceties of life, and the meals he served came as a shock to Alex. Salt pork, or "sowbelly," beans and bread or, in its frequent absence, a gray mass of unleavened dough fried in the frying pan and called bannock, were the regular menu. If anybody wanted something fancy, there was a can of syrup in the middle of the rough board table with a spoon sunk almost out of sight in the sticky depths.

Alex earned twenty dollars a month. It was good pay for a young lad just starting out. He saved part of it for his grubstake and sent part of it home to help the family. He learned much about the West that first year with Abbey, seeing the crop harvested in the fall and caring for the horses and livestock throughout the winter months, a job he particularly liked.

Alex worked for Moses Abbey for four years with the exception of one summer when he took a job selling trees for an eastern firm at an attractive commission. He soon learned that the farmers of the district could get spruce trees free from forests near Shilo and were not interested in spending time and money on planting shrubs in decorative gardens. With the passage of time his original plan of riding the range in Idaho dimmed.

In 1893 his dream was extinguished for good. Homestead land had long since disappeared but by a lucky chance a farm became available south of the Abbey place and near to the town of Chater. Alex MacEwan put his grubstake down as the initial payment and contracted to pay off the rest. He was now a landowner and a farmer with a quarter section of land untouched by the plow, and the immediate challenge appealed to his nature and physical stamina. The first summer, with a team of horses and a ten-inch walking plow, he broke the whole quarter section and was ready to plant a crop the following spring, a crop which he harvested in part with ancient tools, the cradle and the flail.

Within two years the land had produced enough to enable the prosperous young farmer to travel to Guelph for a visit to show relatives

Alex MacEwan's threshing outfit, 1903   *(MacEwan Collection)*

and friends that he had done well out West. It was upon the return trip that he demonstrated what was to become known in the district as the MacEwan stamina.

As the train headed west out of Winnipeg and toward Brandon, a sudden March blizzard swept the country. At Belmont, fifty miles from his destination, the train became hopelessly snowbound. Alex MacEwan sat immobilized in the train for two nights and two days, surrounded by drifts ten feet high. The CPR served free meals. Finally, on the third day, after the noon meal, he had had enough of inactivity. Checking his suitcase at the baggage car and arranging for it to be dropped off when the train eventually arrived in Brandon, he set out on foot, shod only in leather shoes. By nightfall he reached Wawanesa where, after a brief rest, he set out, on foot once more, across the lonely snow-covered prairie. By noon of the day after he had left the train, he reached Brandon. Fifty miles in twenty-four hours through mountains of snow!

All his life Alex MacEwan would be inventive, adventuresome, and prone to taking speculative ventures whenever the opportunity to improve an operation or make money, preferably both, presented itself. He demonstrated these tendencies early on new land, which he had added to the original plot, by breaking the native sod — this time with a twelve-inch gang plow. On seeing MacEwan at work, a skeptical and less progressive neighbor volunteered that "it was neither practical nor respectable to farm in such a hurry."

The remark fell on deaf ears, for Alex MacEwan was one who would always be a member in the advance guard of a new breed — western pioneers who worked to revolutionize agriculture as the world knew it. Not content to become a subsistence farmer producing merely enough to feed himself and family, he was open to new ideas for improving his land and the beasts he raised on it, reducing the time and labor required and, at the same time, increasing the yield. This was the spirit, the initiative, that turned western Canadian farming into an industry wherein the labor of one produced enough to feed fifty. By their efforts Canada would export a flow

Nurse Bertha Grant (top center) on graduation, 1897   *(Foran Collection)*

of golden grain in unheard-of quantities and quality, earning for the Prairies the sobriquet "breadbasket of the world." Alex and others like him would continue to experiment.

*   *   *

In 1898, with his farm well established, a two-story frame house erected, barn and outbuildings standing surrounded to north, west, and east by a broad belt of promising young spruce trees, he saw an opportunity to speed his farming operation and that of his neighbors. This one was on a grand scale.

Every western farmer at that time had learned that, although there were many others, the major hazard facing him and his crop was early frost. Many, too, saw crops ruined by wet weather while they stood helplessly awaiting the arrival of the threshing crew with their machines. Alex was as aware of the danger as anyone else, having had one of his own crops damaged by fall rains soon after he had started farming.

Thus it was that in 1898 when he read an American advertisement for a new steam threshing outfit complete with self-feeder and blower, he invested heavily and brought one into the country to do custom threshing, the first of its kind. He reasoned that it would speed up the job of harvesting the crop, would lessen the possibility of being caught by bad weather and would thus be in great demand, making money hand over fist. The results were mixed, to say the least; much later they were described by Grant MacEwan in *Sodbusters.*

Homesteaders came for miles to see the monster in action, to see a separator building its own stack and eating up sheaves which didn't have to be forced into its throat. The only trouble was that the new feeder didn't work and had to be discarded. So instead of having four men pitching sheaves into the automatic feeder, they had to be satisfied with eight men at the feeder end, four pitching from the loads to the tables, two cutting bands and two forcing sheaves into the cylinder. When noon time came and the threshing crew descended upon the farmer's kitchen, 23 ravenous men sat down to test the food resources and the patience of the good wife. But when things were going well, that big outfit threshed a lot of wheat. It threshed 1000 bushels in three hours one time, to say nothing of the bushels that went into the straw pile. That record stood a while and when the big outfit had to move from one farm to the next, it broke another record, a record for slow motion. And it usually broke a few bridges, because bridge builders hadn't reckoned with any such mechanical monstrosity. Indeed the same outfit went through the 18th Street Bridge at Brandon on one occasion and after that if the river was to be crossed, the outfit was placed on a flat car at Chater and sent across on the rails. Strangely enough the big outfit didn't ruin Alex and it didn't drive him crazy. Some who bought threshers weren't so lucky.

*   *   *

When Bertha Grant first arrived in Brandon, her brother James, with the strong Scottish sense of family solidarity and also possibly because he was still a bachelor with no other family to worry about, took it upon himself to care for her. On one occasion when she was in training at the hospital, James heard that she had attended a dance in company with a young man of whom he didn't approve. Early the next day he presented himself at the hospital and, when she appeared, said to her, "Bertha, get your things, I've come to take you home."

Bertha Grant stared at her brother momentarily and then, when she realized what was going on in his mind, she laughed until the tears rolled down her cheeks. James knew his mission was a failure and he had the good sense to leave the scene as soon as possible — alone. The story became part of the family lore and was a favorite, especially among those who had come up against fun-loving Bertha's high principles and strong will.

It was not long thereafter that James had other things to occupy his mind along with the well being of his sister. He married Bella Smith in 1897 and the following year she presented him with a daughter. Bella Grant and Bertha Grant took to one another at first meeting, and just as Bertha visited her brother John's farm, she now spent weekend leaves at James's farm as well. It was on such a visit she arrived at a turning point in her life.

A young farmer by the name of MacEwan had taken land just two and a half miles from the James Grant farm, and James had been impressed with him. He was a hard worker and had made great strides in getting the land under cultivation. He was industrious, intelligent, and had a wry sense of humor, although not given to much talk. Most important of all, the young

Alexander Hedley MacEwan in 1899   *(Foran Collection)*

man drove a fine team of Clydesdale horses and took great care of them, always turning them out for work or for the road as if they had been groomed for show, which to James's way of thinking was the highest recommendation of all. MacEwan was a bachelor, James's sister Bertha as yet unmarried.

By this time he knew better than try to oversell the young man to his sister, but as a daughter of James Grant, Maria Nelson, explained years later, "one evening when Bertha was out at the farm, father saw MacEwan driving along the east road, so he went out to the road and invited him in. Thus Alex MacEwan met Bertha Grant and this was the beginning of a romance for which father always took credit. Alex and Bertha were married in Uncle John's house in January, 1900."

Chapter 2

Birth and Childhood

When the Grant and MacEwan clans were joined through Bertha and Alex, the future of the young couple looked promising. Indeed, there was even something prophetic in the time selected for the marriage — the first month of the new century, the beginning of a new life together.

Seldom had the mood of the country been more buoyant and, although there was great movement and expansion, whatever changes there were, came in orderly fashion. A natural evolution carried out within the accepted framework of society. As the new century opened, the city of Brandon was a thriving young metropolis, surrounded by rich farmland — all of it long since taken up and turned into well-developed and solidly established farms surrounded by shelterbelts, the land producing rich crops and supporting good livestock.

Twenty-five years previously the first 850-odd bushels of wheat had been shipped eastward out of western Canada; in 1900, the West shipped out 5,000,000 bushels, much of it produced in the rich lands of southwestern Manitoba with Brandon as its hub and distribution point. The benefits flowed into the communities.

It was the era of boosters and optimism. Their spiritual values were solid and safe from question, the prevailing mood was one of progress and prosperity. All were boosters and proud of it. Everybody was out to make a million and nobody was ashamed to admit it. A touring senator, after listening to Western promoters, was heard to mutter to a companion, "well, they've either got the richest soil in the world or the biggest liars in the world and I'm damned if I know which it is."

During the first dozen years of the new century, approximately 400,000 homestead entries were made. Some of the newcomers brought their own capital and equipment with them — mainly from eastern Canada and the United States — but thousands arrived with little or nothing and required outfitting almost from the ground up. The benefits of this newly created demand accrued to centers such as Winnipeg and Brandon, both being in a position to supply tools, implements, seed, wagons, good horses and oxen to provide the indispensable power.

* * *

Alex MacEwan brought his bride home to his farm within sight of that of James and Bella Grant's. It was four miles from the town of Chater, then a thriving railway delivery point, with store, post office, hotel, lumberyard, blacksmith shop, and most of the essential services required by the farmers who drew their wheat to the elevators standing alongside the railway tracks.

It was as comfortable a home as a bachelor would tend to make it. There were two rooms downstairs, the kitchen, which was the main center of activity, and the parlor, which was reserved for special occasions, and two rooms upstairs. Heat was supplied by the wood-burning Great Majestic cooking stove in the kitchen and by a wood-and coal-burning heater in the parlor. Pipes from each ran up through holes in the ceiling and through the bedrooms, thus providing the only source of heat they enjoyed. In a short time Bertha MacEwan, adding the woman's touch, had transformed a house into a home.

A year after their marriage, Bertha gave birth to a baby daughter, christened Agnes. Tragedy struck soon after in the form of the scourge of pioneer settlements — diphtheria — and the MacEwans lost their first-born within a short time.

It was in the middle of summer the following year that the next child was due at the MacEwan farm. This time Bertha MacEwan gave birth to a boy on August 12, 1902. The baby was christened John Walter Grant MacEwan after his maternal grandfather in Nova Scotia. (There were a number of John Grants in Pictou County, so all his life the grandfather had been addressed by his full name to distinguish him from others and it came out as one word something like"Jnwaltergrant.") Two summers after the boy's birth, Bertha took him to see his grandparents at Pictou.

Young John Walter Grant MacEwan spent his most impressionable years on the farm eight miles northeast of Brandon. It was a pleasant location on the uplands above the Assiniboine River Valley. From the farmstead looking south on a hot August day under a blue sky, Brandon was easily visible. Over the rolling land covered with golden wheat, an almost imperceptible drop in elevation toward the valley exposed the tall chimney stack at the Mental Hospital and its water tower. There, Mental Hospital Hill dropped down into the valley and beyond, and as the land rose again across the river, one could see grain elevators and church steeples against the sky. At fair time fireworks lit the heavens, making Brandon the

Four generations: Grandmother Christie Gray Grant, Great-grandmother Gray, Bertha (Grant) MacEwan, and Grant MacEwan at about age two years, photographed in Springville, N.S., about 1904   *(Foran Collection)*

Mecca for all children. Beyond that, in the blue distance, the Brandon Hills rose over the country by a thousand feet.

Here it was that the universe gradually unfolded and expanded before young Grant's eyes. Nature had favored the boy, who had inherited outstanding characteristics from both father and mother. He early revealed the quiet, almost shy, mien of Alex MacEwan, head tipped slightly forward as if to shield somewhat the piercing blue eyes that peered beneath a high brow and seemed to be trying to unravel the mystery of anything and everything that came within their scrutiny. At the same time, he had inherited from his mother the sense of humor and love of fun, often expressed by the explosive "Grant laugh."

As his range increased with the years and he gained freedom to move about the farmyard and the adjacent fields, he learned from everything he saw and heard; his father at work from before dawn until dusk, the hired man at work in the fields, his mother in the kitchen and at the church, the birds and animals in the shelterbelt and on the rolling land, conversations between men weighing the value of this horse against that one, this beast against another — the countless fresh experiences of a beginning lifetime which he seemed to absorb silently and without effort. Everbody worked hard, it was the way things were.

Grant MacEwan was brought up in no doubt as to Whom he owed all things. Brandon and district for miles around were almost completely populated by people of British descent. The inhabitants were largely fundamentalists in religion, and the Presbyterian faith prevailed, followed closely by Methodists, Baptists, and when the movement grew, the Union church. In a few districts there were enough Anglicans to build a church. The churches functioned not only for religious purposes, but for community social activities as well.

To Bertha MacEwan, her faith and her church were the foundations upon which her life rested and this she communicated to Grant at an early age. Alex MacEwan was not without faith, but his was of an informal nature and did not depend upon the ritual or theology of any special sect and his association with Bertha's was a loose one. Each parent accepted the other's attitude with sympathy and understanding.

Nevertheless, as Grant MacEwan's early training fell mainly to his mother, it was in the church that he was brought up. In transporting Presbyterianism from Scotland to Nova Scotia and then to Manitoba and the West, much of what gave it its early grim reputation as a dour, strict, and austere faith seemed to have been modified to suit the openness of the new country. At any rate, there was much more room in western Canadian Presbyterianism for fun and humor than there was in the land of its origin. After all, it was written in Proverbs that "a merry heart does good like a medicine." It would be wrong to assume from all this that basic beliefs had been altered, for this was not the case; they had been carved out of granite and so they would stand.

For entertainment in the district there were house parties, barn dances, ball games, and picnics. Many years later Mrs. Wesley Gordon Nelson (Maria Corlette Grant) recalled that "any outing could develop into a picnic whether it was school closing or berry picking or a baseball game." It was the era before the automobile ruled, so "10 miles was a trip and 20 miles a day's journey. Since people did not go great distances, their gatherings were intimate community affairs, where everyone knew everyone else." The annual Sunday school picnic, next to Christmas, was the most important day of the year for the young ones such as Grant MacEwan.

Grant MacEwan was to spend the impressionable years in a community that was confident of its standards and did not hesitate to enforce them. Such an occasion transpired one Sabbath, when a wrongdoer was seen to be stacking wheat sheaves in his fields at the time other good folk were on their way to church. Following the service, there was a brief meeting of the Church Session and John Grant and Mr. Brownridge were delegated to approach the wrongdoer and "set him straight."

They set about their duty with dispatch and, approaching the man in his field, found him still at work. Greeting him in the usual fashion, they recalled to him the fact that it was Sunday, the day of rest, lest he had lost track of the passage of time. As he knew the day, they then asked him to

The MacEwans and Grants on a picnic: (left to right) Nettie Grant, Alex MacEwan, Grant MacEwan (up a tree), Maria Corlette Grant, her father Jim Grant with Christina in his arms, Bella Grant, wife of James, a friend, and Bertha MacEwan   (MacEwan Collection)

stop profaning the Sabbath by his labors — but they said they would return the following day and help him catch up on time lost through reverence for the word of the Lord.

It was on the occasion of a sad and solemn event that another facet in the nature of the community was graphically revealed (and described years later in MacEwan's book *Hoofprints and Hitchingposts*). One of their number was to be buried and the usual procedure — the service at home and burial two miles down the road in the cemetery — was to be followed. This day the livery firm in Brandon that provided the horse-drawn hearse was not able to send the usual docile team, which happened to be performing similar duties in Rapid City the same day. The driver did the best he could and hitched a Standardbred, which had done some racing in its time, alongside a young bronco whose training had been cursory to say the least.

The pick-up team became restive as the service in the farm house dragged on and the driver held them in with difficulty. Finally, the service ended, the coffin was loaded into the hearse and the slow procession left the yard turning toward the cemetery in solemn order, the hearse leading, the Presbyterian minister next with his pacer and buggy, the chief mourners and a long procession of grieving friends following in an assortment of buggies and wagons.

Feeling freed of restraint, the bronco began to stretch its legs, moving ahead at a pace much too brisk for the occasion, but there was little the driver could do. The minister thought it best to keep up, and similar

*Above: Bertha MacEwan's church, Humes-
ville (Elton Historical Committee Collection)*

*Right: Grant at five or six years, with friend
at the North Brandon farm
(MacEwan Collection)*

sentiments swept back through all drivers in the solemn procession. Having
gained a measure of freedom, the bronco wanted more.

The minister's pacer was not to be outdone and drew abreast of the
Standardbred on the high side and would pass. The Standardbred would
have none of that and, previous training asserting itself, kept ahead of the
minister's pacer.

Those who retold the tale over the years were in some doubt as to just
when the competitive spirit of the horses overcame the grief of the drivers,
but with half a mile to go, the entire procession was thundering pell-mell
down the road for a good view at the finishing post — the graveside.

Fifty yards from the turn-off, the minister's entry made a tremendous
lunge, gained the lead, turned into the cemetery on two wheels and pulled
up at the graveside accompanied by the shouts of those close enough to
witness the finish — the winner by half a length.

With studied calm the triumphant clergyman performed the solemn
funeral rites for the dear departed. When all had paid their respects to the
bereaved, they joined the admiring crowd surrounding the minister's pacer.
When a horse trade was suggested, the good man replied: "No thanks, not
even if you throw in the Pearly Gates."

*   *   *

In a close community the Grants and the MacEwans formed a tightly
knit family group which drew them together to the point where aunts and
uncles became almost interchangeable among the children for their own
mothers and fathers. If the weather was agreeable and the roads good,
seldom a Sunday went by without the families of John and Martha Grant,
James and Bella Grant, and Alex and Bertha MacEwan, visiting one another

after church, or on anniversaries or other special occasions. Despite the strict rules of behavior, church and Sunday school, discipline, deportment, and obedience that governed these Presbyterian families, there was no shortage of joy and laughter when they assembled.

Alex and Bertha MacEwan were always welcome at any of the houses in the neighborhood. Although Alex was a man of few words, his taciturnity was not taken for lack of interest or friendliness toward those around him. He was accepted as he was for what he was. As one who knew him well said years later: "Alex MacEwan didn't talk very much, but when he spoke you listened, for he usually had something to say." Coming from a large family, Bertha was used to much chatter about the house, and, if there was less in her own home from day to day than she was accustomed to, she got her fill on the Sunday visits with the other Grants.

Some years later Maria Corlette Grant wrote: "there was a great deal of laughter in the home of my childhood. When relatives gathered . . . and their children, the house would echo with songs and laughter. Aunt Bertha would sing Italian songs (brought to Pictou County by Italian crews working on the Intercolonial Railway) and father would recite Robbie Burns and everybody would sing Scottish songs and tell Nova Scotia stories."

*   *   *

Although Alex MacEwan said little it was not because he was unaware of what was going on around him, for he was an observant man and an understanding father in most things. As his son grew older, among other things he began questioning the existence of Santa Claus. Alex was first to notice these signs of doubt.

Grant had always been a manageable boy, getting into no more mischief than other children save for the occasional sleep-walking incident that set him apart slightly from the others, yet was not a matter of great moment. However, from the questions the boy was asking, Alex knew that he was going to have trouble over the myth of Christmas as his son neared his fifth year.

Despite convincing appearances by the jolly old gentleman at church concerts, doubt lingered in Grant's mind and Alex was aware of the problem with which his son wrestled. How could a rolly-polly man such as that come down the chimney? On that particular Christmas Eve, Grant was tucked into bed by Bertha while Alex went to work outside. Just before the lad dropped off to sleep the sound of distant sleigh bells could be heard. The next morning, when he got up and went down to the parlor where the tree stood, he noticed that the rarely used front door had been opened. Upon further investigation he discovered footprints leading away from the door in fresh snow. They went in one direction only; none had come in. It was enough to protect his belief, shaky protection though it was, for another Christmas.

*   *   *

When Grant MacEwan was five years old, the reality of life taught him there were other things besides picnics, Sunday school, and Santa

Miss Marion Grant,
"Aunt Marion" to all
(Nelson Collection)

Claus. His lovable Aunt Bella, James Grant's wife, had brought three girls into the world and with the increased family, she and James had been planning the dream home they would build on the farm one day. During this period Bella ailed and needed constant help with the work of a farm wife. In 1907, the year the home was being built, she was taken into Brandon General Hospital where she continued to waste away despite rest and attention.

Eventually James brought her home where she spent her last weeks in bed in the dream home she helped to plan. She died at the age of thirty-four. Thus Grant felt for the first time in his youthful way the wing of death brush over the community and descend to take one of those he loved.

James wrote to his unmarried sister who was in domestic service in Providence, Rhode Island, to see if she would fill in for a time until he could devise a permanent solution. The sister arrived, and with one glance at the three motherless girls, she knew her fate was sealed. She remained in James's house for the rest of her life and became Aunt Marion — a leader in

Provincial Women's Missionary Society affairs and a strong influence and example to all, including Grant MacEwan.

*   *   *

The year 1906 was an eventful one for the MacEwans. On April 16, Bertha MacEwan gave birth to a third child, a son, christened George Alexander. Four-year-old Grant now had a brother.

In this same year the Canadian Northern Railway had opened up a branch, the Carrot River Valley line, 400 miles to the northwest in the newly formed province of Saskatchewan. To promote the new district, the railway took out a whole trainload of prospective buyers, Alex MacEwan among them.

Land deals were the topic of the day. Almost every new center, no matter how tiny, aspired to become "the Chicago of the West" and told everyone about it. The new district, Melfort, was no different and Alex, for purely speculative reasons, bought a section of good black loam before returning to Brandon.

That was the year a Prince Edward Islander came to the MacEwan farm to work as the hired man. He was attracted to the bright, elder son. Ronald Lamont was thought to be somewhat of an eccentric by the neighbors, but before he left he uttered words that became part of MacEwan family lore. He predicted that the handsome young lad would go far in the public life of his country and that one day he might even become prime minister of Canada.

The boom which swept the country between 1905 and 1913 was astounding. Towns and cities sprang up and prospered. Real estate prices soared and investors made small fortunes. Alex MacEwan was making money farming, but as was his disposition, he was on the lookout for ideas to expand and improve agricultural operations. He was also aware of what was going on in town.

His reputation for keeping good livestock had increased with the years. His cattle were admired by all, his Tamworth pigs were known for their quality and found ready markets for breeding or slaughter. Above all, he liked good horses and knew quality when he saw it. So it was in 1905 he felt that much could be done to improve the quality of horses in the district to the advantage of the farmer and to the profit of those who undertook the task.

MacEwan advanced his idea to a number of others he knew to be interested in horse breeding and they agreed to form a syndicate and bring into the district the best their pooled resources could purchase. The result was the arrival in the North Brandon district of Flash Baron, sired by the world-renowned Baron's Pride. In a few years, Flash Baron began winning championships in horse shows throughout the country and the quality of horsepower available to farmers in the district was greatly improved. The syndicate did well — but there were other worlds to conquer.

As Grant grew, his world expanded. On rare occasions when he was taken on the long trip toward the valley, down the steep descent at Mental

Hospital Hill, over the bridge and up into Brandon on the south bank of the river, his curious eyes drank in the sights. To him it was a large metropolis filled with towering elevators and chimney stacks, soaring church steeples, streets crowded with horses, carriages, vans and wagons of all kinds. Best of all was the CPR depot where the huge steam locomotives, belching clouds of smoke, traveled through Brandon many times every day going east and west. Each time they stopped they attracted what seemed to be the whole city population to the platform, where people poured down the pullman steps, where fathers and uncles picked up important parcels from expressmen wearing peaked caps and black sleeve guards, who said "sign here."

*   *   *

As they prospered during the first decade of the twentieth century, farmers could be roughly divided into two groups: those who used the money to improve their farms and to make life on the farm more amenable and by so doing elected to stay on the farm: those who built up a bank roll and sold out, often retiring and going "back east" or "down south" to more salubrious climates or, at least, moving into town and possibly going into business of one sort or another.

The Grants fell into the first category. John had long since declared himself a farmer for life and had built Balsam Place into a showpiece and the hub not only of family life but of a good part of the district social life as well. James had done the same and, although tragedy intervened, had established a comfortable home where he would, with his sister Marion's help, bring up his three daughters.

Such were not the ambitions of Alex MacEwan. By 1908 his mind was made up. Nineteen years before he had stopped at Brandon merely to make a grubstake so that he could continue on in search of the far horizon. The temporary pause had become permanent and he ended up with a farm, a wife, and two sons. He had prospered through hard work — his lifetime habit being to rise at four o'clock in the morning and be about his chores long before others — and now he had a bank roll large enough to sell out and retire. At thirty-seven years of age he wasn't ready for the quiet life, but felt it was time for a change — change was good for a man.

Alex's inventiveness and his earlier revealed tendency to take fliers when the spirit moved him came together and he made a decision. He would sell the farm, move into Brandon and enter business. Money was to be made in manufacturing. Others were making money speculating in city lots. Furthermore, the boys would get better schooling in the city than in the country.

March 26, 1908, found neighbors gathering from far and near at the farm of Alex MacEwan. Much earlier in the day, friends had arrived to help him prepare machinery and livestock for the sale, the women to help Bertha prepare the food. In his book *Between the Red and the Rockies*, Grant MacEwan described an incident that became part of the family lore:

Sometimes this neighborly spirit warred against individual interests. When Alex MacEwan sold his farm north of Brandon, he announced the customary auction sale of stock and implements. On the morning of the sale pioneer neighbors gathered to help. Bob Walker and the McCallum boys brought brass-fitted harness, top collars, and rings in abundance, to dress the horses for the sale. When Auctioneer T. C. Norris (later Premier Norris of Manitoba) arrived and saw the stylish display he enquired if there was a ring factory in the district. Bob Walker, instead of talking down the team he himself wanted to buy, braided tails, plaited manes, and so adorned the animals that he was obliged to pay the high price of $525 for the pair. It was a just reward that both of the two horses he bought lived to be more than 25 years of age.

It was on this occasion that the first public pronouncement of young Grant MacEwan was reported for posterity, his sentiments more than likely those of the MacEwan family. When asked what he thought of selling the farm and moving to the city, he piped up for all to hear: "This is the most important day of my life."

Following the sale, there was much in the way of business arrangements for Alex to do in Brandon so Bertha took the two children on a train trip to Nova Scotia, Alex to join them later. Such trips were the custom of the day — those who had left home returning to show all how well they had done "out West," and also to introduce new and old family members to one another for the first time.

Even as a six-year-old, the forests, rivers, and lush countryside of Nova Scotia made a deep impression on Grant. He would carry in his mind the memory of the visit for many years.

He would also carry in his heart a lasting friendship that developed almost instantaneously between John Walter Grant MacEwan and John Walter Grant. They were to be seen many times during his visit with bait and fishing rod making their way to the East River. It was there, under the tutelage of his grandfather, that he caught his first fish.

When the time to depart for Brandon came, his grandfather was reluctant to see the young lad leave. In an expansive gesture, he waved his arm toward his farm and offered him anything he wanted to take with him. It was later recalled "the selection was quickly made — it was a modest gimlet that had proven effective in making tiny holes in pieces of board."

On the return trip the family, by this time joined by Alex, paid a visit to Guelph, Ontario, where Bertha and the children met the MacEwan relatives.

The trip was symbolic of the influences that would shape the boy's life — the Grant blood would predominate with the exception that their tendency to enjoy a moderate measure of the good things in life would be replaced by the MacEwan frugality. Casting his mind back years later he said, "Mother was so clannish I thought I was a Nova Scotian." However, there was the belief in hard work, drive, and stamina on both sides that would serve Grant MacEwan well in the life ahead.

Chapter 3

Move to the City

The MacEwans moved into Brandon with a spirit of optimism that was a reflection of the times. Things were prosperous in the West in 1908, particularly in Manitoba. The waves of settlers moving across the country produced benefits that accrued to already established communities in a position to help supply many of the needs that arose. Brandon participated and was then called variously by her enthusiastic boosters "The Wheat City," "The Wonder City," "The Horse Capital."

The boom that swept the country came to be known as the Manitoba Boom. Growth was everywhere and by that time the city had reached a population of approximately 11,000, with expansion continuing. Alex MacEwan had made arrangements to get in on it. He would do it two ways.

Observing the frenzied building that was going on throughout the country, he conceived the idea that hundreds of wooden structures being constructed would need fire protection. With this in mind, he plunged into the business of manufacturing and selling fire extinguishers. At the same time, with the prices of city lots soaring, he invested some of the spare cash from the sale of the farm to get in on that particular bonanza.

Bertha was content with the move although it was her nature to be concerned somewhat with all the talk about spending and making easy money. It was she who taught Grant the little jingle "Willful waste brings woeful want, and some day you may say, oh how I wish I had the crust, that once I threw away." However, it was not her habit to interfere in matters customarily left to the men in those days, and besides, she was fully occupied with bringing up her two boys, looking after the neat two-story

Above: Brandon street scene in late 1800s
(Daly House Museum Collection)

Right: MacEwan residence at 1316 McTa-
vish, Brandon, as it looks today
(R. H. Macdonald photo)

clapboard house at 1316 McTavish Avenue, and working for Knox Presbyterian Church mission society and ladies' aid.

*   *   *

On September 1, 1908, Grant MacEwan started school. He was to attend two schools, Alexander and Park, transferring on one occasion in order to take a basic carpentry course, then referred to as manual training. He liked school and was a bright student which became obvious when, in 1914, he was promoted from grade six to eight.

Two teachers stand out in his mind. In grade six he studied under Miss Bertha Pilling and in his final year under Mr. J. Johanson, an excellent teacher of Icelandic origin with the Icelander's respect for words. Years later he was to look up Miss Pilling and recall the debt he owed her.

Perhaps the greatest disappointment experienced at public school was in the history class. He soon discovered that, for a boy who had been brought up on "Nova Scotia stories" and tales of stamina and courage in the pioneer periods of both eastern and western Canada, there was little but boredom in learning lists of dates and names of kings and far-off wars. He came to detest the history classes. Where were all those thrilling tales he had heard at his grandfather's knee?

However, if he lost a bit he also gained at school. Early in the junior grades one such advance was made when students were introduced to what was called "the penny bank." Monday morning was "banking day" over which the teacher presided at her desk. As the student's name was called, he came up and deposited whatever money he had saved from the previous week. Before his eyes it was marked down, he saw how the total grew and returned to his desk resolved to keep it growing. It also presented an opportunity for the teacher to explain the mystery of interest on money. Saving was a lesson the young MacEwan grasped more readily and completely than most students, so much so that at times his family had to restrain him.

Grant MacEwan at school in Brandon (second boy from teacher)   *(Foran Collection)*

Young MacEwan also learned early how to handle matters other than money. Family lore has it that, when still a young boy, his Uncle John called upon him one winter day to go with him in the sleigh and help load purchases he was to make for the farm from a lengthy shopping list, including a most generous supply of Mrs. Shanks' excellent German sausages. Having completed the job, John deposited his nephew at his McTavish Avenue home and presented him with a large parcel of the sausages in appreciation of his company and his help. It had grown bitterly cold, and, as Grant stood motionless clutching the sausages, his uncle advised him to run into the house quickly lest he freeze. "No," said the precocious youngster, "I'll wait until you leave because mother will make me give back part of the sausages."

It would be erroneous to think for a moment that Grant MacEwan appeared at the city school in the guise of a farm boy in bib overalls and bare feet. From contemporary photographs he appears among classmates as the best-dressed kid in school, with Eton collar, white shirt, and tie — the tie slightly askew to suggest the normal boy.

*   *   *

The MacEwan family was much like most Brandon families with small problems to which the children contributed from time to time. Not long after he had started school, Grant was playing with matches and put one behind a lace curtain to see how the flame shone through. The experiment ended in disaster when the curtain caught fire. Completely forgetting one of his father's extinguishers on the wall nearby, he managed to tear down the hangings and stamp out the flame before the rest of the house caught fire. Bertha cuffed his ears and left him in no doubt as to the error of his ways.

On another occasion, when he was nine, he felt that things were not going too well at home and that George was getting far more than a fair share of attention. For whatever reason, he decided to run away in search of more amenable surroundings, so off he went to his savings bank from which he drew $10. In the interests of survival he went to Fitton's store (little thinking that three years hence he would be in charge of the shop), presented the $10 bill, took three cents' worth of sugary food for the trip, and went off with his supplies and $9.97 in change. He headed westward for a mile or so, but by this time he came to the conclusion that in the future he would wait for a more favorable excuse to spend his own money. He returned home, much regretting the fact that the graph of his savings had dipped three cents.

*   *   *

There were ways of wasting money in the city and there were also ways of making money, which the young student was quick to discover. The moment he was big enough to carry newspapers he got half a paper route, which was all the newspapers he could carry. The *Brandon Sun* paid him $1.25 a week. Later, as he grew taller — which he most certainly was doing — he was able to take on a full route. Every penny he made went into the penny bank at school on Mondays, for to his way of thinking, the attraction of seeing his bank balance increase far outweighed the attraction of spending money on boyish whims.

Although he played his full part in school life, he early demonstrated an ability to cram two lives into one so that the one activity was not necessarily carried on at the expense of the other. Considering this period of his life, he later said, "during boyhood years in Brandon, I was as active during the out-of-school hours as in school. Athletics attracted me and although time for frivolity seemed limited, I was able to take a leading part in local baseball and hockey . . . but there was always some business afoot."

During the Brandon fair he had discovered that traveling carnival people constituted a ready market for surplus fresh vegetables from the MacEwan garden, so he picked them and hauled them each day the four blocks to the exhibition grounds where he sold them. His overhead was little or nothing, for he knew a place, if one kept to the north end of the grounds, where one could sneak in free.

He was alert for new opportunities to expand his services too. As Brandon fair was primarily a livestock show, a large number of animals had to be housed and tended in the exhibition barns. Consequently, a manure pile to dwarf all others rose behind the buildings. It was this that attracted the young, commercially minded MacEwan one morning.

A heavy rain had fallen the preceding evening at the end of a hot day and the atmosphere was humid. As he made his way about the exhibition grounds, he noticed a change in the manure piles. On closer inspection, he found that they had turned into one vast mushroom bed.

Working quickly, lest discovery reveal his valuable find, he picked as many mushrooms as he could and went hawking them to the carnival people. They proved a much-sought-after delicacy and sold at a higher price than the other vegetables. For the duration of the fair, following a circuitous route to throw any spies off his trail, he harvested mushrooms and multiplied the return on his vegetable business considerably.

Another business opened up when, in 1910, his grandfather and grandmother Grant, accompanied by another daughter, Florence, came out from Nova Scotia to live in the West with their son James in the Humesville district. John Walter Grant brought with him a carload of settler's effects and livestock, mostly all good breeding and milk-producing cows. The MacEwan family fell heir to one by the name of Polly.

In those days, when riding and carriage horses were stabled in residential districts, it was not unusual for families to keep milk cows within the city limits, tethering and grazing them on vacant lots. Soon, Alex MacEwan built a barn to shelter Polly at the back of his McTavish Avenue house. Polly more than lived up to her reputation as a good producer.

She kept the MacEwan family in milk and each day produced a surplus of from two to eight quarts. It was one of Grant's early forays into the business world to deliver Polly's surplus to customers in the neighborhood, impressing on his youthful mind the importance of the words "increase" and "yield." He learned other lessons — some not so pleasant.

*   *   *

Wise and ever-alert Bertha MacEwan revealed to him what it meant to have a conscience, and the bitter experience cost him money. It happened when he discovered a whole roll of wire in the grass near a fence that had been built in the exhibition grounds. As it remained attached to a strand stapled to a post, he broke it off by hammering it between two rocks. Seeking out a trustworthy friend, he paid him five cents for the use of his wagon and together they loaded it and hauled it to the MacEwan barn.

Bertha was not long in discovering what her son had been up to and had much to say about the morality of the act, warning him he would be in trouble with the law. There she left the matter, leaving her son to think about it and arrive at his own conclusion. And think he did. What had begun as a lucky find, turned into a nightmare of guilt.

Not long afterward — whether or not it was collusion between his parents and the police — a big policeman happened to ride his bicycle down the back alley near the MacEwan house. Whether or not he was looking for a roll of wire and a boy, Grant saw him and a guilty conscience did the rest.

No words were exchanged with the law officer but Grant anxiously waited for the cover of darkness, then heaved the wire onto the wagon and quietly hauled it back to the exhibition grounds, leaving it where he had

Brandon street scene in early 1900s   *(Daly House Museum Collection)*

found it. He later confessed that the experience had cost him "five cents for cartage, a lot of worry, and some tired muscles — but it was worth it."

There is little doubt that Bertha MacEwan picked the proper text for the regular evening prayers that night. As was her habit, she read the Bible to the boys, seated at the kitchen table, often choosing verses with the day's events in mind. After that she would hear their prayers — during which the thrifty mother turned down the coal oil lamp — and it was off to bed.

*　　*　　*

Church and Sunday school played an important part in Grant's young life. For years he had a perfect attendance record at Knox Sunday school; he was also an active member of the Mission Band and the Boy Scout troop, being picked to become a proud member of the guard of honor during the brief visit through Brandon in 1912 of the governor general, the Duke of Connaught.

Life at the modest McTavish Avenue home progressed at an even tenor and was surrounded by the average number of comforts and conveniences but no luxuries. There was an abundance of simple but wholesome food. The days ran smoothly into one another with little differentiation save for Sundays, Christmas, and New Year's, when the old year was often "prayed out" and the new "prayed in" at church.

Christmas was perhaps the only "real and undisputed holiday . . . Summer holidays and travelling further than Forrest or Chater [to visit the Grants] were practically unthought of. My father was devoted to his fire extinguisher business and my mother was devoted to her boys and church." Nevertheless it was not all chores and hard work.

The automobile had arrived in the West and with it James Cowan, a cousin of Alex MacEwan, who came to work in the new industry. The MacEwan boys were extremely proud of James, "a big strapping fellow with 'fine carriage and good personality." In their eyes he was a mechanical genius, a driver, and a hero, just as some years later aircraft pilots and then astronauts would appear to the youth of their time.

James Cowan gave Grant his first automobile ride and it left a vivid impression on the boy's mind.

It was a big day when Jim took me for a ride in the country, perhaps to test a car or maybe to get away for an hour. One occasion stands out above the rest. That was in 1913 when Jim wished to test a car recently overhauled. I accompanied him out First Street to the mental hospital and a trail leading toward Eighteenth Street was selected — the speed a marvel to me. It was a week before I got over the thrill of travelling thirty miles per hour in a car.

He went through a period during which he was musically ambitious and aspired to play in the Alexander school orchestra which was sponsored by the principal, Mr. Hunter. He was attracted to the cornet or the trombone but, when he got a catalogue of instruments, he was appalled at the prices. Following a close and canny search, he found an instrument which, although still costly, was more in keeping with what he thought he should pay — he sent away for a B-flat flute at five dollars.

However, Grant was no musician. After practicing religiously for two years, his ambition cooled. It would be many more years before he would touch a musical instrument and then (if it is permitted to stretch the appellation) he taught himself to play the bagpipes — and performed on a number of public occasions. Back at the Brandon school of his youth, Mr. Hunter's orchestra would have to go on without a flutist.

Business ventures were more to his liking, for he certainly caught the spirit of the Manitoba Boom and it became his ambition, much more so than most other boys, to work and to make money. In 1914 he scoured the city for a summer job, finding one just around the corner from his home at George Fitton's grocery store, 610-12 Fourteenth Street. He worked from eight in the morning until six at night on weekdays and until after ten on Saturday nights. As clerk and errand boy he earned three dollars a week and underwent his first real test of responsibility to someone outside the family.

Fitton let him carry out regular duties for the first week or so, and then began thrusting more responsibility on to the shoulders of the twelve-year-old. Eventually, at noon, it became Grant's responsibility to take Fitton's money to the bank, riding his father's bicycle. As the First Great War had broken out by that time, it also became part of his job to swing around by the *Brandon Sun* building, read the news bulletins that were posted up outside, and return to the store with a summary of the latest war news.

Before summer was through, Grant MacEwan had taken charge of the whole store, not only looking after the money, but running the entire store when Fitton saw that he was capable of taking charge on his own. Years later Grant MacEwan recalled, "it gave me a little money, considerable experience and a wealth of satisfaction."

*   *   *

Just as he was precocious in business affairs, so Grant MacEwan was far ahead of many of his contemporaries in considering the choice of a career. At eleven years he resolved to become a medical doctor and began collecting medical and first-aid books, some of them his mother's nursing textbooks. Whenever one of the boys stubbed a toe or cut a finger, he delighted in taking charge and performing first aid.

His mother, who would rather have had him aspire to the clergy, nevertheless looked kindly on medicine as an alternative vocation. His father ventured that he didn't much mind what future his boys pursued "as long as they become neither preachers, lawyers or bartenders."

Other advice was near at hand and it came from one to whom the boy had grown steadily closer since his move to the West. When he confided his ambition to Grandfather John Walter Grant, the beloved old man offered advice Grant would never forget. His words were simple and honest, like the old man himself. "John," he said, using Grant's first name as was his habit, "I would rather see you an independent farmer, than the richest doctor in Pictou County."

The old patriarch hit the mark. From the age of twelve years onward, Grant MacEwan's goal was to farm and to raise the best livestock in the country. It was an ambition that would serve him well through a bleak period in his life.

*   *   *

In the buoyant years of 1912 and 1913, few thought the boom would ever end. Life was exciting in Brandon as it was in most western communities. There was money to be made everywhere, most certainly in the real estate business where investment was flowing in, even from Great Britain and European countries such as Germany, speculators seeking to enter the rising market early. Alex MacEwan was not standing idly by.

Manufacturing was profitable but, as there was more money to be made dealing in land, that was where most of the profits went after providing for the family. As the year 1913 turned into 1914, Alex MacEwan held a large number of lots in the booming city of Brandon.

It was then the drums of war were heard far off in Europe and, like early morning mist in sunlight, foreign capital vanished from the Prairies. Within a short time, soaring land prices leveled off and began to drop, building slowed and almost ceased altogether, and what had come to be called the Manitoba Boom was a thing of the past.

Alex MacEwan was caught with too much land on his hands. The drop in building had also reduced sales of fire extinguishers alarmingly, and he had no reserve to fall back on to tide him over the slump, as everything had gone into the purchase of city lots.

George and Grant MacEwan about 1912   *(MacEwan Collection)*

After the declaraton of war in Europe, things went from bad to worse. Freight rates rose, workmen became scarce, wages increased, and — a particularly stiff blow to a CPR town such as Brandon — 2,000 miles to the south the Panama Canal had opened, reducing the amount of material being shipped to the Pacific by transcontinental rail in Canada. Early in 1915, Alex MacEwan's business venture went on the rocks, along with many others. Seven years after arriving triumphantly in the city following the sale of his farm, he faced bankruptcy.

If the European war had played havoc with businessmen in Brandon, its effect on the farmers in the surrounding district and elsewhere in the West was the opposite. The *Brandon Sun* was full of it. In the issue of February 18, 1915, Hon. Martin Burrell, federal minister of agriculture, issued "the call of the Empire to the farmers of Canada," pleading with them to stay on the land and produce food in ever-increasing quantities. "Patriotism and Production" was the slogan as he explained that with mobilization of armies in Europe "millions cease to be producers, they have become consumers — worse they have become destroyers of food."

The price of wheat rose rapidly; in March it was $1.32¾ per bushel and by April it reached $1.60. Britain was in the market for 40,000 horses and their price was rising. Stockyards reported vast increases in business; swine volume up more than 600 percent; sheep up 98 percent; horses 52 percent and cattle up 22 percent. Had Alex been on his farm he could have recouped his losses with a good crop in one year.

Amidst the gloom, a ray of sunlight broke through. Early in the year when figures were tumbling and businesses failing, he met another like him — a land-poor man who was willing to trade farmland in Saskatchewan for all of Alex MacEwan's unsalable Brandon lots.

The man's description of what he had to trade sounded ideal. The farm had 250 acres cultivated and ready for seed in the spring; it had good buildings, a house, sound fencing, nine horses and harness ready to work. The countryside was dotted with lakes which provided good fishing.

Deep in his troubles, Alex MacEwan's mind had returned to the land. He yearned to be back on a farm working for himself. He needed a going concern, a farm with land ready to grow a crop the same year so that he would be both producing food for the country at war and selling on the rising wartime market to pay off his debts. He made the trade on the spot — sight unseen — a package of Brandon city lots in return for 800 acres of farmland and buildings at Margo, Saskatchewan.

Grant would go to Saskatchewan with his father, Bertha would stay in Brandon with George and follow along after allowing Alex time to move furniture into the house on the new farm and generally get things in running order.

*   *   *

It has not been recorded what Bertha MacEwan thought of the move. Clearly, however, there appeared no other alternative unless they were to throw themselves and their boys on the mercy of Bertha's brothers and, as they both were possessed of firm Scottish pride, this was the last thing on earth they would think to do. Nevertheless, the prospect could not have been a pleasant one. They had both done their pioneering at a younger age. They had worked hard to build up one farm, had failed in the city among relatives and friends, and now, each at forty-four years of age, they must start all over again, almost from the beginning on land that was 400 miles northwest in a new frontier. With all the understanding in the world, a woman in Bertha's position was bound to have second thoughts.

On the other hand, Grant rather looked forward to the move as an adventure. He had taken his grandfather's advice to heart and had set his sights on becoming an "independent farmer" and this seemed to be a start. He withdrew from Principal Johanson's grade eight class. Knox Church Mission Band presented him with a copy of the book *Souls in Action* suitably inscribed by Mrs. F. McKenzie, Mission Band president. He withdrew a small sum from his savings account — by that time having reached approximately fifty dollars — and went down to City Square to shop for farm implements. He made a deal for an old scythe and a pickax for seventy cents and these, together with the family lawn mower (to cut the grass around their new farm home) were all the farm equipment they would take with them.

It is a measure of the family's reduced circumstances that their Presbyterian scruples bowed before necessity and they accepted a game of deception for the trip to Margo. In those days settlers were given reduced rates on a carload of "settler's effects", one person traveling free, when going by rail to take up new land. It was decided that Grant would accompany his father in the car as a stowaway to save money, of which Alex had pitifully little.

Money or no money, Alex managed to assemble a carload of settler's effects. Included was all the furniture, dishes, bedding, and utensils necessary to make the new home livable. Polly, the faithful cow, was loaded along with a crate of hens, a pail, lawnmower, scythe and pickax.

The greatest shame of all came when Alex MacEwan, always the proud possessor of the finest Clydesdales in the district, was forced to buy two old "fox meat" horses for fifty dollars each, in order to start working the land at Margo. He loaded them hurriedly as darkness fell.

They had hope, but it was a long way off, and the words of Alex's lawyer who said, when told of the move, "What, you going to township forty-four? Should be the best place in the world to grow icicles: but what else can you grow?" ringing in his ears.

Regardless of friendly skepticism, Alex had no choice and the father and his thirteen-year-old boy set out on Saturday, April 17, 1915, aboard a freight train, their car billed for Margo, Saskatchewan, which neither had even seen. Their objective: to get on the land and seed a crop in the hopes that at harvest time the family would be lifted out of hard times by good markets and good prices, and set on the road to the recovery of their fortunes.

Chapter 4

Move to Saskatchewan

The journey into the Northwest was of significant importance in Grant MacEwan's life as he headed toward something entirely new and different. Here he would grow into manhood tempered by the heat of experiences he had escaped as an infant on the North Brandon farm and as a junior schoolboy in the city of Brandon. Through the varied and intensive training provided by the farming activities, the youngster would become more self-reliant and capable than he had become in the city.

It is doubtful if the boy, precocious as he was, could fully comprehend the nature and extent of the defeat his father had suffered when land prices came tumbling about his ears. Alex was not the type of person to air his problems at home. However, if young Grant MacEwan did not fully realize the gravity of the move when they set out, he was soon to find out.

With stops along the way to water the livestock, clean the boxcar and put down fresh straw bedding, the trip to Margo took most of four days. It was on one such stop at Dauphin that, the livestock tended to, Alex set off to replenish their supply of bread and cheese from a grocery store near the freight yards. He cautioned Grant, the stowaway, not to show himself.

The boxcar was quiet save for the clucking of the hens and the sounds of Polly and the horses munching on hay. Soon sounds of approaching footsteps sent the boy to his hiding place, his attention fixed on the open door. It was the train conductor who peered through the open doorway and whose eyes swept the contents of the car. Grant feared he had been caught, but the man's attentions settled on the crate of hens momentarily. He heaved himself into the boxcar, selected two prime specimens from the crate, and thrust them — squawking, wings beating, feathers flying — into a bran sack. The thief left with his booty before the eyes of the frustrated youngster.

On April 20 their boxcar was shunted onto a railway siding at Margo and the day was spent unloading and making contacts in the small village. The residents proved friendly and of much help, particularly a Mr. De Galliers and old Mr. Chapman who, among other things, saw that Alex MacEwan had the loan of a wagon to transport his possessions to the farm.

The arrival of a new family was something of an event and soon most of the children in town stood watching the operation. Grant made friends easily with boys his own age, inquiring about public school facilities as he was anxious to complete the grade eight term without losing a grade. The boys were delighted to hear that he played baseball — they had a team but no catcher, and they hoped Grant would fill the gap.

It was raining the following day but there was no time to be wasted; they hitched the two old horses Alex had brought with him to the heavily laden wagon, tied Polly to the rear, and set out to locate their new farm.

Land surrounding Margo was not as level as the North Brandon countryside; it was hilly with sloughs here and there in the depressions and much of it covered with ragged poplar bluffs. Alex MacEwan had seen better land.

Toward the middle of the day they found survey stakes and located their farm. They followed what had once been a trail leading to the farmstead. On the top of a slight rise, they caught the first sight of their land of promise.

Alex reined in the plodding horses and the little entourage came to a stop in the drizzle. The shock of discovery was deeply imprinted on Grant's mind. "To our horror the fences were down, the house was a shambles and uninhabitable, the horses didn't exist, the land was not ready for crop — nothing was as represented."

On the wagon seat at the rain-soaked Margo farm the young MacEwan experienced major failure for the first time in his life. Alex MacEwan had been outrageously taken. The vision of a farm ready to work vanished like a desert mirage.

After a long period of silence, broken only by the drip of the rain, Alex spoke. "Well Grant, this is a failure."

"What can we do?" the boy asked. Alex turned the horses and headed slowly back toward the village.

There was ample time to think during the dismal return drive but whatever thoughts were going through Alex MacEwan's mind were not communicated to his dispirited son. However, by the time they reached Margo, he had evidently come to a decision.

Almost forgotten in a far corner of his mind lay a section of land he had bought nine years before. It had been purchased when he had taken the Canadian Northern Railway land promotion trip on their newly opened line through the Melfort district. A purely speculative buy, he had never intended using it himself but would hold it and sell when the price was right. Events had changed all that now.

At the time he knew what he was buying. It was rich black soil — much better than they had seen at Margo — but it was untouched, unimproved, not a building on it and certainly no land broken. It was as if he had lost twenty-two years from his life, for he was exactly where he had been when he started breaking his first land north of Brandon. But he had been much younger then and full of hope. Now he had a wife, two children, and no shelter for them. He was older, and Bertha too. What was more, it would be another year before they could expect to harvest any sort of crop at all.

"We'll reload and bill for Melfort," said Alex as they neared Margo.

It was much to be preferred to an inglorious retreat to Brandon. Neither he nor Bertha could have stood it, no matter how rocky the trail ahead. If there was a positive element in his situation, it was that there would be no further disappointment upon arriving at Melfort, for he knew it would be untouched land waiting for him. He had no high expectations to be dashed once more.

When the next westbound train pulled out of the village of Margo with the two MacEwans aboard, it was a sad little knot of boys who waved good-by to their departing ball catcher.

* * *

It was a roundabout trip from Margo, taking them about 125 miles to Saskatoon, 100 north to Prince Albert and 50 miles east again to Melfort. By the time they stopped in Prince Albert to water the stock and clean the car, they were out of bread and low on pocket money. It was here that Grant's enterprising spirit came to the rescue. Despite the rough trip, Polly had continued to yield copious supplies of milk, more than enough for the two of them, so he took the surplus and peddled it up and down the streets near the railway tracks in the strange city. There was little sale, but one woman with a fresh batch of baking just out of the oven — its smell reminding the boy desperately of his mother's cooking at home — was willing to make a trade and he returned to the boxcar with more than enough fresh bread for the remainder of the trip.

On Saturday, April 24, 1915, Grant and his father arrived in Melfort after spending a whole week in the boxcar. During that time they had lived on bread, cheese, Polly's milk, and twenty-five cents' worth of fancy biscuits.

* * *

Melfort was a much larger center than Margo and its surroundings more pleasant to look upon. It was situated in the Carrot River Valley which consisted of large expanses of almost level ground, tracts of open meadow, and scattered forests of poplar trees. Where the land had been cleared and broken, it appeared black and rich; where there were trees, they too suggested nutritious soil, being large and well formed.

The town itself was about as old as Grant MacEwan, having been surveyed in 1902. With the building of the railway and the addition of branches, Melfort prospered and grew, expanding its services to become the major supply point in that part of Saskatchewan. Incorporated as a town in 1907, it continued to thrive between the years 1910 to 1920, during which settlers flooded in to claim virtually all available land.

Grant's welcome to the town was warm but not propitious. As he stood guard over their carload of possessions while his father was away making arrangements, two town boys walked through the freight yards playing with matches. As they passed the MacEwan car they tossed a lighted match through the open door. The flame exploded in the tinder-dry straw and it was some time before Grant could stamp it out successfully.

The next day was a fine spring Sunday. Leaving their furniture and livestock in Sparrow's barn, they walked through the smells of awakening vegetation and meadowlark song south of town and located their land. The MacEwan section was four miles south and west of Melfort on a gentle prominence with a good prospect to the south. It was in its natural state, no buildings of any kind, no breaking. Here and there clumps of aspen dotted the open meadow and trembled in the gentle spring breeze. It made a pretty sight, but not to the man from the open Manitoba prairie who would have to cut down the trees, pull out the roots, and clear away the underbrush to make a farm.

The day after Sabbath, they began moving. "We borrowed a wagon and hauled a load of the crated furniture to the place and led the cow. The crated furniture was stacked in a bluff of poplars in the form of an enclosure and inside we set up a table and called it home." Isaac Poole, a neighbor, permitted them to use a granary as a place to sleep.

*   *   *

Alex MacEwan sent a message advising Bertha that she and George were to stay in Brandon until he could prepare shelter for them. But the message was ignored and in a few days they arrived to share the poplar bluff and granary with Alex and Grant. Sixty years later the writer discovered that the other members of the tightly knit family in Brandon knew nothing of Alex's failure in Margo, and indeed, knew nothing of, nor ever heard of such a place. It appears that a proud wife would rather act as if the original plan were working smoothly and, instead of making sudden changes that would arouse curiosity, she carried on as if nothing had happened and she and her son left for Melfort where they knew no shelter had been prepared.

The relative comfort and convenience of city life had switched abruptly to the unremitting drudgery from which no homesteader's wife could hope to escape save through desertion, death, or madness. It would be Bertha's nature to deem any work necessary to lift the family fortunes out of the mire as more of a challenge than drudgery. This she would do with the aid of her strong ally, her God.

Grant feeding cat straight from the source at Melfort farm   *(MacEwan Collection)*

By this time, Grant MacEwan, the thirteen-year-old boy, was showing signs of MacEwan, the man to come. He was growing rapidly, having begun to outstrip most of his contemporaries in height; he continued to play his part in school sporting activity, while at the same time carrying on a number of commercial ventures of his own. He revealed characteristics inherited from both the Grants and the MacEwans, including unusual strength and stamina. These were put cheerfully to work on the farmstead, as he was impatient to prove himself by doing a man's work.

There was much to do and Grant worked alongside his father to get it done. Alex, who was short of money when it came to incidental human requirements such as food, produced fifty dollars and with a good part of it bought a secondhand wagon which was to serve them well for years to come.

Another neighbor, James Durnin, who lived to the south of the MacEwan land, invited them to use a log granary on his land. It was accepted with gratitude and served as sleeping quarters until other arrangements could be made. For a time, they stored some belongings in one granary, slept in another, and cooked and ate camp fashion under the sky in the enclosure formed by the furniture crates and trees. It was there that Bertha, upon arriving, cooked her first meal for the family. Years later Grant recalled: "I'll never forget how acceptable was that first mess of potatoes we cooked over an open camp fire in the bluff."

Alex MacEwan was no longer the failed businessman but a settler with a section of rich black loam to turn into a farm. On the strength of that, the bank loaned him $3,000. As it had done throughout the country at the time, credit started things moving. He bought a shack measuring 16 feet by

18 feet, borrowed another wagon, and with Grant as helper and using the two wagon beds, moved it from Melfort to the farm. It took them from daybreak until nightfall to move it to within a mile or two of the farm and on that day Grant provided the lunch: "It cost us a total of five cents and consisted of four buns which I purchased in town at fifteen cents a dozen."

The shack was a great improvement over the bug-infested granaries and in short order Bertha's touch turned it into a home. It was to serve them for three years until she laid down the law to Alex.

Together Alex and Grant cut poles from the trees on their land and, with $100 worth of shiplap, they built a stable. Drilling by hand with a seven-inch boring auger, they struck water at thirty feet, to the joy of all, and dug a well. Additional horsepower was badly needed and Alex purchased a third horse at an auction sale. Grant recalled: "The new horse was Bill, widely known for his great age, his chronic indigestion which made driving behind him a hazardous business, and his high tail. Nevertheless old Bill, light and old as he was, served us well for several years." The next purchase was a sixteen-inch sulky breaking plow suitable for turning over unbroken sod.

*   *   *

Work was endless. Alex rose at four-thirty each morning, except Sunday, the rest of the family two hours later. Having established a farmstead in which were gathered all their hard-won belongings, they set about protecting it from the scourge of early settlers — the prairie fire. Alex plowed a fire guard around the lot in which they planted a crop of potatoes. He then began to break the first sod in a relatively open field south of the house and, by May 20, had a plot of seven acres seeded to oats — not quite a month after starting. It was on this occasion that Grant's younger brother George went on the family record for the first time, saying: "Pa, you've done pretty well today."

The statement reveals the singleness of purpose and pride in accomplishment with which the MacEwan family worked, and were to continue to work, throughout the early Melfort period. They were brought together as never before, their minds focused on the one thing — to break land and seed a crop. In all this Grant played a part far beyond his years at a period of life when boys of his age in different circumstances might well be riding bicycles, playing games, and flying kites.

With all the energy and stamina in the world there were limits to what a man could do, even with the help of his family, and Alex MacEwan made judicious, if grudging, use of his credit at the bank to "hire work done." He bought barbed wire and he and Grant cut pickets from willow brush but, to free them for more important tasks, he hired a man to string the fence. Grant remembered him as "bad tempered and a marathon cusser," but he got the job done. Later, Alex bargained with Jack Curtis of Mount Forest, a few miles north of Melfort, to come with his tractor and five-bottom breaking plow, to break fifty acres of land at three dollars per acre. It was a heavy job for the old one-cylinder International Harvester machine "and the district had seen better breaking," but the MacEwan farm advanced. It fell to Grant's lot to disk the new breaking during the summer holidays. In reconstructing the scene for his daily journal, he recorded:

> Disking our 50 acres of tractor breaking and it is very rough. Three horses on the disk. The load was too heavy for three horses but it could not be avoided. The pioneer man and the pioneer's wife have been extolled but the pioneer's horse has frequently been forgotten. I would like to suggest that if somebody wants to erect a memorial, there would be none more suitable than to that noble creature who has played such a great part in the development of the country. Would suggest that the "Pioneer Horse" be depicted in a half-starved state, gaunt, ribs projecting, head low and back end partly submerged in bog.

The harvest of 1915 was a heartbreaker for the MacEwans. "It was the West's biggest year to that time — but we missed it." It was one of those crop years farmers dream about; reports circulated of crops yielding thirty, forty, or even fifty bushels to the acre, and Alex MacEwan had only seven acres of oats to harvest. But, with the Westerner's eternal optimism, he said, as countless farmers had said before and would say after, "maybe next year." There was work to do and little time to spend pining for the impossible.

Grant, too, had been endowed with his share of irrepressible optimism. He shared in the work of harvesting the small plot of oats and recorded for September 30, 1915: "stacked 10 loads of oat hay from the seven-acre plot. Seeded on fresh breaking south of the house. We worked until after dark to complete the stack. I was a tired helper that night, but very proud of our first lowly harvest."

*   *   *

It had not been all work for the MacEwan boys. After the first week or two of intensive labor necessary to provide shelter and the basic elements of a farmstead, they were sent to Spry school two miles from their home. It was a one-room frame schoolhouse in which Miss Olive Durnin presided over about thirty-five pupils in eight grades.

Owing to the lateness of the season Miss Durnin found it impossible to continue Grant in grade eight, where he had left off at Brandon, and so he was dropped back to grade seven. If the start had been disappointing for him, he would have cause for gratitude to the teacher later.

Miss Durnin, too, was to discover very soon that the tall MacEwan boy had a mind of his own and no fear of expressing his opinion when he felt it necessary to do so. It was near the end of the term, summer holidays were approaching, the class work was ahead of schedule, and she needed something to keep the students occupied. She proposed to the class that part of their time be devoted to raffia work and that each pupil bring fifty cents to school to purchase the necessary material. In Grant's own words, "that was a large sum for us boys. We talked it over at home and the next day when the matter was again under discussion in school, I took the bit in my teeth, arose in my seat and explained to teacher and all that the money would only be secured with difficulty in our home and perhaps others, and it would be more satisfactory for us if the time were devoted to something less costly — I suggested physical training or something equally novel. The raffia work was never started."

Grant and George walked the two miles to school, carrying lunch. Bertha usually prepared egg sandwiches, sometimes a jelly sandwich for a treat, if the berry crop had been good, and Grant always stood in awe of his mother's ability to prepare simple, wholesome, and palatable food from very little. In winter when walking was hazardous at best, the boys were allowed to take one horse drawing a small cutter.

Cyril Ede, who was to serve as a Spry school trustee for many years, gave an eyewitness account of Grant and the MacEwans in relation to the school. He remembered Grant as a tall boy and a good ballplayer. He was a good student and capable of mischief from time to time "but he was too smart to be caught." Alex was a fine man who "taught us a lot and after he got a good start on the farm, always seemed to have money for anything when the need arose — not that he spread it around." Alex's inventive streak revealed itself when winter set in and it was necessary to send the boys to school in a small cutter drawn by Bill, the horse with the upset stomach. He tied a log behind the sleigh runners so that the snow was spread each trip and it did not pack and build up into the high, curved, and slippery crown that upset sleighs toward spring. The walks to and from school were productive. It was then, with observant curiosity, that Grant studied the flora and fauna of their new countryside and laid the foundation for a deep knowledge and appreciation of nature that would never leave him.

The Spry baseball team made good use of a broad, level stretch of land on the MacEwan southwest quarter section of land that made an ideal ball diamond before it was broken. The first summer they challenged the Melfort High School team, and with Grant as catcher, they beat them in a hard-fought game, despite the fact that they were only public schoolers.

* * *

Grant returned to school in the fall of 1915, but by the second week in December, it became apparent that their shack was no place for Bertha and the boys to spend the winter, which was proving to be one of the coldest on record. So Bertha took the boys to Brandon where they stayed with their Uncle James, Aunt Marion, and their three daughters, Janetta, Maria Corlette, Christina, in the Grant's large, brick farm home. It was here that the older MacEwan boy revealed qualities that would characterize him for the rest of his life.

His upbringing had instilled in him a strong sense of the value of time and even as a boy he was not disposed to fritter it away. Apart from doing his fair share of chores around the Grant farm, helping Bill Chapman the hired man, he kept up his studies at Turriff school two miles distant. As

Christmas approached, he wrote Miss Durnin for the examinations, as he was in the crucial eighth grade leading to the all-important "departmental examinations" that would give him the coveted Grade Eight Certificate.

Evidently he had impressed his teacher with his trustworthiness, for she sent him the examination papers, instructing him to set his own time so that he would not enjoy any advantage over the students who wrote under her surveillance at Spry school. He passed high in his class, saving the results of half a year's work. After Christmas he continued school but also managed to crowd in extracurricular instruction.

Taking a week off, he went into Brandon to attend a course on the internal combustion engine sponsored by the International Harvester Company. At the age of fourteen, he became one of the most enthusiastic supporters of the machine age. "I was sold to engines in general and to IHC engines in particular. I was amazed to discover that engines were not complete mysteries after all and that I could really grasp the fundamental principles without much trouble."

During the sessions at the engine school, officers recruiting for the army addressed the gathering, imploring members of the class to join up, but Grant was not moved. There were a number of reasons, the first being that his age was against him — but not his height, for he looked much older than he was. He had also heard the pleadings of other governmental officers for farmers to stay on the land and produce food — "food will win the war" rang in their message. In addition, he had inherited a strong thread of pacifism and aversion to violence from his mother, and, during one fling at cadet camp while living in Brandon, his nascent individualism had rejected attempts at regimentation. He was destined, despite an easy affability he would develop, to be pretty much of a loner.

* * *

They returned to Melfort in April, Alex meeting them at the station with the sleigh. Grant, bursting with newly won knowledge, had to hold himself in and ride silently behind his mother and father as Bertha filled her husband in on the news and happenings in Brandon. Even Alex, normally silent, had something to say about the past winter. Finally, upon arriving home, he could contain himself no longer and burst forth, giving his father the principles of internal combustion and describing what the engine could do for farming. Alex MacEwan, the Clydesdale man, was no instant convert.

Returning happily to Miss Durnin, Grant plunged into his studies to make up for lost time and the differences between the Manitoba and Saskatchewan curricula. He studied three and four hours a night, doing his farm chores as well. Miss Durnin did all she could to help. He wrote the examinations in June, determined to do the best he could — then followed the long wait for results from Regina, which, to a degree, overshadowed the joys of summer and the freedom from school.

Finally the day came when the results were posted at Melfort Post Office. Teet Arnold, a so-so student, also a ballplayer and a grade eight student, rode out to the MacEwan farm with the news and seemed comforted to have company when he blurted out: "Grant — we both failed. Our names aren't on the passed list."

Grant was shattered. Miss Durnin drove into the yard in her buggy to see if they had heard any results. Grant was beyond speech, and for once in his life it is recorded that tears flowed. When apprised of the situation, Miss Durnin was appalled. It was beyond comprehension. She immediately wheeled the horse around and headed for Melfort to see for herself.

In due course she returned, but Grant could not bear to face her and ran for the barn. For what seemed a dreadfully long and quiet period he hid, until he heard a voice calling, "Mrs. MacEwan — where's Grant — he passed his departmentals — with HONORS! The only one in the whole northern school division to get honors!"

The tears dried instantly and Grant came out of hiding to rejoice with the others. They then reconstructed what had happened when Teet Arnold read the results. It was true that neither his name nor Grant's appeared on the "passed" list and he, being an indifferent student, would never think of looking elsewhere — let alone in the "honors" section, where Grant's name stood alone among all the results of all the schools in the northwestern Saskatchewan school district.

Teacher was invited to dinner. The excitement carried through the happy occasion, for it was not only a mark of distinction for the student, it reflected honor on Spry school and certainly on Grant's kind and understanding schoolmistress.

Among the most elated was Alex MacEwan. Seeking the best way to express his jubilation, he burst out: "Grant — if you say so, we'll buy that purebred Clydesdale mare in town!"

Showing control and judgment far beyond his years, Grant didn't "say so." Later, he confided to his journal: "I knew we weren't ready for that yet."

Any hope for future schooling for Grant MacEwan was dealt a cruel blow by the harvest of 1916. Throughout the summer they cleared land, cutting the trees, digging out roots with grub hoes or tearing out the larger ones with the aid of the horses. They also kept an eye on the fifty acres of new breaking seeded to wheat. For a time it was an encouraging sight and looked as if it would yield upward of forty bushels per acre, which on clean new land was bound to produce first-grade kernels "as big as beans," commanding top wartime prices well above two dollars a bushel. If one permitted himself to hope, he could see the debt against the land wiped out and money to spare for badly needed machinery and livestock.

But as harvest neared something mysterious plagued the ripening grain. Farmers in western Canada that year were introduced to the devastating effects of what would come to be well known to them as "stem rust." For miles around farmers harvested nothing but a straw crop, the kernels in the heads having literally rusted away.

The only income that year came from the sale of surplus eggs, and the milk from three cows. There was no question of Grant going on to high school in Melfort. It appeared as if his formal education had come to an end.

Chapter 5

Melfort, Tractors, Trading

Alex MacEwan saw to it that there was work for the boys to do on the farm. The boys found rare moments for play, usually a baseball game. Bertha saw to it that the spiritual side of life shone as brightly in Melfort as it had in Brandon.

It is not unusual for men of similar background to look back on their youth and write scathingly of the harsh Presbyterian upbringing to which they were subjected — but not Grant MacEwan. He embraced it, admired its austerity and discipline and its fundamental absence of frills. Under his mother's guidance, prayer became for him the same source of strength and encouragement that it was for Bertha.

With regularity, Grant and George accompanied their mother to St. James Presbyterian Church services in Melfort. In order to do so and walk the distance (letting the hardworked horses rest on the Sabbath) they would arise early and leave by nine-thirty in the morning to walk the four miles into town. Usually they remained after the church service to attend Sunday school and so they would not return home until around three in the afternoon — ravenous for food!

Grant never doubted the need for a solid religious background. Years later he recalled: "It meant something to have a mother whose faith was as firm as Gibraltar and who thought sufficient of her God and her church that she, with her two boys, would walk eight and one-half miles, in addition to her regular housework, that the benefits of church service would arise."

*　　*　　*

After his school years, there followed the steady round of work on the land and chores about the barn and farmstead. Clearing trees and scrub brush, breaking new land, double-disking it, building granaries, repairing machinery, feeding and watering livestock and cleaning barns, were all duties in which Grant took a full-time part. The second crop headed out in mid-July 1917 and was ripe for cutting within a month, an early harvest.

When it came to harvesting, his father cut the wheat and Grant and his mother stooked it. Rod Reid, from down south, moved in with his Case steam outfit to do the threshing and that meant a crew of thirteen or fourteen men to be fed. Grant did his share and felt a rush of pride when he was entrusted for the first time with one of the grain teams, hauling the loads to the country elevator at nearby Pleasant Valley. He was caught up in the excitement and tension of it all, especially the threshing operation, which he described years later in his book *Between the Red and the Rockies*.

In that season all social intercourse ceased. Cows went dry because nobody had time to milk them. School attendances dropped to the point where the teacher was almost alone. Threshing season brought out the best and the worst in people. Some loved it and some went insane.

Getting and holding a crew was not always an easy matter, especially late in the season when cold weather and snow added to the hardships. Frequently the teamsters were neighbors or homesteaders who left their land to make some extra money. Often they were the hard-hitting, hard-drinking men who worked in the lumber camps in the winter and came to the farming districts at harvest time. They received a dollar and a half a day and all they could eat.

A little later, harvester excursions were instituted and many young men from eastern Canada got their first glimpse of the prairies from the window of an excursion train. Some of the easterners remained in the West and took up farming for themselves. . . .

The acknowledged hero of the harvest season was the steam engineer. He had special qualifications, he held a certificate, and he commanded the biggest wages and the greatest respect. If he had a good outfit, he wasn't very busy. As he stood with folded arms on the great drive wheel of the tractor, and surveyed operations, he knew that he was the envy of everybody. When he placed his hand upon the throttle and the mighty wheels responded, young hero-worshippers resolved on the spot to become steam engineers. It took a good man to resist the virus of conceit.

For a normally susceptible engineer, probably the biggest thrill of all came when he pulled the cord of the steam whistle and human ears tingled for miles around. The single long blast that meant quitting time was always welcome. There was one mule team that positively refused to move a load or tighten the traces after that quitting signal. Two long blasts brought a special message to the tank man, who was pumping at some distant slough or creek, that water was low. Three blasts reminded teamsters on the grain wagons to hasten along so there would be no delay for want of a place to deposit the grain, and a series of short toots warned the workers on the stook wagons to speed up or the machine would be left "to idle." . . .

Another distinctive character was the old-time separator man. His dusty and dirty job was not glamorous. But he commanded the second highest wage and upon his skill depended the success of the season. He was expected to have untold knowledge about bearings and concaves and pulleys, and at lacing belts he was a master. Such knowledge came not from books but from years of experience. For fully half of his time he was squirting oil into holes which nobody but himself would have any hope of finding. . . .

All in all, those big threshing crews represented a perfectly co-ordinated effort and each of the fifteen or twenty-five members had his part to play on the team. More than that, it was a strictly co-operative undertaking in the community. The wagons, racks, and horse teams were assembled from farms about, chiefly from those which would be served by the outfit. And some of the dishes and pans used in the kitchen were requisitioned from willing neighbors. Thus the job of keeping the accounts was often difficult and complicated. If a man had a big crop and depended upon much outside assistance, all one side of the barn door might be needed to carry the figures and balance the account. It was an argument in support of bigger doors on barns.

One might marvel at the fortitude and stamina of the farm women who fed those big gangs of ravenous threshers. When threshers were coming, the kitchen table was extended by strange and ingenious means until it would seat fifteen to twenty-five men as the occasion demanded. There one learned to eat with elbows "in his pockets," and there one learned, by the necessity which comes from competition, to eat in a hurry.

It wasn't much wonder that the thought of a breakdown or delay occasioned by wet weather terrified the farm women. Meals were provided as usual whether the weather was fit for threshing or not and it was common for the woman of the home to serve a total of 400 or 500 man meals before the fields were finally cleared of stooks.

Alex marketed approximately 2,500 bushels of wheat, graded Number Two Northern, at about $2.00 per bushel, with a harvesting bill of $318.16. Entries in the farm records reflect the changed circumstances and bespeak of cash on hand for essential additions: in August, they purchased a new Frost and Wood binder from Jack Stewart, farm machinery dealer in Melfort — no secondhand deal this time. On September 22, they vaccinated eight head of cattle against blackleg. Four days later "traded the Billie Engles horse 'Ted' to R. Kellet for 'John' plus $15.00 and began plowing with a new John Deere plow ($130.00)."

*   *   *

There was great jubiliation at the MacEwan farm save from one quarter. Bertha was strangely silent. For the first time in his life Grant MacEwan sensed a tension in the otherwise even-tempered atmosphere that had prevailed in their home for as long as he could remember.

It had been a long stretch for Bertha MacEwan in the old shack, although she seldom complained no matter how difficult things were. When she saw money going for machinery and livestock and no sign of a move toward improvement of living conditions for the humans on the MacEwan farm, she began letting her husband know in her own way that

The MacEwan farmhouse, Bertha standing near front door
(Jarrett's Photo Art Studio, Melfort)

she expected something to be done about it before machinery, horses, and outbuildings claimed most of the cash that came into the farm from the sale of their first good crop. What was more, she did not look forward to spending another winter away from the cold shack in Melfort, with relatives in Brandon, no matter how congenial such sojourns were. That was a move she would avoid repeating at all costs, not only for the sake of her own pride but for that of the man she had married. Alex was a good man, a good provider, and he must be seen to be such.

Alex MacEwan got the message and it is typical of the man that he altered his plans at once, the justice of the claim having been revealed. Grant recorded in his small pocket notebook that on October 12, 1917, Charlie Van Camp and his crew of carpenters from Melfort arrived to begin building one of the finest farm homes in the district. It was to be a two-storied frame house, 30 by 30 feet, with a 12-by-16-foot kitchen added; dormer windows offered an elevated view of the country on all sides from the second floor. A second story in a strange house could constitute a hazard to a sleep-walking youth but such occasions were now quite rare and gave rise to no more than a fleeting thought in the excitement. It was too late in the season to pour the concrete for the foundation so the house was mounted on blocks, the excavating to be done the following summer whenever time permitted, as was the case with the finishing work inside.

Grant recorded that it was merely a shell when they moved in "but it looked like a million dollars to us."

* * *

Grant MacEwan was both a witness to, and a participant in, the transition of a farmstead from the open-air campfire stage to fully developed farm with horsepower, a growing herd of cattle and other livestock, barns, outbuildings, a good line of machinery, a modern two-story house, and all that went with it. From the beginning he had played a part far beyond his age and, at sixteen years, was now capable of performing all the tasks side-by-side with his father. Now, he was about to play an active part in another transition, this one of historic proportions, that would sweep the West and lift it into a new era.

With a larger than normal measure of natural intelligence he learned more through observation than direct instruction, which was just as well, given his father's minimum use of words. Not only did he learn the current methodology of farming but he often devised in his mind what he thought would be improvements leading to greater efficiency. They were not always accepted by his father who had a mind of his own and did not sway easily.

He early learned the importance of good nutrition, especially where the horses and heavy work were concerned. A journal entry, made when he was fifteen, states: "The crop in, we prepared to do more breaking. We had five horses in that season and my father and I worked together all summer. Feed was scarce so we made only seven or eight miles per half day with the teams (two drivers, one plow) and utilized all spare moments (while the horses were resting) cutting and grubbing along our lands. The flies were nothing short of terrible."

But no matter how well the horses were fed or how hard the farmers worked, food production for a nation at war was a matter of major concern and men's minds inevitably turned to the then relatively untapped source of power — the internal combustion engine. Being constantly urged by the federal department of agriculture, and its minister, Hon. T. A. Crerar, to stay on the land and double and redouble production (and in the face of shortage of manpower as more and more joined the army), a few farmers had already switched from horses to tractors and were reporting good results. Figures on an American farmer's experience were widely published: he had done twice the work using a tractor; the work had been done better; the plowing had been deeper and the seedbed much improved; his production had doubled.

"We required more power to operate our holdings adequately," Grant's journal of the time states. "My father and I were somewhat interested in the advisability of purchasing a tractor. . . ."

And so the argument had begun. Grant had kept up his interest in tractors since his 1915 sojourn in Brandon and had attended a number of short courses in Melfort, including one sponsored by the Happy Farmer Tractor Company, and was a natural spokesman for the machinery side of the debate. Alex tended to agree with him, much as he loved his fine Clydesdales. Bertha was anti-tractor and pro-horse.

The fact that a man could handle much larger tracts of land himself, using tractors, was dismissed as the points in favor of the horse were brought forth; tractors did not reproduce themselves, horses did; the farmer using horses could grow his own fuel, the tractor farmer lost control and must buy fuel from outside sources — and for cash. When tractors worked,

Above: Alex MacEwan with six horses hitched to cultivator   *(MacEwan Collection)*
Right: Grant MacEwan driving Fordson tractor in 1918 on new breaking, Alex standing behind with ax   *(MacEwan Collection)*

they produced only evil-smelling exhaust products where the exhaust product of horses, manure, was used to enrich the soil and increase production. The discussion was heard around farm kitchen tables throughout the entire West.

The matter was settled on the MacEwan farm in 1918, when the federal government, in order to increase production and compensate for lost manpower, announced that the import tariff on tractors under $800 in price would be dropped and further, the government would bring in what it called "The Greater Production Fleet" of 1,000 Fordson tractors and lay them down at the farmer's shipping point at cost. In April, Alex put in his order for one.

*   *   *

It was a memorable day in Grant MacEwan's life when the tractor arrived the following month. On the farm, life was grim and life was serious and Alex MacEwan frowned on the notion of others taking a holiday when there was always so much work to be done. Later, when they had livestock to show in the judging ring, one could almost justify taking time off to go to the fair, but to be acceptable in Alex's eyes, there had to be that double purpose. The arrival of the tractor was a welcome change from all this and it brought a touch of novelty to the endless rounds of the fields — at least until the novelty wore off.

The cost of the machine, unloaded at Melfort, was $795. Grant drove the machine home and, as he put it later, the Fordson seldom stood idle long enough to cool off. So enamored of the new power unit and its potential was he, that he took only one holiday that year, and even on July 1, Dominion Day, when there were picnics aplenty, sports and ball games, he remained on the farm tearing up scrub brush, picking stones, and breaking new land. Where his journal had spoken of horses up to this point, the tractor now appeared so much that it almost became a personality.

An entry in June 1918 says: "The Fordson's first job was breaking 15 acres on the southwest quarter for late oats. I ran the tractor and Dad cut scrub ahead of the breaking."

Another in June states:

The Fordson's next job was breaking on the northwest quarter. We began to break on the east side of the quarter and while the brush was not the big kind, it covered the east side of the quarter. Furthermore, that part of the farm had about 25 acres of stoney ground and we found the combination of bush and stones was very bad. Dad cut scrub and I did the breaking and handled the stones. Every stone that was touched by the plow was taken out and we finally took over 100 loads of stone off. We broke 50 acres on the quarter that year and did all our disking with the tractor.

* * *

The relationship between Grant and his younger brother seemed to be all that fraternal affection permitted, although little is recorded in the MacEwan journal about George. This is possibly due to the fact that, to them at the time, the four-year difference in age constituted an unbridgeable gap, thus eliminating any possible danger of collision. Grant later recalled that they got along well, that he had a real affection for his brother and that he suspected it was reciprocated. On rare occasions they had their differences but they didn't amount to much: "We would probably settle things by heaving a clod of earth in one another's direction and leave it at that."

Grant was to continue his business ventures in order to build up his bank account and, as George grew older, he would take him in as a partner on a deal or two. There was little similarity in the opportunities available to a boy with an enterprising turn of mind between Brandon and Melfort. There were extra chores to be done on neighbors' farms, but that was usually on the basis of "swapping work," no cash being involved, only an invisible entry made on a mythical balance sheet that somehow always seemed to come out right in the end. However, there was solid cash to be made raising cattle.

He had been a precocious trader and stockman. In Brandon at the age of about ten or eleven, he had bought a calf for two dollars and brought it home to put it in the small barn behind the house. When his parents learned of his plans, they made it clear to him they weren't about to tolerate a feedlot operation on their limited patch on McTavish Avenue and told him to take it right back. He was crushed, but obeyed without a word. He sold it for three dollars, clearing a dollar on the deal.

In Melfort, it was a different thing. They had space and feed and were expanding in the livestock business themselves. As was the custom on countless prairie farms, the children were permitted to make the occasional deal. This constituted acceptable practical education and a way for the boys to make a little pocket money.

The "practical education" proved to be a hard one. A year after their arrival at Melfort, Grant made a deal with his father whereby they would each put up a sum to buy a Holstein cow. The family would get all the milk she produced and Grant would get the calves. As it turned out, she calved in May but the calf was born dead. On the other hand, she proved to be a record milker, producing over a period in June 150 pounds a day, on three-times-a-day milking. She never calved again, and when she dried up and was seen as a breeding failure, Grant got a portion of his investment back when she was sold for slaughter.

On another occasion, he bought a likely looking cow with calf at foot from Malcolm MacPhail for $100, the calf revealing all the marks of an animal suitable for showing in the judging ring. Unfortunately, for the young investor, the calf proved to be so wild all its life that it ran itself skinny, never reaching the peak of fitness necessary for the show ring. The calf's mother was bred again but when her time came she got into trouble. Grant called a veterinarian to tend her. He killed the calf, the cow died and — the crowning insult for the parsimonious young cattleman — he charged $10!

All was not failure. He and George went together to buy a red cow in calf to Alex MacEwan's own Aberdeen Angus bull and owned by Ted Frank. She calved without mishap, producing a fine bull calf that was fattened successfully, used as a show steer, and sold at a tidy profit. It also contributed a touch of humor to the MacEwan family lore.

They were feeding the calf for show and, as Grant was otherwise occupied on the farm, he instructed George to go into Melfort and purchase from the A.E. Code establishment, three gallons of Cane Mola, a popular brand of molasses used to top up feed for special animals. George went to Code's all right but got tangled up in the instructions, asking Mr. Code for three gallons of Coca-Cola. The surprised man sent the boy to Graham's Confectionery, but this time he got the name right and duly requested three gallons of Cane Mola. Mr. Graham told him he would get what he ordered only at Code's feed store. Upon returning to Code's, the embarrassed boy once again became tangled and ordered Coca-Cola. He returned home in disgust without the molasses.

* * *

Whatever the failures amounted to, there were successes and the boys learned much. The ventures taught them both the lessons of industry and self-reliance — not that Grant required much instruction in that direction. They also learned the fact that money does not grow on trees. There again he needed little guidance — as he said himself, "I have always had an abnormal respect for the dollar." The respect for frugality would persist during the remainder of his life despite changes in fortune for the better.

Chapter 6

Willa MacPherson — Catalytic Agent

The year 1918 was to be an eventful one in the life of the young farm boy. Indeed it, and the two succeeding years, would give rise to events of fundamental importance which would alter the shape and direction of his career.

That summer John Rayner, of the Extension Department of the University of Saskatchewan, visited Melfort to conduct courses in weed identification and livestock judging for young farmers. Each day during lectures, Grant walked to town to learn all he could and he was one of the three top students chosen by the Melfort Agricultural Society (in which his father was later to play a leading part) to attend the Farm Boys' Camp at the Regina Exhibition. "The Fordson was idle for one whole week and thankful I was to be away from it," he said.

At Regina, military movements were the order of the day and "the poor farm boys were drilled and marched beyond all reason," but regimentation was a small price to pay and was to be overshadowed by the main purpose of the camp. He scored highest in the weed competitions and stood near the top in horse and cattle judging, bringing honor to the Melfort team.

Most of his spare time was spent in the barn housing the beef cattle entries, and it was there he saw Beau Perfection 47th, owned by the Curtis Cattle Company. He was attracted by the beast's conformation and general appearance, his youthful judgment proving sound when Beau Perfection worked his way through the preliminaries and was awarded the Grand Championship ribbon for Hereford bulls. By that time the owner, Curtis Martin, had been attracted by the tall young lad from Melfort who seemed

Above: Grant and Willa pose for the camera   *(MacEwan Collection)*

Right: Dean W. J. Rutherford
(University of Saskatchewan Archives)

honored to perform the smallest tasks about the animal's stall. He met Grant and shook his hand. On the final day when the champions were paraded before the Regina grandstand, it was Grant MacEwan, a few days before his sixteenth birthday, who had been chosen to lead Beau Perfection before the largest crowd he had ever seen. In the years to come he would play other parts in such parades.

* * *

That one experience was enough to lift the camp out of the ordinary for any boy, but there was yet another that would prove to be of fundamental importance in his outlook for the remainder of his life. On the last day of camp the boys were taken on a tour of the legislative buildings. In the legislative chambers they were permitted to sit in the seats of the members where they were to hear an address from the dean of agriculture of the University of Saskatchewan.

Grant chose the seat of G. B. Johnston, the sitting member for Melfort, and waited expectantly to see a man measuring up to the impressive title of Dean, speaking on the subject of agriulture. Later, he recalled that there were two surprises in store for him — the speaker wasn't big and husky and he didn't say anything about farming. In Grant's own words:

It was assembled in those buildings that I first saw and heard Dean [W. J.] Rutherford of Saskatoon. He talked for a few minutes on a topic I have not forgotten. A lot of water has passed under the bridge and a lot of topics and addresses have been heard and forgotten, but Dean Rutherford's text lingers green within my memory. It has lost none of its value and loftiness in the years. Few texts could be found more suitable for a talk to a bunch of boys and indeed I have used it myself a few times. It was this: "The boy increased in wisdom and in stature, and in favor with God and man."

Grant MacEwan had listened to a man who would prove to be one of the formative influences in his life. He left the building that day resolved to emulate the boy in Dean Rutherford's text, to grow in mind, spirit, and body, and to make the text a governing principle in his life.

On November 2, 1918, a parcel arrived at the Melfort post office addressed to Grant MacEwan, from Eaton's mail order office in Winnipeg. It was a great moment in his life as he carried it home and unwrapped his first pair of long pants.

*   *   *

The year proved to be an outstanding one on the farm. They harvested one of their largest crops and, although the grade could have been better, at wartime prices it brought close to $6,000 into the MacEwan coffers. This figure did not include income from eggs, poultry, livestock, and the sale of surplus hay.

Not long afterwards, on November 11, 1918, Armistice was declared. The War was over.

*   *   *

Had the young aspiring farmer needed samples of the harsh reverses the Prairies would deal him from time to time if he continued to farm, he experienced them in the first year of peace. As if to test him, Nature threw everything she had at the western farmer, and the MacEwan farm suffered with the rest.

In 1919, following the success of the preceding year, the MacEwans sowed the biggest crop in their short history in Melfort, doing everything that was humanly possible to assure a successful outcome. The land had been carefully prepared; they purchased the best wheat seed they could find, paying the bonus for registered seed; they were on the land early and had all crops in — 198 acres of wheat, 40 acres of oats and 10 acres of barley — early enough to catch the first spring rains.

The rains did not come. Only half the seed managed to germinate and thrust slender shoots above ground. Then in early July, one of the heaviest hailstorms ever experienced in the district, with hailstones the size of hen's eggs, cut down whatever shoots had managed to pierce the parched earth.

Nature began its cruel cat and mouse game. Following the hailstorms, the prolonged drought appeared to end and periodic showers alternating with hot sunny weather surprisingly germinated kernels that had lain dormant until then. It seemed likely the grain that had been cut off by hail would be replaced by a crop that grew rapidly under ideal conditions. To the experienced eye it held promise of yielding eighteen or twenty bushels to the acre.

However, the promise did not materialize; rust attacked the fields. By August 20, the MacEwans had plowed down about half of the headless straw the scourge had left standing. They then turned to the oats and barley which would at least provide feed for the livestock, and cut it. However, before they could gather the newly cut sheaves, late rains bedeviled them, preventing the crop from being threshed; so it lay in the fields.

There it stayed, as winter arrived early that year and the rains turned into snow, burying the whole district for miles around to a depth of four inches, to be added to throughout a bitter winter. They were forced to thresh what little they could by use of sleighs.

That year the only potatoes they ate were those lifted from the frozen ground by crowbar, the old pickax Grant had brought from Brandon, and a shovel.

If more were needed to cap a cheerless fall, news came that Grant's inspiration and the man he venerated, Grandfather John Walter Grant, had died at his son James's home in Brandon.

They had taken in close to $6,000 from the fields the previous year and now they did well to scrape $1,000 from the land. Chicken, egg, and milk money supported their existence. They had been hit by drought, hail, rust, late rains, early freeze-up, heavy snow and a bitter winter — but Grant MacEwan was to be tested even further in other ways.

* * *

Postwar influenza had swept the world like a forest fire, flaring up and dying down, only to flare up elsewhere. In the winter of 1919-20, the epidemic swept into the Melfort district and both Alex and Bertha MacEwan were stricken. The two boys were left to care for their parents and run the farm, which had by now a large herd of Aberdeen Angus cattle. With George still attending school, the main responsibility fell on Grant's shoulders.

One tumultuous March night, when the weather appeared intent on getting in the last cruel licks of a bitter winter, Alex appeared near death. His ailment was accompanied by excruciating headaches, forcing groans of anguish even from him. The doctor had prescribed headache powders but the supply was exhausted. Alex became delirious.

Leaving George at home to feed the fires, Grant fought his way through six-foot drifts to the stables where he harnessed a team for a trip to Melfort in search of help. The willing beasts floundered out of the farmyard, but when Grant turned them into the teeth of a furious nor'wester, they insisted on turning away and putting their tails to it. Forced to take pity, Grant yielded, returning them to the barn where he unharnessed and gave them a double ration of oats for their noble effort. He then set out on foot to summon a doctor and replenish the supply of medicine.

Where his own feats and accomplishments are concerned, Grant MacEwan is deceptively brief, tending more to flippant dismissal as if speaking of the ordinary. When asked about his eight-mile journey on foot breaking trail through a blizzard horses could not face, characteristic understatement is clearly revealed. "I wondered once or twice if I was going to make it," he said. Make it he did, and with medicine Alex lapsed into merciful sleep and, although still pronounced gravely ill by Dr. Hawke, he was out of danger. Bertha was much improved by the time the good doctor was able to fight his way to the farm with horses and cutter the following day.

Ill luck dogged them to the end when, in early spring, faithful Polly, the milk cow, dried up and was sold for slaughter.

From what had been a most trying and dispiriting winter and spring, the MacEwans and their eldest son were left only two pleasant memories. Telephone service became available early in 1920, and with the dreadful isolation of the winter fresh in their minds, the MacEwans were among the first farmers to install a telephone. At one stroke they were linked to nineteen neighbors on the party line, and through Central in Melfort, with the rest of the country.

That same spring another symbol of coming manhood arrived by parcel post for Grant MacEwan. It was a Maple Leaf Dollar Special pocket watch, guaranteed for one year. It greatly pleased the young man, for even at that early age, he had developed a healthy respect for time and a critical attitude toward the tardy.

* * *

The year 1920 was to prove much kinder to the fortunes of the MacEwans than the previous one had been. It was also to introduce into Grant's life an experience, brief though it was, that would have an important influence on the future course of his life.

Work was never ending, but was taking on a different character. The back-breaking chore of hacking a farm out of bush-covered land was almost finished and it was more a matter of operating a farm that was now a going concern. All the land had been cleared and broken, so much so that in future it would be necessary for Alex to negotiate with neighbors to go on to their land and cut firewood. The only trees standing were those left for the purposes of shelter, windbreaking, and appearance.

As he had done in Brandon, Alex MacEwan was building a reputation for his purebred cattle but this time Grant shared some of the honor. The feeder cattle he had purchased the previous fall had been left in Grant's care during a visit Alex had paid to Brandon and later, out of necessity, during his prolonged bout with the 'flu. The boy had managed well, for in the spring they were fat and fit, averaging 1,500 pounds each, and were sold at a good profit. That summer Grant showed MacEwan cattle at the Melfort Fair and came away with first prize for a herd of four — his first recorded victory in the show ring.

The crop was early, and a good one, without a touch of frost. Despite falling postwar prices, the yield from grains alone brought in over $5,000. This position of relative plenty, coming on the heels of a disastrous year, was to be marked by music, when at Christmas the MacEwans awoke to strains coming from a brand-new Edison Victrola, Alex's surprise for the family.

However, the biggest surprise as far as Grant was concerned, came in the form of Willa MacPherson, who arrived in Melfort with the spring in 1920. Snow was still on the ground, but her visit would last far into the hot summer months, much to his satisfaction.

Willa was the daughter of Alex MacEwan's sister. Her mother had married a man who became a successful executive in the National American Biscuit Company and she moved with him to the United States where Willa was born. Mrs. MacPherson died prematurely, leaving her husband with a growing daughter. Mr. MacPherson also died young and Willa, with a small competence, was returned to Canada to live at the MacEwan home in Guelph, visiting whatever relatives she had across Canada in the process.

Willa MacPherson was everything a young man could want. Contemporary photographs show her as tall, willowy, and though perhaps not beautiful, most certainly pleasant for a man to look at. She was energetic, vital, and full of fun, being ready at a moment's notice to don moccasins and go snowshoeing, to take long rambles through fields and forests bursting with new leaves, searching for the first wood violets, playing tag in the meadow and ending up wrestling tomboy fashion in a stack midst peals of laughter and flying handfuls of hay. The girl was an entirely new experience for the eighteen-year-old farm boy.

It was not that Grant had been blind to the attractions of the opposite sex before that. Indeed, he was as active in that respect as any other farm boy in the district, which wasn't saying much, as work and distance conspired to reduce the possibilities of socializing to a minimum. Still, there were occasions — such as the time of his first kiss. It was after a box social at Silver Park school one winter night. He had bid on Mamie Argall's box and won the honor of eating lunch with her and seeing her home. It was one of those fairy-tale frosty nights when the full moon was so bright it cast shadows on the diamond-speckled snow. As their horse ambled along, drawing their cutter through the milky-blue frost haze, the two were warmly wrapped together in blankets and buffalo robe. Too soon the horse turned in to the farm where Mamie was staying. A long pause followed as the beast rested, puffing steam into the midnight air. It was then that Mamie Argall gave Grant MacEwan his first kiss. The brief contact short-circuited his nerves and he tingled from head to toe. "I would have married her on the spot," he recalled. That had been three years before Willa. The farm had kept Grant busy, and the bachelors in the district who were in a better position than he, kept Mamie busy. The one magic night with her had been the only one.

Willa MacPherson was a different matter. She came to the MacEwan household imbued with the mystery and manners of the distant United States, using an unusual inflection here, an attractively different phrase there. More important, she was staying in Grant's own home, seated across the table from him at mealtime. It was an unsettling experience which set in motion an entirely new train of thought for the otherwise serious-minded young farmer.

As it had been in Mamie's case, so it was with Willa. Eligible bachelors in the district were also attracted to this fun-loving and unaffected girl who took an active interest in all that went on about her, and they came calling. It was their right, for they were not blood relatives and girls were scarce. Five bachelors to one eligible maiden was the usual ratio. Blood relationship notwithstanding, Willa MacPherson's presence taught Grant MacEwan the meaning of jealousy. It also produced one overriding thought in his youthful mind that had never occurred before: if a man were to "leave his father and mother and cleave to his wife" he had better have a place prepared to receive her.

*   *   *

Grant MacEwan had much to think about following Willa's departure for Guelph. His work was well suited to thought as he drove the tractor on its endless rounds in the field, and his mind was more and more occupied by thoughts that doubtlessly would have occurred eventually but were there now, with Willa the catalytic agent.

By May he had formulated a plan. But he waited until spring seeding, with all its pressures and long hours, was completed before approaching Alex. In the barn one evening, as they stabled the horses, he finally spoke to his father, blurting out his plan and supporting arguments in a tumble of words as Alex stood in the growing dusk, listening silently.

He was ready to go on his own — indeed, he was one year older than Alex had been when he first set out for the far West — and he had proven himself capable of looking after land and animals. He had a little money in the bank to make a start, and if Alex would let him have the northwest quarter section (he chose neither the best, nor the worst), he could buy a nearby quarter from the Hudson's Bay Company, develop it, and pay both Alex and the company off from the proceeds of his own operation in a few years. George was now fifteen and finished with his schooling and would replace Grant as his father's assistant on the MacEwan place. The need was urgent, or the elder son would not have asked.

His father's answer was simple, short, direct, and unequivocal. "No," he said, and walked into the house without giving reasons or inviting further discussion. As far as Alex was concerned, the matter was closed. It was not for Grant. The collapse of his plan was to have far-reaching consequences.

In the weeks following, there were no recriminations, sulks or confrontations from the youth. Grant, too, had inherited his fair share of Highland Scottish aversion to unseemly displays of deep inner feelings, and he went about the daily routine much as before. All appeared the same on the surface, but there was great activity in the boy's mind. He did not agree with Alex but he accepted his decision and went on from there. He had inherited other traits including a full measure of self-confidence that had been strengthened in the atmosphere of self-reliance imposed on him by the farmstead, and a buoyant spirit. With all this, and with God's help through prayer, a way would be found perhaps in an entirely new direction. Whatever he thought of his father's attitude, filial piety sealed his lips.

However, once having been refused land, he would henceforth never lose the desire to possess it.

* * *

Family life at Melfort continued that summer without rupture. Conditions were good and were to remain so until they had harvested the best crop seen in the district since the bonanza of 1915. The MacEwan farm advanced a step into the machine age when Alex traded the Fordson tractor plus $1,100 for a brand-new tractor and a Model T Ford car for the family. The car revolutionized social life on the farm, extending horizons greatly. On a memorable day, August 4, 1921, Grant drove his mother, Mrs. Ted Frank, and George on a blueberry picking excursion, thirty miles north to Star City and back — in the same day! With horses the trip would have taken at least two and possibly three days. The following day he began building a garage.

* * *

Attractive addition to life though it was, the new car was not sufficient to distract Grant's mind from his main problem. Quietly on his own, he had canvassed the situation and come to a conclusion. Working the land was not to be his destiny. He would take further education in the field of agriculture and trust to God to guide him from there on. The boy would "increase in wisdom and stature and in favor with God and man."

It had not been an easy matter to resolve. Grant had been six years out of school and needed high school to continue on to higher education. He was not about to return to school, a six-foot-three young man among immature boys and girls, to get it. The best that prairie universities could offer, he discovered, was a short course or "associate" course in agriculture at Saskatchewan and Manitoba. It was a two-year course only, and ended with the award of a certificate, but no bridge existed between it and the degree course which was a secret ambition best kept to himself for the moment. Although they usually took their advice and usually profited from it when they did, it was customary for western Canadian farmers to look upon men with university degrees in agriculture with something akin to amused derision. In the farmers' eyes, they were "white-shirted agriculturists" — many fine and unselfish men among them, mind you, but figures of fun none the less. For that reason, Grant kept his full plan to himself.

For that matter, he could not with certainty conclude that he actually would be able to achieve a university degree, for the road ahead was formidably steep. He had learned through the mails that the Ontario Agricultural College (OAC) also offered an associate course leading to a certificate, but there was a bridge at the end. Those in the associate course who achieved a very high standard in their final examinations were permitted to continue in what OAC called an "intermediate" year, wherein they could cram the four years of high school they had missed into one. If they did so, and passed with a set standard, they could then enter a course

Melfort as it looked in early 1900s   *(Saskatchewan Archives)*

leading to a Bachelor of Science in Agriculture degree, with credit for certain classes taken during their earlier years. It was a possibility designed for just such farm boys as Grant MacEwan who, because of their remoteness from secondary education facilities, had missed high school and could not qualify for entrance straight into the degree course. Indeed, Dean Rutherford himself had been a beneficiary of the arrangement one year before Grant was born. It offered a challenge MacEwan was eager to take.

It was also not an inconsiderable coincidence that OAC was situated in Guelph — where Willa MacPherson now lived.

*   *   *

Grant broke the news to the family on September 12, 1921, and recorded the fact in his journal, which now becomes studded with fuller, more discursive entries. Whether to ease the news that he planned leaving the farm, to leave the door open in case the intermediate year proved too much for him, to avoid community ridicule on aspiring to the position of "white-shirted agriculturist" or a combination of all, he let it be known only that his plan was to take the two-year associate course at Guelph.

The reaction of the family upon hearing the news was neither one of opposition nor of great jubilation. If he were to go on for higher education in agriculture, Bertha saw her hopes of having a clergyman in the family fade. Alex tended to share the community's view of agriculturists, but the boy was taking an associate course, so he went along with the plan.

Having made his decision, Grant MacEwan went about implementing it, showing signs of an ability to get about the country efficiently and cheaply — an ability that would serve him well for the rest of his life. Foraging about the community, he learned that Malcolm MacPhail was shipping a carload of cattle to Toronto stockyards and he applied for the job of herdsman. Shipping regulations required that such a person accompany livestock to tend to them during the long train trip. MacPhail gave him the job and Grant traveled free to eastern Canada.

When the stock train pulled out of Melfort, Grant carried with him nothing but a "telescope" suitcase that was adjustable in length as its contents diminished. It contained enough food for the trip, an extra shirt, a pair of socks, and a pair of cheap dress boots "which gave me pain every time I moved." The only suit of clothes he had was the one he stood up in. He would eventually buy another "that never fitted me" at Eaton's store in Toronto, along with "a hat 10 years out of date."

His bank account in Melfort's Bank of Commerce remained untouched, to draw upon if necessary, but he left town with $20 in his pocket and a cheque from his father for $100 to cover fees and board and room for the first part of the year. All in all, he had estimated that the full year would cost him somewhere in the neighborhood of $400.

As the father and the cattle drover stood watching the train disappear down the track, MacPhail turned to Alex and said: "Well, there he goes to that Eastern college — and he'll come back a damned fool."

Chapter 7

A Freshman at OAC

Had he chosen the right college? How was a farm boy from the far West to fit into the campus of an old and established eastern institution? Questions and doubts flooded his mind upon his arrival.

It was an awe-inspiring sight, his initial view of Ontario Agricultural College, and he had momentary qualms when he first turned into the campus from Dundas Road. Long, tree-lined avenues curved up to the main building at the foot of which was situated a geometrically arranged fountain flowerbed. Rows of tall trees embraced playing fields and tennis courts, and between the greenery and rising above it, he could see in the vast expanse of lawn and shrubbery, Victorian residence buildings three stories high, laboratories, professors' halls, greenhouses, farm buildings, silos, and the tallest water tower he had ever seen.

For a brief moment, Grant MacEwan experienced a sudden flood of homesickness amidst these strange surroundings, yearning to be back in Melfort close to his own familiar fields, trees, and livestock. The feeling soon passed and he was drawn into his new environment.

No evidence appears in his journal to suggest that he doubted his choice of college apart from that one fleeting moment. Indeed, it seemed that OAC could not have been better suited to his needs and temperament had it been specifically tailored for him. The college had been founded in 1874 to teach sons of farmers practical farming and, a few years later, their daughters in domestic science. Later on it moved in the direction of the academic and, being an affiliate of the University of Toronto, offered degree courses, the degrees being those of the latter institution.

The year MacEwan registered was a watershed year for the college. President George C. Creelman, who had governed policy since 1904, ended his term of service and handed control to Joseph B. Reynolds. During the Creelman regime the relationship between college and farmer remained close and very active. His extension policy, an extroverted one, took the college out into the country, or brought farmers in to the campus at every opportunity. On the other hand, the new president emphasized the scientific and academic. While the extension program did not suffer, the merits of independent research and scientific method were brought to the fore.

MacEwan soon found himself drawn into an active round of registration, initiation, and familiarization with the schedule of the associate course. It was of two years' duration and consisted of practical farm training on a truly farm timetable.

* * *

Journal entries, made in the heat of the moment, recall some of the atmosphere on campus in the 1920s and reveal Grant's early introduction to the ways of college life: **September:** "Enrolled at OAC. Paid $63.00. Took up residence at 32 Upper Hunt at old residence. Wilf Weber of Wallaceburg is my roommate, He is a degree man and I 'just' an associate." **October:** "Freshman initiation a brutal affair. We received the roughest initiation in the history of the college." **October:** "having a difficult time to make my restricted clothing take care of me. Two pairs of sox are hardly enough for a man."

There were difficult moments arising from the incompatibility of Grant's sleeping habits with the exigencies of campus life. All his life he would object to sleeping in anything but his own skin and, despite the occasional embarrassing moment, would refuse to do otherwise. When the campus initiation committee demanded that all freshmen present themselves suitably attired for a pajama parade through the streets of Guelph, he wrote:

This presented a dilemma for me because I did not own pajamas. Under the circumstances, I was informed I could wear a nightgown. But I didn't own one of those either. However roommate Wilf Weber, who was much shorter, came to the rescue; he had two nightgowns and would lend me one. His nightgown on my long body resulted in more exposure than the streets of Guelph had seen to that date, but I got away with it.

The students enjoyed self-government, a full sports program, with many opportunities for mixing at informal activities such as toboggan and skating parties, hay rides and campfire gatherings, church socials and others. There was also ample opportunity to take part in religious activities, and it was at Guelph that Grant was first introduced to the Student Christian Movement, in which he was to take an active part. In addition, most disciplines taught at OAC had formed societies, the purpose of which was to bring faculty, outside scholars, and students together away from the

MacEwan pinning "house to rent" sign on Macdonald Hall, the women's residence at OAC, with the support of men-about-the-campus   *(MacEwan Collection)*

classroom to further their knowledge of the subject in a more social atmosphere. The Animal Husbandry Society was one such group and in this, too, MacEwan took a part.

OAC offered MacEwan the chance to continue his education; it offered him the opportunity to live on campus and partake to the full in residence life, the sports program, and the social life — with seemingly throngs of charming girls for company. In short, the farm boy from Melfort found at Guelph everything he had dreamed college life could provide. He plunged into every aspect of campus life with all his zeal, talent, and energy.

It is just as well that he had been stricken dumb by the emotions Willa MacPherson had unconsciously given rise to during her visit to Melfort, for had he declared his feelings at the time he would now have found himself in need of a diplomatic retraction. Although they would continue dear friends and relatives and would see one another when Grant visited the MacEwans in Guelph, in one week they had been thrust into two different worlds, miles apart.

*   *   *

With the same intense application of energy which had become a MacEwan characteristic in the Melfort homesteading days, he now sought to extract every last drop of experience from college life. In later years he confessed: "I tried everything once." Whether it was the value he placed on hard-won dollars or determination to do the best he could in his classes —

or a combination of the two — he had little difficulty in discarding the more expensive campus frivolities for the more productive pursuits. This did not necessarily mean the total exclusion of fun, for he was to enjoy his full share of that while managing to keep it securely in a subordinate place on his list of priorities.

Whenever he found a spare moment, he put it to good use in ranging the countryside wherever there was good farming and good livestock to inspect. Once having made the acquaintance of a first-class herd sire, he would never forget it, A series of journal entries begun when the main body of students were away on Christmas holidays and continued into the 1922 term reveal such activities combined with others:

Jan, 2, 1922 — Box of Mother's homemade candy from home. Along with McIntyre of Chilliwack, BC, I walked out to Jas. Bowman's farm and saw his Angus cattle. Saw the bulls Prince of Good Hope, Rosadore Lad, and Elm Park Elford.

Jan 3. — Back to College. Paid $47.00 in college fees. Along with Irene Carter I saw the picture *The Four Horsemen of Apocalypse*. I have been nursing a sick eye for several weeks, must continue to wear a shield on it. Have two ulcers on my right eye and Doc W. O. Stewart, the college doctor has certainly not helped it any.

Jan. 5 — With Beatrice Byers I saw Ralph Connor's *Sky Pilot* on the screen. Very good.

Jan. 9 — At a box social at Chalmer's Church I got a box belonging to Jean McPhail.

Jan. 10 — First of a two-day break in classes on account of the Experimental Union (a faculty symposium). Bill Dyer, "Alkali" Bill Reaves and I walked out to Gordon Auld's farm to see the cattle. We were impressed by the red Browndale Monarch and the roan Ambassador by Burnbrae Sultan. Told that Burnbrae Sultan weighed 3,000 pounds at the time of his win at Chicago.

Jan. 11 — Reaves, Wilson, Dyer, Lawrence and I walked out to J. J. Elliott's farm to see the $30,000.00 Millhills Comet. It was a 14-mile trip out and back and by the time we got back we were ravenously hungry. All we had on the tramp was one frozen turnip, which agreed with me but gave the other boys a bad attack of diarrhea. Elliott has 80 head of Shorthorns. Millhills Comet is a grand individual and his other bull Maxwalton Manager by Revolution, is also very good.

Jan. 16 — At Brooklin Young Peoples meeting. Took the shield from my sick eye.

Jan. 23 — Gave my first class speech — Topic "The International Livestock Show of 1921." At Young People Society at Congregational Church.

Jan. 27 — Out with Jean McPhail.

Jan. 30 — Cheque for $100.00 from home.

Feb. 1 — Paid board for February — $22.00. Our year beat the Third year at Volleyball. I was playing.

Feb. 4 — Tobogganing behind Mac Hall. The hill is icy and dangerous.

Feb. 6 — Skating at Royal Rink, auspices of Chalmers YPS.

Feb. 7 — The Girls Club held a sleighing party. Lasted two hours and we went to Mr. and Mrs. Benam's home for lunch. The evening's events were quite respectable until Monahan bit his girl's seat and caused tears to flow. But she should have known better than to sit on a man's head.

Feb. 11 — *Annonias and Doughnuts* was the topic of a skit put on at the Delphi Lit by Tubby Felton, Vic Elton, Shorty Kerstine and myself. Word from home reports purchase of two Aberdeen Angus cows from Billie Wood. Received cheque of $40.00 from Spry School Board for work I did last summer. Didn't expect it.

Feb. 11 — Took part in inter-year judging competition. Got second in beef cattle.

Feb. 16 — At Prof. Baker's for supper. [Baker was professor of entomology and zoology. His home was to become a home away from home to Grant.]

Feb. 18 — Cavers and I out for stroll with Dorothy Bruce and Jean McPhail. Took some snapshots.

Feb. 21 — At practice for mock trial at Chalmers YPS.

Feb. 25 — Saw a carcass demonstration in which a choice carcass from a well-bred steer and one from an ill-bred cuss were cut up. [The instructive impact of the demonstration was to be remembered and to be put to use years later.]

Mar. 2 — Executive of the College YMCA on which I serve was invited to spend the evening at Mrs. Galbraith's rooms. We had to be accompanied by an inmate of Macdonald Hall so I took Miss Sloan. Very good time and champion grub. I can't get my collar off tonight so may have to sleep with it on.

Mar. 11 — At athletic concert supervised by Musgrove.

Mar. 13 — The poultry department has about 2,700 spring chickens, 1,000 of them since Feb. 4.

Mar. 14 — Got bushel of OAC No. 3 oats from New Liskard. These early oats should do all right in Northern Saskatchewan.

Mar. 15 — At Animal Husbandry Club to hear Prof. Geo. Day.

Mar. 16 — At Annual Indoor Athletic Meet. Was second in hitch and kick. I kicked 7' 11" and the winner 8' 2". Appointed to Initiation Committee for next fall.

Mar. 18 — [a Saturday] — Bill Reaves and I caught 12.30 bus for Elora. We visited J. A. Watts farm first of all and saw the great old bull Gainsford Marquis now in his 13th year. He has outstanding width and size and still looks very well. Weighed 2,785 pounds when he won the Grand Championship at Toronto in 1917. Were attracted by Lawfton Toff, an imported 2-year-old, and Fairlawn Red Lion an imported 5-year-old. Visited Alex Watts herd and then Gearry Bros. — returned to Guelph by bus at 7.30 pm.

Mar. 21 — Vicious snowball fight between 1st and 2nd years.

Mar. 23 — Elected vice-president of my year for coming season.

Mar. 31 — Lectures stopped. Went down to the MacEwan house and made a trunk out of a box. [He had a bag of oats to take back with him.]

Apr. 3-12 — Wrote exams on Soil Physics, Farm Engineering, Zoology, Rural Sociology, Mechanical Drawing, Literature, Horticulture, Field Husbandry, Farm Economics, Mechanics and Hydrostatics, Materia Medica, Chemistry, Geology and Animal Husbandry.

Apr. 12 — Ticket for home $56.75. Left at 7.45 pm.

On the way home he made a brief stopover at Brandon and, as was his nature, every hour was accounted for. He visited all the relatives; inspected livestock; attended services at Humesville Church; sheared sheep for his uncle Jim Grant; attended a missionary thank offering.

He arrived in Melfort at five-thirty in the morning; walked out to the farm; strode into the house as Bertha and Alex were eating breakfast;

deposited his suitcase on the floor and greeted them. George had just got up and was "too sleepy to be even friendly."

* * *

Spring work had begun in earnest and Grant changed clothing and was back on the tractor working the Melfort farm. He planted thirty-one test plots with OAC seed he had brought with him. All but one plot failed to produce satisfactory crops and that plot was the one seeded to OAC No. 3 oats — Alex was to make good use of this early-maturing feed crop in the years to come.

Thus the summer went by following his first year away from college, almost as it had in preceding years with one exception, the livestock. His opinion was being sought out. He advised a neighbor, at his request, on a flock of sheep the man was considering buying and he took some of the MacEwan Angus cattle into the Melfort Fair for showing. On August 14, 1922, he drove D. N. Jameson to the Tisdale Fair, where Jameson was to judge cattle, sheep, and swine. Jameson invited MacEwan to share the task of placing the livestock and thus it was at the Tisdale Fair that Grant MacEwan did his first real public judging of livestock outside the school.

* * *

In the fall of 1922 MacEwan's second year at college took on the same shape as before, allowing for events which were the natural result of scholarly evolution. However, there was one exception toward the end of the year when he faced the possibility of a break with the family at Melfort.

To prepare for the year, he discarded the short mackinaw he had worn the previous winter and bought his first long coat in Toronto for $18. In the annual flag fight between the freshmen and sophomores, Grant's sophomores took the flag in eight minutes. On another occasion in an inter-year battle he came out with a bruised hand, a cut head, black eye "and a general soaking." However, the blasé sophomores did more than fight with the freshmen — as all old-timers at any college were wont to do, the second-year students made a great thing studying "the incoming crop of freshettes." Following a freshman reception dance at Macdonald Hall, Grant carried out an operation somewhat different from his usual activities and narrowed the field down to three, one of whom came from Indian Head, Saskatchewan, and "looks very likely to me," he confided to his journal.

The year before, he had been selected by fellow students for executive office and this continued the second year when, among other positions, he was elected secretary of the Animal Husbandry Club. He also began to show ability in sports, placing in the pole vault at a track and field meet and winning the position of center on OAC's second-string basketball team. Active though he was in all that went on at campus — including a raid on the college orchard for apples during which he came within an ace of being caught — his studies were never neglected, and at Christmas examinations

Grant as mustache-wearing OAC senior basketballer with 1924 Intercollegiate Championship winners — MacEwan on extreme left beside J. E. Ridley   *(MacEwan Collection)*

he wrote fourteen papers and came out with an average of sixty-seven, standing fifth in a class of thirty-four.

Typical of young men in his stage of development he began to show evidence of a desire to shape his own destiny. For a time it manifested itself in the form of a mustache. However, a journal entry for February 14, 1923, states simply, "I cut off my mustache. Regrets." In similar fashion, he began toying with the spelling of his surname and wondering if a "Mac" wouldn't look better than a "Mc" as it had been spelled up to then.

*   *   *

At the beginning of the last half of the 1922-23 term, he considered his position relative to the family at home. Was he to reveal his secret plan to continue on to a degree in agriculture if OAC officials accepted him into the intermediate year? Was he to return home summer after summer to work on the farm, or should he consider broadening his experience by seeking work elsewhere? He did a lot of thinking and praying for guidance over these questions, for it could amount to a break with the family. No matter that George was sixteen, through school and obviously dedicated to the home place, his mother and father were over fifty years of age and could use whatever help he was prepared to give them.

In time he arrived at a conclusion and, for the first time in his life, applied for a job — to the Civil Service Commission as livestock promoter in the Peace River country of Alberta. Nothing came of the application but it was significant for it marked Grant MacEwan's first impulse to move away from the home farm at Melfort.

With heavy heart he wrote a letter informing his parents that he would not be home in time for spring seeding but that he intended staying in eastern Canada for the summer to make enough money for a return to OAC and a degree course. He knew he had done well on the final examinations and, having stood near the top of the associate class at Christmas, he had every right to expect that his application for the intermediate year would be accepted.

He then joined classmates Ian MacKay and Len Cavanaugh to make a killing in the Toronto early potato market as they had planned. MacKay's home farm was at Woodville and there was land to spare. Using all the techniques they had picked up in class, they seeded a large tract of land to potatoes and did all they could to promote early maturing and capture a chunk of the city market.

The venture yielded a return, but owing to unforseen problems, nobody made a killing. Anticipating the gloomy outlook, Grant settled his share of the venture early and took a job selling nursery stock on commission (as his father had done briefly more than thirty years before). He worked for a horticulturist by the name of Howard Downham of Strathroy. His partners in the potato venture did the same, but their efforts failed to pay off in any way similar to those of Grant.

MacEwan bought a 1918 Model A Ford for $150 and started selling — and selling and selling. He never looked back. To his great surprise, he discovered he was a first-class salesman. Having sold as much the first week as the average experienced salesman, his sales record soared each week from then on. Not only was selling profitable but Grant found it enjoyable and so rich in human experience that he began collecting short character sketches in his journal, a habit that would continue throughout his lifetime. In one of his moves throughout the country, he boarded with a woman in Stayner, Ontario, whose husband was "a great character — big, deaf, eats enough for a horse, and drinks enough for a cow."

By the end of July, Grant, having covered all of the most promising territory in his section of the country and with the gardening season pretty well over, decided to call it quits — and well he might. He had made more money than he had ever made in his life; he had ample to cover complete expenses at college the next year with a generous amount to spare. When he reported back to Downham at Strathroy, the owner tried to persuade him to leave school, sign on with him full time, and make his fortune. Grant resisted the temptation, collected his commission, and left with a promise to consider a lucrative offer the following summer. All this was done — but not before Grant had sold the man his Ford car for $150, the same amount he had paid for it at the beginning of summer!

Between the time he left his job and the reopening of the fall term at Guelph, Grant took the offer of a motor trip with a college friend, Tubby

MacEwan back on farm for the summer, "spike pitching," a tough job he particularly enjoyed as a challenge (MacEwan Collection)

Tolton, and his parents to Winnipeg in their Columbian Six — an exceedingly adventurous excursion for the times — a trip from which he extracted all the experience possible. He studied the Americans and their country, swam in the Mississippi River, and toured as much of the Chicago stockyards as he could. Taking a train from Winnipeg, he was back home in Melfort by August 9, well in time for an early harvest. So, having missed seeding in the spring, he arrived in time for the harvest in the fall — he had not quite left home.

*   *   *

On his return to OAC he found that he was one of nine from the associate course to register for the degree course and he also found that he was to have one of the least likely roommates he had drawn to that time. His room was at 300 Mills Hall and his roommate was J. J. Brickley, "a fat Irish Roman Catholic from Marysville, Ontario." It was the long, lean, western Canadian Presbyterian's "biggest worry in going back for this year." There was doubt on both sides whether they could manage together. "The first day was a trying experience, but 'Brick' and I grew to accept one another and then to enjoy each other and ultimately, I had to confess that the association was the richest one in University years."

Not only did the two develop a lasting friendship, but each being the possessor of a strong enterprising streak, they became partners in a number of ventures. Their judgment wasn't always that good, as was shown in the case of their trousers, which they discovered to be worn thin at the same time. The short Easterner and the lanky Westerner went shopping. They called on a clothier and discovered he had two suits of clothes, the same size, that he was anxious to get rid of. After a period of haggling, the two agreed to take both suits if he would cut the price in half. This he did, and the two walked out with a new suit apiece. The only trouble was that they fitted neither. Most important to both — the suits covered them and they were inexpensive.

As the skating season approached, Grant and Brick pooled their resources and bid on the catering service at the rink. They won the bid and went to work. By the end of the season they had made a tidy profit.

*   *   *

In his third term at College, 1923-24, Grant was independent of the family. From that year onward there is no record in his journal of receiving "a letter from home with a cheque for $100.00." News of the family and farm arrived from time to time, including a letter saying that his brother George had registered at the University of Saskatchewan for the associate course in agriculture.

Financial independence from home did not reduce the moral and spiritual advice that came through the mails from his mother. If there were no words of advice in her own hand, then there was often a clipping carrying messages she felt were timely and which Grant valued enough to save and paste in his journal. One such clipping, possibly from *The Presbyterian Record*, dealt with prayer, already firmly established as a source of strength from which he drew regularly as part of his daily existence. The clipping read:

The greatest thing any one can do for God and for man is to pray. The great people of the earth today are the people who pray. I do not mean those who talk about prayer; nor those who say they believe in prayer; nor yet those who can explain about prayer; but I mean those who take time and pray. They have not time. It must be taken from something else. This something else is important. Very important, and pressing, but still less important and less pressing than prayer.

These are the people today who are doing the most for God; in winning souls; in solving problems; in awakening churches; in supplying both men and money for mission posts; in keeping fresh and strong these lives far off in sacrificial service on the foreign field where the thickest fighting is going on. *S. D. GORDON.*

Chapter 8

Final Year at OAC

The intermediate year, 1923-24, at OAC was unlike the first two. It had MacEwan breathing hard at times but it did little to curtail his activities. "The intermediate classes are heavy — there are about 10 of us who were associates taking the year and we are finding it very stiff." Despite the academic load, he donned his first football uniform and made the senior team as lineman. He was also lifted from the second- to first-string OAC basketball team as their jump center for the season, which ended in the winning of the league championship.

Although he had taken a rising position among student government leaders and was destined for more, he was, nevertheless, still "one of the boys." Ample evidence of this fact arose when St. Patrick's Day came along with the associated tomfoolery that had become traditional on campus. Grant and others roped Blewitt, an Irish freshman, into his bed and smuggled him, bed and all, into Macdonald Hall, where they left him beneath a stairwell for the girls to discover in the morning. Visiting privileges at Mac Hall were canceled for a time.

In the inter-year livestock judging competitions he came second in judging pigs and at Christmas he passed all the tough intermediate year examinations with flying colors.

Previous to that time Grant had "played the field" as far as women were concerned, but, possibly because he was now spending his own money and not that of his hard-working parents, his social life took a different turn in 1923-24. At the first victory dance for the football team he met Gladys Eaton from a farm near Campbellford, Ontario, who was a student in domestic science. They were to see much of one another over the

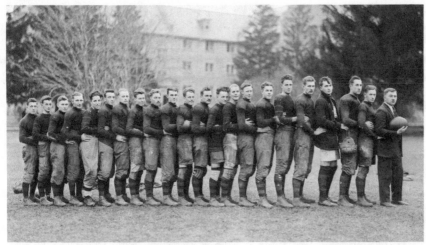

The OAC football team with lineman MacEwan (sixth from right)   *(MacEwan Collection)*

next two years, and although they went out with others from time to time, the young lady from Campbellford had become what could be termed as Grant MacEwan's first steady. However, as in the case of many such college friendships, it came to an end two years later when Gladys left Guelph to take a position in Toronto as a household science consultant for a utilities firm. At the time Grant had one more year of college to put in.

*   *   *

As examinations for the crucial intermediate year neared, when it would be determined who would continue in the degree agricultural course and who would fail, Grant MacEwan received a telegram from home dated March 26, 1924: "George seriously sick. Dad," The next day he received another: "George died last night."

Grant sent a reply: "Leaving tonight."

Brick and other friends in residence looked after his packing while Grant went off to speak to his physics professor and the bursar to notify them of the situation. Clearly the professor, W. C. Blackwood, had been impressed by MacEwan's ability and his contribution to student life and thought it a promising career worth saving, for he allayed any fears about the student's standing in the forthcoming final examinations. He advised him to leave immediately and tend to his familial duties in Melfort while the professor looked after his academic interests at OAC. Aunt Annie and Aunt Aggie came up from town for a short, sad visit. Grant left by train to go to his brother's funeral, four hours after receiving the news.

*   *   *

When their youngest son succumbed to spinal meningitis, the MacEwans were dealt a severe blow. "Mother and Dad are completely

Photographed on a Sunday stroll: (left to right) Bill Young, a young lady from Vernon. B.C., Grant, Gladys Eaton, another young lady   *(Eaton Collection)*

broken, their very life seems snatched from them." Mercifully, spring work was soon upon them, forcing their minds away from the tragedy of the untimely death, and with Grant's help, they managed to seed the crops early that spring.

By this time, Alex and Bertha held an undoubted position in the community and their farm and the line of livestock it supported constituted one of the show places in the district. Alex had become established as a purebred Angus breeder and his cattle sold at a premium for breeding purposes. Indeed, his operations had expanded to the point where, even with George alive and helping, he had to engage two hired men. Established though Alex was, Grant felt he must remain close to home for the summer, and as it happened, the following summer as well.

Word arrived from Guelph that Grant had been awarded full intermediate year standing on the basis of his showing in the Christmas examinations. He was now a degree student. Professor Blackwood had done a good job of looking after his interests at OAC.

*   *   *

Having finished the spring work, Grant saw to it that Alex and Bertha were kept busy enough to keep their minds diverted from George's death as much as possible. He drove his mother about the country to visit friends

Marked for leadership, MacEwan was OAC Students' Council treasurer for the 1923-24 term. (Front row, left to right) MacEwan, F. K. B. Stewart, S. L. Page (president), N. Jones, D. B. Blair: (back row) D. W. E. Donaldson, W. J. A. Stewart, J. Marshall, E. T. Goring, F. Morwick, H. G. Bamforth, J. H. Matthews   (Kennedy Photo, MacEwan Collection)

and packed his father off to Winnipeg on business while he ran the farm.

Neither did he neglect his own career and, to earn money for the following year at OAC, he signed on with the Rural Municipality of Star City as weed inspector for five dollars a day. He was later to declare that he hadn't been able to eradicate the weeds completely "but we gave them a bad scare." With his three months' pay for weed inspecting, prize money earned showing cattle at the Melfort Fair and his by now firmly established habit of spending only minuscule amounts on himself (that summer "no more than enough to buy a cheap hat"), he returned to Guelph with sufficient cash to see him through the following year.

*   *   *

The pinnacle of success at OAC, the highest ambition any student could aspire to and the one upon which all eyes were focused, was to win a place on the college livestock judging team in the final year of the degree course. When the time came to choose the five who would represent their college at the Toronto Winter Fair and then the Chicago International Exposition, the entire graduating class stepped forward to compete.

In football formation: (Front row, left to right) Ainsley Berry, Jim Simpson, Grant MacEwan, Joe "Brick" Brickley (Grant's roommate), Russ Sneider: (back row) Frank Baird, Ed Bonneyman, Wilf Rogers   *(Eaton Collection)*

An entry in his journal, dated September 14, 1925, records Grant's feelings:

> Beginning today we pursue a position on the OAC livestock judging team to Chicago in no uncertain way. We will first of all take a 10-day tour of livestock establishments in Eastern Ontario. Throughout my college career my hopes have focussed on the Chicago judging team more than anything else and it was this and lower living expenses and tuition that motivated me to OAC rather than some other institutions. Today our senior class, every member of which is keen to make a place on the team, left Guelph in five autos to broaden our knowledge of types and to score among the top five if possible.

This expedition out of Guelph must have been among the most grueling and extended tours of herd inspection and livestock judging of the day. During the first week on the road they visited twenty farms and institutions noted for fine horses, cattle, sheep, and swine. On one record day they paid five such visits and judged at each — handling seven classes at one particular stop. Neither were they through when they stopped for the night, for after supper they gathered in hotel rooms or the lobbies, "giving oral reasons" for the judgments they had made during the day. Wade Toole was their respected coach — "one in a million" — assisted by Jack Steckley, Bill Knox, and George Raithby.

On returning to Guelph, they resumed regular classes but most minds were preoccupied as they waited for word from Wade Toole announcing

OAC International Judging Team 1925-26: (left to right) George Cruickshank, Herb Hannam, Herb Knox, Archie McGugan, Grant MacEwan, Arnold Kennedy, Jim Simpson
(MacEwan Collection)

the team roster. Seven were selected, five regular judges and two spares. Those named were Jim Simpson, Herb Knox, George Cruickshank, Herb Hannam, Archie McGugan, Arnold Kennedy, and a jubilant Grant MacEwan. Further judging was necessary to separate the spares from the regular team. The pressure was even greater and the pace faster on this second round because of the greatly reduced number of contestants.

They set out on the second tour, this time in western Ontario. There were days when Grant could do nothing wrong, other days when nothing went right. "Yesterday my judgment was rotten and I could see my chances of Chicago fading."

On November 11, the day they were to leave to compete at the Toronto Winter Fair, their standing on the team was revealed. Wade Toole gathered the seven together and read out the names of four of the five to be regular judges. The names were: H. A. Knox, G. Y. Cruickshank, J. A. Simpson, and J. W. G. MacEwan. He then tossed a coin to see if Herb Hannam or Archie McGugan would be the fifth man. Archie won the toss.

At the Toronto Royal Winter Fair, OAC competed with teams representing the University of Manitoba and the University of Alberta. Out of a possible 5,000 points, OAC scored 3,861; Manitoba scored 3,745, and Alberta, 3,734. Thus OAC carried off the Farmers' Dairy Trophy, emblematic of the Canadian Intercollegiate championship. Although he won no firsts in any of the classes, MacEwan's scores in each event were consistently high and he came away with the highest aggregate score of all contestants.

From there it was on to Chicago to test their ability in international competition against twenty-two entries from American colleges and universities. The experience is best revealed in a letter Grant wrote home:

> We have been away nearly two weeks now and it will be two weeks before we get back. We have had quite a trip. . . . We went from Guelph to East Lansing, Michigan, where the state university is. We worked there all day Saturday judging hogs, horses, sheep and beef cattle, and travelled all Saturday night to Lafayette, Indiana. That's where Perdue University is. We slept all day Sunday [an understatement for, as was his habit, Grant sought out a church and attended the service] and worked Monday and Tuesday at the university. (The change of diet did little for Coach Wade Toole who developed a bad case of diarrhea aptly described by Bill Knox who said he took enough essence of wild strawberry "to block a sewer.") They have some wonderful stock there. We went from there to Danville by bus and from Danville to Champaign by electric car. We were two days at Champaign [where among other things they traveled with the West Virginia team and judged livestock at Urbana, Illinois State College]. Then to Chicago Thursday evening. Rested Friday (among other things visiting the Lincoln Zoo where Jim Simpson saw the stork and promptly left an order with it) and went into competition Saturday.

It remained for *The Farmers' Advocate* to report the results of the competition and place them in true perspective in its December 17, 1925, issue:

> Every agriculturist has reason to be proud of the record made by the Ontario Agricultural College stock judging team at the judging competition, Chicago, over a period of years. The team this year, coached by Professor Wade Toole, while ranking third, made the highest score yet made by an Ontario Team and besides had the high man. The following resume will be of interest to our readers:
> There were 22 teams in the competition and the scores were the highest ever made. The Ontario team stood 3rd, just 43 points behind the winner out of a possible score of 5,000 and had a score of 4,416 which is the highest score ever made by a Canadian team and was 110 marks more than had ever been made by a Canadian team. The top score of 4,459 made by Oklahoma, was the highest score ever made at Chicago. . . . Ontario produced the high man of the competition, with a score of 924, out of a possible 1,000, which is the highest score ever made at Chicago and had two other men in the first 6, one with a score of 905 and another with a score of 903. No other team ever had three men in the first six with such high scores. . . . The Ontario team consisted of A. McGugan, 924, 1st: H. A. Knox, 905, 4th; J. W. G. MacEwan, 903, 6th; G. Y. Cruickshank, 858 and J. A. Simpson, 826. . . .

Returning to Guelph, the team received a hero's welcome. At the railway station the entire student body, and a good part of the city as well, turned out to meet them. The band played and the victorious judges were carried on sturdy shoulders to waiting cars. They rode through city streets lined with crowds of townspeople who displayed a traditional proprietorial interest in their college and its achievements. The jubilant reception continued on into the night at Mills Hall.

When Grant MacEwan graduated that year, he found that membership on the livestock judging team had lifted his name into national and international prominence in a way no other endeavor could have done. As with most such publicity, it faded in time, but one thing was certain — his name would be remembered where it really counted.

And so it was that talent-scouting teams in search of agriculturists interviewed the graduates, most of whom thought that the highest attainment they could aspire to would be acceptance in government service as a district agricultural representative. MacEwan emerged from the interviews with a firm offer of a job buying livestock for Gunns Limited during the summer and another promise that there would be an opening for him as district representative in Ontario when he returned.

*　*　*

The boy, of whom it had been said "he will return to Melfort a damned fool," returned a champion and his parents were proud of him. On his arrival home, they presented him with a gold Waltham watch in recognition of his graduation on May 28, 1926.

By this time, no one would expect Grant MacEwan to take a well-earned rest, like an ordinary person, after a job well done. He immediately went to work alongside Alex's hired man and then proceeded to fill the summer with a solid round of productive and — mostly — profitable activity, while he waited word from the East.

Col. J. G. Robertson of the Saskatchewan provincial livestock branch invited MacEwan to join the staff on a touring display of three weeks' duration, devoted to cattle improvement. It was made to order. It paid well and meant movement by train about the countryside. He took the job.

*　*　*

It was on such a train that an incident occurred revealing clearly MacEwan's method of living as a young graduate fresh out of college. It was recalled by Tom Devlin, himself to become a widely known judge of good horses and contributor to the advancement of agriculture in western Canada. The trains were staffed by young agronomists full of fun, energy, and mischief. On one occasion, at the end of a long day when most people would be retiring for the night, two of them got into a friendly tussle which ended in a chase through the aisles of the cars. They plunged through the door of the caboose at the end of the train, where the sleeping quarters were located, to find it in darkness — but the chase continued and they tripped over a pair of long bare legs extending across the aisle between the bunks. They were those of Grant MacEwan, who they saw to their amazement was kneeling beside his bunk, so deep in prayer that he had not noticed the invasion. The two tiptoed sheepishly out of the caboose.

Grant MacEwan, B.S.A.   *(MacEwan Collection)*

MacEwan with Bessie Bell of Willowdale Brae, junior champion at Prince Albert Fair, 1925 (MacEwan Collection)

"We all looked at Grant from then on with a deep respect," Devlin recalled years later. "He wasn't one to make much of a show of his inner convictions, and although we knew that he was a good churchman, we hadn't realized to what extent until that night."

* * *

After that job ended, he won $142 and two trophies showing MacEwan cattle at the Melfort Fair and then received an invitation from John Rayner, director of extension, University of Saskatchewan, to judge livestock at summer fairs in southeastern Saskatchewan. He took the job and the Canora Fair, July 26-27, 1926, marked the MacEwan debut as an official judge, the first in what would prove to be hundreds of such occasions spread over more than fifty years.

Judging duties completed, he returned to Melfort to help with the harvest. It was an early one and work was pretty well finished by the end of August. Then a new experience loomed for the young graduate.

* * *

That summer had been one of bitter constitutional crisis involving Governor General Lord Byng and Prime Minister Mackenzie King. A Dominion election was called for in the fall and throughout the country party workers of all persuasions were working diligently.

O. D. Hill, a tireless worker for the Liberals in the Melfort constituency, recruited the, by now, well-known OAC graduate to work for his party. It was a foregone conclusion that his political sympathies lay in that direction, for his father had always been a Liberal supporter. Hill took MacEwan to his first rally at Fairy Glen and from then on Grant played an increasingly important role in the campaign to elect their man, Malcolm MacLean of Eldersley. When the votes were counted MacLean had a majority of approximately 3,000 over his Conservative rival, Herb Keown, and the Pleasant Valley poll where Alex MacEwan was returning officer and Grant was MacLean's agent, produced a majority for the Liberals for the first time in its history. Nationally, King was returned to power with the added support of eleven Liberal-Progressives who swung to his side after the election.

From that point on, Grant waited in vain for word from Conservative Ontario about his appointment as a district agriculturist. Years later he speculated: "I guess word must have got back East that I worked for the wrong party." For whatever reason, the possibility of Grant MacEwan returning to Ontario, and the further possibility of his finding a satisfactory career that would hold him in eastern Canada, was put off for good. His career was to remain in the West and take an entirely different direction.

Chapter 9

Back in Saskatchewan

From an early date Grant MacEwan had a strong sense of mission. Whether it rose from his mother's teaching, Bible reading, his Presbyterian upbringing, memorable and formative utterances of those whom he admired, or a combination of all of these, it would be impossible to say.

One thing is certain — whatever the source of inspiration, he firmly believed that he had been placed on this earth not to indulge himself in "the pursuit of happiness" but to carry out a task legislated for him by a Higher Power, and that it was through prayer that he must seek guidance in order to carry it out. Once having found direction, he would advance, pouring into his efforts the prodigious energy and stamina with which he was blessed.

However, for almost two years following his graduation, he was far from confident. He had made a triumphal return to Melfort and the world seemed to be at his feet. As time wore on and no summons came from out of the East, his future became a matter of concern. There it would remain until a chance meeting on the steps of the Saskatchewan legislative building revealed a new challenge, a new direction. Until then he seemed destined to spend a period of "wandering in the wilderness."

It would be no aimless wandering, despite the lack of direction, for that was not the MacEwan manner. If the way ahead seemed to be enshrouded in fog, it would no doubt clear and, in the meantime, he must make the best of it.

*　　*　　*

Grant worked on the farm and showed MacEwan cattle at fairs with the usual good results. He accepted temporary work with the livestock branch of the provincial government, and moved to Regina, taking a room in a boarding house: "I'm dying for sleep. If the lady next door whose bedroom faces mine would either pull the blind down or go to bed early it would be alright, but no, she won't do either." He coached a junior rugby team: "It is a discouraging business, rugby players in this city appear to believe that to play the game one must drink, and smoke and fight and swear and practice on Sunday mornings."

One lesson he learned and wouldn't soon forget. He began forming a picture of the kind of work he would enjoy doing, as well as the kind he would not. The first few days in Regina, he discovered that the civil service tended to be wastefully overstaffed and that a man trained in animal husbandry could be employed for days on end at the simple task of hanging pictures in the halls of the legislature. He also discovered that he enjoyed the work out in the field but could hardly abide being closed in an office.

Welcome and sometimes comic relief came when he joined a Better Farming Train on tour in the northwestern part of the province. It was staffed by agriculturists of his own bent and there he met men he would come to know well in the years ahead dedicating themselves to the improvement of agriculture: Dunc Stewart, Hugh Ross, O. A. Cooke, Harry Follet, Frank Baker, and Tom Devlin.

A. S. Morton, in his book *Saskatchewan, the Making of a University,* describes the trains and their purpose thus:

> One of the most colourful means of carrying information to the farm population, dating from 1914, was the operation of Better Farming Trains. This could almost literally be called "carrying the College to the country." The trains were equipped jointly by the Saskatchewan Department of Agriculture and the College of Agriculture and operated free of charge by the railways. The technical staff was provided mainly by the College. Each train, usually of fourteen cars and coaches, carried livestock demonstration cars, exhibition cars, displaying farm products and equipment for the farm and home, lecture cars, a nursery car for small children, and sleeping and dining accommodation for the staff. Two or more stops were made each day; a well-organized lecture programme was offered; and the visitors were given an opportunity to look through the exhibition coaches and discuss their particular problems with the staff. The spectacular form of this service attracted large audiences and focussed attention on the problems of agriculture during the years of rapid development on the Prairies. In the first year of the Trains 40,000 people attended over a period of five weeks; in addition two dairy specials, running for two weeks, held 103 meetings and drew 6,500 people.

On a Sunday as the cars stood idle on a railway siding, one of the staff went swimming in a lake separated from the train by a broad open expanse and a distant clump of trees. A prankster among them took his clothing while he was disporting himself, leaving only a pair of boots. In the meantime, a carload of young ladies who had been invited down during the week drove in and parked by the train on the open area, waiting to take several of the young unattached men for a drive. The swimmer, clad only in

A horse demonstration being given from the Better Farming Train
(University of Saskatchewan Archives)

his boots, sought to return to the train, but on seeing the situation, searched desperately for something to cover his nakedness. He eventually emerged from the bushes inside a wooden barrel he had been fortunate to find, clutching the middle loop to hold it in place. Gaining confidence, he made his way past the tittering females. As he approached their car, he came to a full stop, clicked his heels and bowed. The barrel was old, the staves were dry, and with the added strain of his maneuver, they collapsed, leaving him no cover save the middle hoop. He turned tail and ran for the safety of the train, still desperately clutching the useless hoop, for whatever cover it afforded.

*   *   *

During this period, MacEwan's parents had not been far from his thoughts. With the exception of an occasional visit to Brandon, as often as not to attend funerals, neither had enjoyed a real holiday in the twelve years since they arrived at the farm in 1915. As he seemed to be marking time himself, it appeared a most opportune time to suggest they spend the winter "at the Coast" while he looked after the farm. With some difficulty they were persuaded to accept the offer.

It proved to be a bitterly cold winter on the prairies and Grant was left to look after 100 head of livestock. All the cattle were stabled in barns, to which he had to draw feed and water, and from which he had to haul manure and dirty bedding, a difficult job in the best of weather. It was far from a gloomy experience:

Batching is going fine. Meals served at all hours — I baked a pan of biscuits and the dog liked them so well I gave him the entire batch. D. N. Jameson has been here twice for meals. I told him that if he took a good dose of salts prior to one of my meals and another after, chances are that the meal would never hurt him . . . 40

below 0 this morning. When I was through milking — I had a pail full of shreds that looked like macaroni. Each squirt of milk froze before it settled.

The neighbors in the district were all in the same boat and they joined together to make the best of it. The Pleasant Valley Church people put on a play, the title defying the weather — *In Hot Tamale Land* — with Grant playing a leading role. It was a smash hit. Despite the bitter weather, people came from miles around to see it. They took it to Pathlow to show it before standing-room-only crowds and then to Melfort, performing before an audience of 300 in the Melfort Theatre — after which the cast repaired to the Ark Cafe "to await the reviews in the *Melfort Moon!*"

It was during that winter MacEwan first wrote for publication. Toward the end of 1927, J. G. Harvey of the International Harvester Demonstration Farms gave a lecture in Melfort. Grant attended, then "stayed up all night to write the lecture up for the *Melfort Moon.*"

Bertha and Alex returned in the spring looking well and rested. It had been a delightful holiday — save for Alex who, up to his old tricks, took a flier and invested what Bertha thought was an inordinate amount of money in a sure thing. A certain group had cornered a source of "medicinal and cosmetic mud that would bring beauty to the plainest of faces." Alex bought a share in the enterprise, which eventually confirmed Bertha's suspicions about the outcome.

*   *   *

At sixteen, MacEwan had been inspired by the man who spoke to a group of farm boys in the legislative chamber. He was at work with the livestock branch in Regina when one day, on the steps of the same building, he met William John Rutherford, dean of agriculture at the University of Saskatchewan. He instantly recognized the dean. There is little doubt that Rutherford knew MacEwan, for he himself was an old OAC man, a fancier of fine horses, and a livestock judge, and no doubt he would be familiar with the younger man's achievements at Guelph and the Chicago International.

During the short exchange, the subject of future plans came up, the dean wondering if MacEwan had ever entertained the possibility of going on into graduate studies. He explained that there were various ways of doing so if one could qualify. For instance, at Iowa State College — a fine institution with a reputation second to none in the agricultural sciences — where the dean himself had taught upon graduating from OAC, there were fellowships to be applied for from time to time that pretty well covered all fees and living expenses, if a person could find his way there.

The two parted, but the thought remained fixed in MacEwan's mind. Eventually, and with grave doubts, he sent an application to Iowa. He had sent other applications, among them one for the job of assistant superintendent at the Lacombe Experimental Farm, but all to no avail. This would meet with the same response, he felt.

The response was far different than he had expected. Even without evidence, it is not difficult to imagine that Dean Rutherford, old Iowa State man that he was, had had something to do with that difference. (Who could tell? He may even have had designs on MacEwan himself, after he had obtained his Master's degree.)

A letter dated July 19, 1927, lifted the cloud of doubt that had hung over MacEwan for more than a year and gave him direction at last:

"We have been looking over your application for our meat fellowship for the next year. Your recommendations seem to be of the very highest type and we have decided to offer you our meat fellowship if you are still interested in it." The fellowship was worth $540.

(The letter was addressed to "J. W. Grant MacEwan." Up to that time in Guelph correspondence, student and graduate lists, he is "McEwan", without the "a", as his father signed his name. Possibly that change, together with the use of two initials and two surnames, appealed to Grant as being more likely to attract the awarding of fellowships.)

Indeed, MacEwan was "still interested." He sent off his letter of acceptance immediately; served out his term in Regina, quit his job, sold his car to Ed Ridley, and returned to Melfort to help with the harvest. On September 16, he left Melfort for the last time. From then on he would return only to visit.

He was due to arrive in Ames, Iowa, September 22, for the next big adventure.

Chapter 10

Iowa State College

The list of Canadian agrologists who, throughout the years, made their way to what used to be known as the Iowa State College of Agriculture (now the Iowa State University of Science and Technology) must be a long one. It most certainly is an illustrious one, as many of the early policy makers of agriculture in Canada followed a well-worn path from OAC to Ames, Iowa, where the university is located.

Rushed though he was, Grant MacEwan was impressed by his first sight of the university. For the first time, a mix-up occurred in his traveling schedule. To conserve money, he sat up during the long trip through Winnipeg, then south across the state of Minnesota and on to Iowa. When he neared his destination late at night, he left a message with the train conductor to call him at the proper stop to make his way to Ames, north of Des Moines. He then fell into a sound sleep. Some time later he woke with a start to find that he had been carried well beyond his stop. One way or another, he found his way back and arrived somewhat breathless and behind the appointed time. However, his preoccupation with keeping his appointment did not blind him to the beauty of his new surroundings and he was struck by the veritable park which the Iowa State campus constituted. Amid the lush green of broad lawns, trees and shrubbery, stately buildings of white Bedfor stone rose to reach a peak in the form of the far-famed campanile with its chimes of thirty-six bells. He knew immediately that he would enjoy living on the campus. It seemed to be the right move for a person in his position but, at that early date, he could not possibly have anticipated the quandary he would find himself in before the end of the year.

On registering he learned that he would be taking eight hours of lecture a week in meat, two hours in experimental methods, and five in comparative physiology. To get as much as possible out of the year, he also signed up for visiting privileges in biometrics and breeding.

He recorded his first impressions October 10, 1927:

> I like the instructors and fellow students fine. Kildee [Dean of Agriculture who exercised a formative influence on MacEwan], M. D. Helser [chief tutor] and Anderson of A. H. [animal husbandry] staff are all 100%. In our group of Animal Husbandry specialists are Robt. Kay from West of Scotland University, Maurice McSpadden from Oklahoma and nephew of the far-famed Will Rogers, Milton "Doc" Staples of OAC '24, Nathan Jones of South Dakota, Hank Walker from Oregon, Larry Kaufman from State College, Columbus, Ohio, Harms from Oregon.

He roomed with Staples.

Soon the postgraduate students were introduced to the character of their work, and as had become customary, Grant began adding to his records of anecdotes. The one he enjoyed most in the first months involved the fellow student from Oklahoma. Professor Stevenson gave McSpadden a pile of undergraduate test papers to mark over the weekend. On top of the pile he put what he intended to be an example of a perfect paper, for McSpadden's guidance. However, McSpadden, not realizing what had to be done, treated the professor's perfect paper as he treated all the others — marking it and giving the professor 78 marks out of 100!

*   *   *

Although most favorably impressed by the university and its institutions, the churches of the United States failed to make a similar impression, at least at the outset. "Oct. 3, 1927 — I went to church twice today. Tonight I was at Methodist church and heard the Krantz Family Orchestra. It was very good, but anything [from] Yankee Doodle up is called sacred here." He also attended Presbyterian churches and College Chapel, where on one occasion he heard a Roman Catholic archbishop "whose theology and mine, in spite of outward differences, appear to harmonize as far as fundamentals are concerned." President Hughes of Iowa State College spoke at the Thanksgiving service, enumerating his blessings. "First of all I am thankful for faith in a personal God and for the power of prayer. That may seem unscientific but it's like listening to a radio which is giving music from Australia. I can't believe it possible, but it works."

On another occasion, accompanied by fellow student Marie Ringle, he drove to Des Moines where they heard the famed evangelist Aimee Semple McPherson.

> She is one in a million, chuck full of ability and most fascinating. She is only human, however, and her tactics are open to criticism, no doubt. Somehow her manner simply gets you. We were fortunate in being at one of Amie's [sic] healing

services. It was a sight never to be forgotten — a hundred humans, some crippled, some moaning, move over the stage. To all appearances they were cured or helped.

*   *   *

Towards the close of the first quarter of the year, ill health of others involved MacEwan in different ways. Professor Helser was called home through a serious illness in the family and he appointed Grant, from among the graduate students, to carry on with his lectures to undergraduate students, to continue the experimental work they were doing together, to set the Christmas examination paper and mark the results. All this along with his normal load of work!

By putting in eighteen-hour days, he managed to keep ahead of the work, finishing everything three days before Christmas, when he, too, was called away by illness in his family.

He received word that his mother had undergone surgery at home but had continued to ail for some time following the operation. Doctors in Melfort then advised Alex to take the major step to remedy the matter, the ultimate treatment current at the time, and he acted on their advice. He took his wife to the Mayo Clinic in Rochester, New York.

Grant set out for Rochester immediately after completing his extra duties at college. He found his father eating breakfast in the dining room of the hotel in which he was staying. He also discovered in a way never before revealed by his normally undemonstrative Scottish father, Alex's true inner feelings for his son. "Poor old Dad was wild with excitement. He thought I wouldn't be able to make the trip. 'This is my boy, this is my boy' he exclaimed with pride" as he ushered Grant around the room introducing his son to people he had come to know during a prolonged stay.

Grant spent as much time with his mother as the hospital staff would allow and it helped. Upon being reassured that his visit had done the world of good for her and that, although Bertha still looked somewhat pale and wan, she was on the mend, the prognosis was favorable and they were confident of a full recovery, he returned to Ames. On the way, however, he found himself within easy reach of Guelph and made the side trip to see the MacEwans, Willa MacPherson, OAC President Reynolds, and a number of others.

He arrived back at the university in time to hear the famed football coach from Notre Dame, Knute Rockne, speak on campus: "The agricultural colleges of the country are the last strongholds of rugged American manhood. . . . The leaders of tomorrow are coming from rural communities, the people of the cities are soft."

*   *   *

Although there was no time for graduate students to take part in athletics, MacEwan extracted everything else out of the experience at Ames, by firmly established work habits of long hours, efficient use of time, and immense stamina. There is no doubt that he had impressed his professors with his ability, having been entrusted with a full professor's duties during an emergency, and there is ample evidence that his scholarly ability was respected within his peer group. Early in the fall term he had been "rushed" by a number of honorary fraternities whose ideals were centered on scholarship and research. It was to have unusual results.

His journal provides ample evidence of close timing and seemingly unlimited energy. For instance, on January 18, 1928, he was guest speaker at a meeting of the Ames Cosmopolitan Club, his subject, "Canada"; later he took Harriet Brigham to a dance held by the Graduate Club; after the dance he returned his lady to her residence, rushed to the laboratory where he set up a rat-feeding experiment, working at it through the night until it was time to leave for classes the next morning. A few days later he spoke to a Lions Club luncheon, dealing with two subjects they chose for him — "Canada" and "Robert Burns," the latter subject one that he would deal with hundreds of times in his lifetime and in as many places.

With no time to actually participate in the events, he nevertheless attended as a spectator as many college football games, wrestling matches, and other sporting events as he could, in company with professors, women students, and his fellow agros.

*   *   *

The end of the term was fast approaching. Deeply immersed as he was in preparing to meet the final examination for his Master's degree in early May, 1928, and in finishing his thesis, a nagging thought kept recurring in the back of MacEwan's mind: What would present itself after the year was up? Would he find a suitable job?

MacEwan had spent more time thinking about the next step in his career and what he wanted to do than he cared to admit. The period of waiting in vain at Melfort for a summons out of the East, while not traumatic, had been unsettling. This time he had made no applications for jobs anywhere. All his life, events would seek MacEwan out rather than MacEwan seeking them, and he preferred it that way. He would pray for guidance in choosing the right path, yet he would seldom attempt to force events himself, believing fully that he was in Another's hands. He was clear in his mind about one thing. After his Regina experience he knew he did not want to spend the rest of his days in an office, nor in the civil service if he could avoid it.

A number of people had viewed the research he set up as the basis for his thesis — a study of the nutritional value of visceral organs based on a record of performance of a colony of white rats he had been feeding. Only recently the director of the Institute of Meat Packing at the University of Chicago, Emery Filbey, had been to Iowa University and had viewed MacEwan's project with interest. So far nothing had come of it.

Then finally, toward the end of April, a letter arrived from F. Hedley Auld, deputy minister of agriculture, Regina. A Mr. Ross had left the employ of the government and his position as chief assistant to the livestock commissioner was available. If, asked Mr. Auld, MacEwan was favorably disposed to the offer he would approach his minister and advise definitely if the job would be open to him. The position would start at $2,100 per year with annual $100 increases to $2,500 for sure, and "possibly up to $3,000 after some years of experience and service."

Gratified though he was to receive Mr. Auld's offer, he hoped something else would turn up. Clearly, further work in the livestock branch office was not as attractive to MacEwan as it might be to others. Dare he take a chance and turn the position down?

He sent a night letter to Mr. Auld: "Thanks for letter. Would like more money but will consider favorably such offer as you suggest. . . ." Mr. Auld acknowledged the telegram and said he would like to pay more money and hoped to do so in the future, but the first offer must stand. And then, as if trying to interest MacEwan as much as possible he added: "your work will be of a more varied character than it has hitherto been and you will be closely associated with the office."

Hard on the heels of the first, another offer came to MacEwan. This time from the University of Chicago Meat Packing Institute. It was wide open. They suggested that he could go to the university either as a fellow working toward a Doctor of Philosophy degree or as a full-time salaried researcher. They set out a number of broad subjects from which he could choose research projects that interested him, or, they suggested, he might have an idea of his own he would prefer to pursue in their laboratories. In other words, they wanted MacEwan to join the institute and they wanted him to be content, working in what interested him most.

MacEwan was in a quandary. One offer was in Canada but also in an office; the other suggested freedom to plan his own work but was in the United States. It was assumed that the Americans, though it was not mentioned, would pay more money than the Canadians, but although it was a factor to be considered, money was not the decisive one for MacEwan.

However, back in Regina, Auld thought it would be, for he apparently got wind of the fact that the Yanks were after his boy. On May 26, 1928, he wrote: "I have advised Mr. Hamilton [Hon. C.M., minister of agriculture] that some others are bidding for your services and I am recommending that we give further consideration to the question of salaries." He added, "if, therefore, we are able to consider a larger initial salary than mentioned . . . you may receive a telegram in the near future. . . ." Mr. Auld appended a handwritten note: "PS — We want, in Saskatchewan, your services if we can make you an attractive proposition but we want more than that — to be sure that you are choosing the right line which will ultimately prove the best."

With his final examination out of the way and his research approaching the point where results could be read, he finally decided to accept Auld's offer despite its reference to office work. On May 21, 1928, he wrote a letter accepting the job and saying that he could report for work in Regina on or about June 20.

If MacEwan thought he had been in a quandary with the two offers, he was to find himself much more deeply involved when a third one came as an utter and complete surprise.

The letter to Auld had no sooner been dropped in the mail than a telephone call completelv changed the situation. It was the Ames telegraph office with a message for MacEwan. He grabbed a pencil and the first piece of paper he could lay his hands on and scrawled the message: "Are you in position to consider offer assistant professor Animal Husbandry at U of Saskatchewan. Wire collect. W. J. Rutherford."

It was an answer to his prayers! However, it turned a quandary into a complicated mixture of sheer joy and gratitude on the one hand and embarrassment on the other. He had accepted Auld's offer — what was he to do now?

He sat at his desk trying to order his thoughts, rereading the welcome telegraph message he had scrawled on the back of a piece of paper. He turned the paper over. It was a mimeographed program for Iowa University's Dedication Day Prayers ceremony at the top of which was printed a quotation from Tennyson's "Passing of Arthur": "More things are wrought by prayers than this world dreams of."

His answer to Dean Rutherford was not long in coming. He sent a telegram as instructed: indeed Grant MacEwan was in a position to consider an offer from the University of Saskatchewan!

With difficulty, he then composed a letter to Mr. Auld in Regina, phrased as best he could. In it he asked him to ignore the letter of acceptance (possibly hoping that by chance the two letters would arrive together) and requesting a few days in which to consider the matter further, not wishing to reject the kindly man's offer too abruptly.

When Dean Rutherford's letter arrived, it revealed that Professor Winters had resigned to teach at the University of Minnesota and that "we are anxious to secure a young man, well prepared to teach and to engage in investigation work and to grow into the position." Salary would be $2,500 for the first year ($400 better than Auld's starting salary), and upon satisfactory performance as a teacher, he would be appointed permanently with a $100 increase each year to the rank of junior professor at $3,200 and beyond that to the rank of full professor. "In the meantime, however, the University would expect you to have advanced to, or well toward your Doctor's degree." He was to report for duty on July 1, 1928.

The Institute at Chicago University was disappointed that they had not been successful in their bid for Grant's services but congratulated him on his appointment to the teaching position at the University of Saskatchewan, where they hoped he would find "some opportunity for research work in line with your major interests." The director left the door open. "If at any time," he wrote on June 12, 1928, "a research position in the Institute appeals to you, we shall be glad indeed to renew the discussion."

MacEwan was not in need of more inspiration than he now had but he was to get it just the same. At closing exercises, the College of Agriculture at Iowa University held its third annual Honors Day Program: Grant MacEwan was initiated into the Alpha Zeta Honors Society for students "in upper two-fifths of their class and judged on their scholarship, leadership and character." He was initiated into Gamma Sigma Delta Honors Society for graduate students "who have shown research ability in Agriculture and related departments." He was initiated into Phi Kappa Phi Society for "outstanding graduate students."

The MacEwan feat created an unusual stir at Iowa that year, Only a very small minority of graduate students succeeded in being named to one such honorary society, let alone three!

In the short time that MacEwan had been there, he had formed a close attachment to his new alma mater which he had grown to honor and respect almost as much as he had OAC during his years as an undergraduate. On leaving Ames, two months before his twenty-sixth birthday, to return to Canada, he wrote in his journal on June 12, 1928:

I left dear old Ames and a lot of fine Iowa friends this morning at 7 o'clock. It was pouring rain and I was soaked to the hide. The Iowa people are hard to leave. Now that my stay with them is past I conclude they are the friendliest and most courteous people that I have ever mingled with.

Chapter 11

The Assistant Professor

The first day in July, 1928, being the Sabbath, Grant MacEwan reported for duty on the second day.

The University of Saskatchewan stood on the high east bank of the South Saskatchewan River, overlooking the city of Saskatoon. It was a far cry from the lush parklike surroundings he had enjoyed at Ames, Iowa. As he left the high end of the bridge and turned toward the university, the whole of the dozen-odd permanent stone buildings seemed set out on the bald prairie as if for inspection, like a number of children's toy blocks on a broad expanse of a linoleum-covered floor. There was evidence of shrubbery and starting trees here and there but, for the most part, the buildings were so open to the prairie breezes that the right angles where stone met sod could be distinctly seen. Houses along the avenue leading to the university soon petered out and the only link with the city was a gravel roadway, rutted from a recent downpour. Streetcar tracks ran alongside for about a half mile to a loop at the main cluster of buildings where streetcars turned back toward the city.

It was not a prepossessing sight but appearances were not important to the assistant professor. What was important was the reputation the young institution had already earned for itself under the guidance of men of his own bent and outlook.

Planning the future university in 1903, Premier Haultain of the Northwest Territories introduced a bill in which he said: "The first principle taken into consideration is to make the university free from all influence of government, sect, or politics; in fact the institution is to be governed by the graduates." The principle remained after the Territories became provinces and the province of Saskatchewan set up its own institution.

University of Saskatchewan campus in 1928   (*University of Saskatchewan Archives*)

Five years later W. C. Murray, the founding president, described the nature of the institution he would seek to build for the people of the province. Dr. Murray said in part that its watchword was to be "service to the state," not only in the things that produce wealth but those things "that make for happiness and virtue," and further "no form of service is too mean or too exalted." Dr. Murray also uttered words with which MacEwan would agree with all his heart when he said: "Whether the work be conducted within the boundaries of the campus or throughout the length and breadth of the Province, there should be ever present the consciousness that this is the University of the people. . . ."

Before MacEwan's arrival on campus, good men and women had taken these words to heart and had established a fine tradition of public service and extension work based upon them. It would be part of his duty to take up the task and carry it forward in his own way.

If the founding principles were sound, the modest start that had been made on the buildings was equally well planned. MacEwan saw this as he made his way to keep his first appointment with Dean Rutherford. The architects called the style "Collegiate Gothic" architecture, and the buildings were attractively fashioned out of hard, honey-colored limestone that had been deposited nearby by glaciers thousands of years before.

The dean's greeting was warm and enthusiastic for the young assistant who came laden with a promising list of achievements. During a short interview, Rutherford restated the conditions of employment and expanded on the terms of reference before turning his new man over to the head of the animal husbandry department, Prof. A. M. Shaw.

Shaw got down to details. For the first year MacEwan would give three animal husbandry classes that would involve over seventeen hours of lectures a week; the remainder of the summer would be taken up in preparation for the fall lectures. There would also be general extension work to be carried out as it arose and some livestock judging to be done at summer fairs throughout the province. The interview over, Professor Shaw drove the new assistant to his home for lunch — becoming hopelessly bogged down in a sea of mud in front of his house on University Drive.

* * *

That afternoon, after he had arranged to stay at St. Andrew's College residence until he could find a boarding house, MacEwan returned to his new office. He was sorting papers and shelving books when he looked up to see a stranger standing in the open doorway.

He was a distinguished-looking man, with deep-set eyes sparkling under a high forehead from which thinning hair receded. Silver-winged temples set off a fresh complexion, and a graying mustache complemented a well-modeled mouth over a firm jaw. He wore a Donegal tweed suit with vest, white shirt, starched collar, and tie. He smiled as he extended a hand: "My name is Murray. If you need anything, let me know."

Years later MacEwan recalled "I didn't recognize him as President Walter Charles Murray at the moment, but I loved him from the beginning and I shall always be indebted to him for giving me an exceptionally good chance to know him."

It was the beginning of a close relationship that would end only at the death of Dr. Murray. The president was to take the young professor into his confidence almost from the beginning and would allow MacEwan to share his mental processes, his triumphs, and his problems, confident that his trust was well placed and would not be abused. This was the man who had said that "the College of Agriculture must be regarded as the sheet anchor of the University." The two were well suited to each other.

* * *

There was little time to become acclimatized. Within two days MacEwan had plunged into a full round of extension duties in addition to his preparatory work for lectures. The second day after his arrival he judged for the Saskatoon Society for the Prevention of Cruelty to Animals, and assisted Professor Shaw in drilling livestock judges at a two-day conference at the university. Then he was at the Yorkton Fair for three days after which he traveled to the Moosomin Fair. In the following six days, he judged at Mortlach, Belle Plaine, Stoughton, Bethune, Turtleford, and Richard. It was an introduction to the way his summers would go for many years — doing a job he liked.

*Dean Shaw (left),
Dean Rutherford,
President Murray
(right), in an early
photograph
(University of
Saskatchewan Archives)*

He later recalled:

It's difficult now to describe the position of a livestock judge in the developing agricultural community of the day. It was the highest calling most agriculture students could aspire to. To get the coveted judge's cane and enter the judging ring carrying it like a field marshal's baton — a symbol of authority — was what a large majority of us dreamed of. You used it to prod the beasts, move them about, to lean on if the entries were thick and the hours long, and sometimes, it was used to defend yourself against ornery bulls.

The judge in the ring was the cynosure of all eyes. In placing beasts as he saw them, the judge established the level toward which farmers throughout the district would strive to raise their own animals back home on the farm.

As in all human endeavor, there was a minority who sought to use their position to their own advantage — but not Grant MacEwan. Allan C. Leslie of Watrous, Saskatchewan, an all-time great in horse competitions, recalled in 1975:

You could never influence Grant. He was the most honest judge I know . . . and one thing was certain, you could never even pour him a drink back in the barn before or after the judging. He might have been a wee bit partial to Clydes, but I think he was aware of it and sometimes might even have leaned in the direction of a Belgian or Percheron to keep the scales honest.

The trips into the country were not without their lighter moments, which delighted MacEwan's sense of humor. Having to go to the small community of Glenbush, he inquired about train connections at the railway station. The ticket agent thumbed through the train schedules for many minutes and finally announced, "one train a week in, none out." The judges went by car.

The judges were a breed unto themselves, and as he traveled with them and served in the ring with them at countless fairs, he came to know them intimately. Among others were Frank Baker, Ken Hays, B. A. Cook,

MacEwan, the livestock judge, giving reasons for his judgment at Climax, Saskatchewan
(MacEwan Collection)

Swanton Haggerty, E. E. "Brock" Brockelbank (a colleague), Tom Devlin, Maurice Hartnett, Jim Burnett, and M. A. "Mac" Collins. Burnett was one of the "old warriors" and it was he who, as Grant registered at a North Battleford hotel, exclaimed: "Why do you want a room with a bath, when you're just a mile from the river?"

At Gravelbourg, he and Maurice Hartnett, another popular judge, were met by a delegation who displayed a fine Gallic sense of occasion. Upon greeting the pair at the station, their spokesman, after delivering a formal address of welcome, said: "And now gentlemen, we want you men to go where you like and come when you like and so we give you the key to our city." Upon which he presented them with a bottle opener of the common type.

As in all such activities, there was an element of risk as well as humor. On a number of occasions MacEwan was berated by losers. At Yorkton he, Ike Beatty, and some others "got roped in" to judge a chariot race the second night of the fair. What they did not know was that trouble was brewing; it was to be the climax of a long-standing feud between two notorious families of the district. Rounding the last bend, the two bitter enemies were in the lead, urging their horses on toward the finishing post, neck and neck, when one driver edged ahead enough to force his team into the path of the other. The second chariot was crowded into the fence. It flipped, throwing the driver out and freeing the horses from the weight of the chariot. The driverless team raced across the finishing line well ahead of all contestants.

Grant and his fellow judges, innocent of the rules of the game, and always more in sympathy with horses than humans, held a hasty conference and declared the driverless lead team the winner. Protests were not slow in coming. The judges quickly retired with whatever dignity remained and, Grant said much later: "I don't know yet who did win the race."

Owing to a tight judging schedule, MacEwan took his first flight in an aircraft in 1928. Following the Radville Fair, he and Hartnett were expected back in Regina, which was due north. Connections were such that they would have to take the train northwest to Moose Jaw and await connections to go eastward again to the capital city. It was then that Pilot Skinner of Willow Bunch volunteered to fly them in his aircraft.

It was a splendid trip. We were one hour on the way, which represented a saving of about six or seven hours over coming to Regina via Moose Jaw. The farms looked like gardens from the air. The Soo Line stations looked about a mile apart as we flew over them. I worried about the gasoline gauge ahead of me which registered empty long before we reached Regina. Skinner advised later it exaggerated.

The first summer left no doubt that the assistant animal husbandry professor was capable in the field, but how was he to prove himself in the classroom?

MacEwan's first lectures began on September 27, 1928. The summer months had been busy due to the demands for extension work, but there were days when he was free to prepare notes for the forthcoming lectures, and he had done so, working his customary twelve- to fourteen-hour days to ensure that he was fully prepared when the time came.

The first lecture was Animal Husbandry 3 — but it was the young professor, not the students, who learned the biggest lesson that day. He entered the classroom with confidence: "I was armed with what I thought were enough notes to last at least half the term but I was very inexperienced and, before the end of that first hour, I was running out of notes." It was just as well that he had become addicted to long hours; the first year he would need them to prepare his lessons.

However, he soon gauged the mental appetite of his classes and gradually began building himself a reputation among his students as a lecturer, but not quite like the ordinary one to be found at the university. H. R. Clark, a professor of extension at the University of Saskatchewan, took several classes from MacEwan and he recalled that by the time most students reached the university, they would more than likely have seen MacEwan in action in the country and would feel that they knew him. Had they participated in 4-H livestock activities, it was probable that they had previously stood before the tall professor to "give reasons" for the way they had judged their event. "We started out trembling and tongue-tied, but with his quiet understanding and his way of saying 'yes, yes, yes' in an encouraging manner, we soon got over it, and ended up talking as freely as if we were talking to our own friends at home."

There were better lecturers than MacEwan but few were as enjoyable to listen to. "He was a good professor," Professor Clark recalled.

MacEwan, the horseman, up on "Laddy," the first Palomino registered in Canada and first Canadian Palomino to be registered in the United States Stud Book   (MacEwan Collection)

We seldom missed classes because we wanted to hear him each time. Maybe he wasn't the best lecturer in the world, in the true academic sense, and thank God he wasn't. He was more of a conversationalist. He would prompt students, draw them out, set up an interaction with them. When he spoke to a student everything in his manner said "I am interested in you" and the student drew confidence from him. You could never get any notes from him — he wasn't that kind of a lecturer — but he was fair and you knew what to study because he always set his examinations on the text. They were hard exams.

Despite his active extension program, MacEwan seemed to manage his time in such a way as to least disturb the classes. "He missed a few, but we always knew in advance. Sometimes [Prof.] Al Ewen would fill in for him when he was away. It is a wonder he didn't miss more for all his travels and activity outside. He was not known for a class misser because he put in twenty-four hours a day." There was no nonsense in a MacEwan class. He was a disciplinarian and yet there was "an easy one-to-one relationship," Clark said. He was accessible and friendly but carried authority that was recognized. "Perhaps it was because he knew them, their names, more than likely where their parents came from, and he would certainly know their livestock if they had anything better than grade stock on the farm." More than any other lecturer Clark knew, MacEwan inspired the student with the importance and dignity of the calling of agriculture.

He treated all his classes the same whether they were filled with students working toward a degree in agriculture, members of an extension class in the country, or those taking the "short course" (the associates in the abbreviated two-year certificate course at the School of Agriculture). Mrs. Joyce (Hodson) Alexander of Olds, Alberta, recalled that when she was a short-course student from Rosthern, Saskatchewan, MacEwan's classes were popular. "He would sit on the desk at the front of the class, with his long legs swinging, talking to us in his easy, chatty manner. He never talked down to anybody and you felt as important as any of the other students at the University." He dealt in practical matters that had application on the farms at home and yet he used each case as an illustration to teach students the basic principles of nutrition, genetics, and management.

Mrs. Alexander's description of a professor sitting on the desk with legs swinging while he spoke in a "chatty manner" may not seem out of the ordinary in the 1970s but it was rare when MacEwan began his career in the late 1920s and 1930s. In those days, it was the usual practice for a professor to deliver his lecture either standing behind a lectern with notes placed as one would deliver a speech, or seated behind the desk with notes spread on the lecture table. The MacEwan technique was accepted by most, but not by all students. There were a few who found his lectures distracting, discursive, and difficult to handle, and who much preferred the traditional and formal delivery to which they were accustomed.

The young professor had other attributes which made him particularly popular with the students, especially in the College of Agriculture. He was a fine horseman, and always had a superior saddle horse in the barn. When mounted — dressed in riding breeches, jacket, and slightly Western fedora — he made a striking picture. Some students called him "our swashbuckling professor" due to the fact that MacEwan could not be long anywhere without commanding attention. "He was colorful, with a hidden but magnetic attraction for people. If he wasn't attracting attention, he would soon be doing something to attract it — not purposely, for he was never conscious of his impact. It just seemed to happen."

His athletic ability and knowledge contributed greatly to his popularity among the students. He was always ready to join in with them. Clark remembers one occasion when the students were playing the faculty in a broomball game. He took a swing at the ball, missed it, and cracked Grant across the shin. In pain, Grant shouted at him, "You little bugger, I'll get you yet!" — to Clark's knowledge, the only time anybody had heard MacEwan use anything approaching a swear word.

As his reputation as a basketball player had preceded him, the Agros were quick to enlist his aid in support of their efforts in the hotly contested interfaculty league. He became the coach of their team and in his second year he guided them to victory over their bitter enemies — the Engineers, Artsmen, and Meds. In 1930, he played center (his alternate Percy, later

Coach MacEwan and his championship Agro basketball team: (left to right) MacEwan, D. Minor, R. Johnston, F. Evans, H. Reusch, L. Purdy, R. Botkin, H. Purdy, N. Foster, W. Foster, manager　　　　　　　　　　　*(MacEwan Collection, Charmbury photo)*

Judge Maguire) with a city team, the Varsity Grads, and the team won the provincial championship over the Regina Balmorals. This endeared him to the students and, at the same time, helped bridge the traditional gap existing between the university and the city.

In those days, when college teams traveled, they were always accompanied by a member of the faculty to maintain order and decorum. On one such trip he accompanied the Husky hockey team to Edmonton (his first recorded trip into Alberta). When the train paused briefly at North Battleford, it was long enough for the students to detrain, decorate the station platform with toilet paper, and return with the local constable hot on their trail. MacEwan, who had been reading in the parlor car at the time, looked up to see the constable towering above, asking who was responsible for this gang of hooligans. Grant confessed. The officer said it would have to be reported. Grant said if he insisted on reporting it to the university, he should write to a Prof. J. W. G. MacEwan, faculty of agriculture, in Saskatoon. That satisfied the constable who wrote the address, closed the book and, without inquiring as to whom he had been speaking, left the train. In due course, MacEwan received a letter from North Battleford and answered it, expressing deep sorrow that such an incident had taken place and assuring them that the students responsible would be dealt with accordingly — there the matter lay.

There were probably few new staff members who accounted for themselves as well in their first year as had MacEwan. He was popular with the students; was more active than most in the extension field; he had ten investigative projects going on during the year (for example: comparative value of frozen wheat grades as pig feed; buttermilk versus tankage as pig protein supplement); he was published in the scholarly journal *Scientific Agriculture*, May 1929 issue.

However, others still had their eye on him; he had not been forgotten by the people in Ames, Iowa. Soon after his arrival at Saskatoon he had received a letter from L. Myron Boozer of the College Presbyterian Church to say "we missed you this year, both in the Sunday School and in other departments of the church — particularly when we were carving up the chicken for the Thanksgiving student dinner, we missed your efficient and cheerful help."

Others remembered him for different reasons and he heard from them as he was entering the second round of judging at summer fairs in Saskatchewan. This time it was in a more serious vein.

In July, he received a letter from Iowa University stating that Professor Holbert had left the faculty of agriculture. Would MacEwan like to join the staff in his position, they asked. MacEwan was tempted. He had fond memories of Iowa and its people. There was no suggestion of a slow progress toward full professorship, for their offer was forthright — a professor had left; would he take his place?

When Dr. Murray heard of the offer, he advised Grant to take no further action until the matter was discussed with others. They wanted him to stay at Saskatchewan — and with good reason.

The year before the young professor had joined the staff, the dean of agriculture had reported that the department of animal husbandry had been involved in judging livestock three times, holding judging contests five times and attending functions at which addresses were given eight times. The following year, MacEwan's individual statistics showed that he had judged at sixteen fairs and exhibitions and seven other gatherings, had given talks and lectures at formal meetings twelve times, and at other gatherings nine times; besides which he had published four articles, and had participated in student activities in a number of ways. He was a valuable assistant professor in a department that was short of staff, a dynamo, generating seemingly endless energy.

A letter from the president speaks for itself. Dated August 7, 1929, it said: "The executive at its meeting yesterday resolved to increase your salary to $2,800.00 for the year 1929-1930, $3,000.00 for the year 1930-1931, and a promotion to Junior Professor with an initial salary of $3,200.00 from July 31, 1931. I have much pleasure in assuring you of their cordial support of the recommendation and desire to retain your services." The letter offered early promotion and raised his salary considerably over the initial offer made by Dean Rutherford. Dr. Murray's offer was accepted and MacEwan began his second term at Saskatchewan.

Chapter 12

Buys First Land

After receiving the official stamp of approval on his first year's performance, MacEwan plunged into his second at Saskatchewan with renewed and increased energy and inspiration.

He assumed additional judging duties, attended lectures and field days in the country whenever they could be fitted in, and he increased his attention to writing, some articles for scholarly journals but most for publications that would reach the farmer and his interests directly.

Busy as he was traveling about the province, whenever he was within reach he always managed to take a day or two off in which to visit his parents at Melfort, and one such visit on August 29, 1929, proved to be a cardinal day in his life. From Melfort, he drove to Nipawin where he called at the office of Charlie Bell, real estate agent. Charlie sent John Short with him to view land across the Saskatchewan River in the White Fox country. He had seen the district some time before in company with Ed Ridley. They both admired the beauty of the newly opened forest country and the crystal-clear White Fox River. On the first trip MacEwan had concluded the land would be worth approximately $1,000 for any quarter section fronting on the river.

The countryside was equally appealing when revisited. After looking at several quarters, he bought one from J. R. Hughes of West Point for $959, right on the banks of the White Fox. This was the first land Grant ever owned.

He had no immediate plans to farm the land or even to pasture livestock in the open meadows. He had seen the benefits of owning land firsthand in Melfort when Alex MacEwan, albeit with years of back-breaking labor, had been lifted out of virtual ruin into a position of respect and relative affluence in the community with the aid of his farm. He would never forget the lesson. Land to him would always represent a sound and wise investment, one he would make on a number of occasions. Land was also a refuge for a man when he needed it badly enough.

Although he did not farm it, he put the land to good use — but it would be over thirty-five years before it was revealed just how he did it. Even then MacEwan would not reveal his secret voluntarily; an inquiring newspaper reporter dug it out.

With his frugal spending habits, his savings would continue to mount in the bank, the more so because of the recent healthy raise in pay. In his lifetime he would resort to a number of ways to put surplus money to work — term deposits in banks, bank stock, preferred shares in blue chip industries, government bonds — but land would continue to be his major investment. Not long after he had bought the White Fox quarter section, he went to look at another a few miles south of Melfort in the Resource district. James R. Aikenhead owned it; the price "with 40 acres broke" and a few log buildings, was $1,600. MacEwan dickered with C. J. Lutes, the agent, and they came together at $1,200 cash.

His pattern of investment had been set.

* * *

As often happens in life, within a very short period in the fall of 1930, MacEwan's path crossed those of three people who had been, or were destined to become, closest to him.

Despite the fact that he has many friends, thousands of acquaintances, and is known to tens of thousands of people, Grant MacEwan in his lifetime has had fewer than his fair share of what could be termed, in the accepted sense, intimate friendships. In Brandon he took as active a part in school society as any but there were none of the long, lazy, hot summer afternoons when two or three pals went fishing, or lay on a riverbank watching the summer clouds float by, exchanging confidences and ideas and growing close in the process. At Melfort, it was the same, only more so, due to the "social cost of space," being laden with chores, and, as most farm boys are, far removed from possible friends his own age. At Guelph, it was somewhat different: he met his first close friend in the person of Joe "Old Doc" Brickley, his roommate; he went fairly steady for two terms with Gladys Eaton; he struck up a friendship with Mackenzie, minister of Chalmers Presbyterian Church, and his wife, "Mrs. Mac," helped with their children and made their home his "home away from home" in a friendship that was to extend to Saskatoon — but this was hardly an intimate association between people of the same age. In the family he had a close relationship with his cousin Maria Corlette Grant (now Mrs. Wesley Nelson), Brandon, in whom he confided as he would with a big sister, she being two years his senior.

He experienced no shortage of people he could revere, for one reason or another: Grandfather Grant, his uncles, John and James Grant, Aunt

Above: Mrs. Wesley G. Nelson (Maria Corlette Grant), 1961
(Brandon Sun photo by Vince Roska)

Left: Phyllis Winnifred Cline, 1933
(MacEwan Collection)

Marion, Dean Rutherford, Wade Toole, the OAC judging coach, Dean Kildee at Ames, Dr. Murray, James Clinkskill, the historian A. S. Morton, to mention only a few, but these relationships were somewhat similar to that existing between himself and his parents — more a filial relationship than anything else.

The simple reason for such scarcity of close friends among his peers is that Grant MacEwan moved too fast and too furiously for anyone — even those his own age and younger — to match. The occasions were rare when he had the time or, more important, the disposition to "put his feet up and shoot the breeze with the boys." To ask his family if he ever went to the beach and dozed on the sand in the sun is to invite an instant burst of laughter. He simply values time too much to fritter it away on unproductive pastimes. He has all the qualities needed for close friendships, save one — he hasn't the time, and that has made Grant MacEwan pretty much of a loner throughout most of his life.

However, three stars in his Heaven gathered in a brief cluster in the fall of 1930.

Joe Brickley wasn't the main one, but he paid a visit to Saskatoon in August for the first reunion of the two old OAC roommates since they had parted and Joe had left for a job in Cuba. Grant walked the legs off him in Saskatoon, showing him all the sights; then with Ab Calbert, they motored to Waskesiu Lake in Prince Albert National Park. The park, having been recently opened, was in its rough pioneer stage, most pleasing to Grant, but possibly not so pleasant to Joe. However, they did a lot of hiking along old trails, looking for Indian artifacts and talking over the old days. It was the kind of warm association MacEwan had had little of since leaving Guelph.

The month after Brickley's visit, MacEwan went down to the King George Hotel at an appointed time to greet the new assistant professor of animal husbandry, A. J. Ewen, who had just arrived from Aberdeen, Scotland, that day. He inquired at the desk with no success. Returning later, he had the Chinese bellboy page Mr. Ewen. Although there were a number of persons seated in the lobby, none rose to the call.

Finally Dr. Murray arrived and by this time, Grant approached a likely looking man, seated in a corner, despite the fact that he had not reacted to the page. It was Ewen, whose ear was not yet attuned to the nasal North American inflections and certainly not to North American pronunciation strained through a Chinese filter.

"He is a big burly Scot, one who would never win a beauty competition, but an interesting and capable type," MacEwan later wrote in his journal of the man who was to become much closer to him, and in more ways, than he could ever have suspected at the time.

The third star in the cluster that came together that fall happened to be a woman.

It was Halloween. The public school teachers were holding a masquerade at Victoria School and MacEwan was escorting one of them. Once there, he became attracted by a pair of large, dark brown eyes flashing over the silken veil of a mysterious Arabian dancer. In time another lady in disguise, Esther Wright, who knew them both, introduced the two.

Grant stood looking down into the dark eyes. "Take off that mask," he said, "so I can get a good look at your face." The dancer complied, at the stroke of midnight. Later, MacEwan confided to his journal that while he had accompanied one lady to the dance, he had "met another who rather caught my undivided attention. The lady was Phyllis Cline, a teacher and singer . . . a very good looking kind to know."

He had written words of a somewhat similar vein about other women he had met, but not quite the same and not quite as many. The professor's social life was certainly picking up.

* * *

If the twenty-eight-year-old professor's social life was accelerating, it was not at the expense of his professional duties. He had already demonstrated an ability to manage a surprising number of activities simultaneously and, with the expertise of a juggler, to keep them all in motion without collision.

For some years before his arrival, the university had conducted a "Radio Farm School" over Regina broadcasting station CKCK, and MacEwan, instantly attracted to the new medium, made his first broadcast over it. He displayed an ability to react to events and come up with programs dealing with current problems facing farmers as in the case when, soon after one of the worst early snowstorms experienced in some time, he spoke on the subject of "winter steer feeding." It was on this occasion that a man who was to tickle his interest in history provided comic relief.

To facilitate the broadcasts, a microphone linking the Regina station directly with the university had been installed in College Building (now Administration) in a small office used by James Clinkskill, then a seventy-six-year-old founder of the university and still vitally interested in its affairs. As MacEwan spoke into the microphone, the old man made a gallant effort to concentrate but eventually fell asleep, snoring audibly and causing Grant to momentarily lose his place. Later, Clinkskill informed MacEwan, "It's the first time I've ever broadcast."

MacEwan's use of the radio to reach the farmer was to increase as was his use of the popular press. While other academics might understandably seek publication in learned journals to enhance their scholarly reputations, Grant was to turn more and more to agricultural weekly newspapers to reach a growing public. He early established relations with the *Western Producer*, the *Saskatchewan Farmer*, the *Free Press Prairie Farmer*, the *Family Herald* and others which gladly published his articles, laden with useful and understandable information.

He made other contributions. Having seen a meat demonstration at Guelph during which a well-bred beef and an ordinary type were butchered, he never forgot how graphically the wisdom of good breeding and good nutrition had been established. MacEwan, Professors Brockle-bank and Ewen, began similar demonstrations at the university. The demonstrations proved so popular that they took them out in the country — the first of such rural demonstrations being held in Wiseton, about eighty miles southwest of Saskatoon. There, farmers saw two beasts, one well bred the other ordinary, slaughtered and the carcasses hung for inspection. It had cost the same to feed each, yet the purebred yielded much more meat. The lesson was clear. The lesson was remembered.

What could well have turned out to be a grisly business was made a smooth and informative operation by expertise. An eyewitness reported that MacEwan's "meat cutting and preparation demonstrations were memorable occasions. He began to lecture and demonstrate at the same time, and he would have the animal killed, pelted and hung up before anyone realized what he had done."

From that time on, and for years, meat demonstrations were held at hundreds of points in the province. In time, MacEwan asked Brocklebank, "How much longer must we continue this business?" They had to keep them up, for not only did the demonstrations improve the meat that reached the farmer's table, thus making life more livable, they also provided the drawing card that attracted many more people than otherwise would have come and exposed them to lectures on other subjects as important to the improvement of their livelihood, if not as dramatic.

* * *

The separation between universities and the communities in which they are situated is so notorious that over the years it has become referred to as the "town and gown" gap. It existed no less at Saskatoon, but there were those among the faculty who were aware of it and who by their actions attempted to bridge it — Grant MacEwan among them.

Soon after his arrival on staff, he had attended a meeting of the local Kiwanis Club with Dr. Murray, and he continued to do so, joining the club later and becoming an active member. In time he was to reach a high level in its organization. Also, through his work, he was brought into close association with the Saskatoon Exhibition, and became a director, contributing much to the livestock shows it sponsored, and eventually to the entire organization as its president in time of need.

The Reverend James Mackenzie had moved his family from Guelph to Saskatoon, where he became minister of Knox United Church, and Grant, who had joined the Unionists with his mother in the great debate of 1924-1925, played an exceedingly active roll, eventually being elected an elder in this church of his close friend. Needless to say, his enthusiasm was not dampened one whit by the fact that a brown-eyed teacher by the name of Cline sang in the choir. On one grave occasion, when Mackenzie was seriously ill, MacEwan sat with him day and night for over a week and finally, when the doctors were taking all steps possible to save his life, he gave blood for his friend. Mackenzie survived and much credit was given to MacEwan for the outcome.

As a horseman, the university professor was inevitably drawn toward the Saskatoon Riding Club and became a founding member and vice-president. A long-time member, Mrs. (J. H.) Muriel Evans, said MacEwan was no ordinary member, but enriched the club and expanded its horizons by his presence, active support, and knowledge of horses.

He judged for the club on numerous occasions and when unable to do it himself, knew the right person to substitute for him; he seldom missed the weekly club rides; he organized and held educational classes at the university for the benefit of horsemen with the assistance of Dr. Norman Wright.

The club acknowledged his contribution when they elected him president for a term. Some years later when their former president rose to higher things, Mrs. Evans accused Grant MacEwan of using the club as a stepping stone, so adept had he learned to become in surmounting its stormier periods.

The local St. Andrew's Society and Burns' Society were also the beneficiaries of his guidance, wise counsel, and — on the proper occasion and before the right audience — his playing of the bagpipes.

* * *

And so it was that MacEwan won a place for himself on the "town" side of the traditional gap. On the "gown" side, accelerated promotion was an indication of his position with the university — although he was not without critics.

Inevitably, a person who applied himself on such a broad front with such an immense display of energy would not endear himself to all colleagues. There were rumblings in the faculty lounge that he was "spreading himself thin," at the expense of work toward his doctorate, and that no professor could keep up such a pace without neglecting his proper work.

An eyewitness said: "He moved with the stride of a hackney, few could keep up. He was more aggressive than most other members of the faculty. On a normal day he would be at the office before seven and have a day's work done by the time the others began showing up at nine. Often he would return from an extension trip and come directly from the train to work at his office whether it was five o'clock in the morning or three. It's important to keep this in mind in assessing Grant's history, his career at the University."

This was the situation when the depression clamped its grip on the country and when the long drought began turning the Prairies into a dust-bowl.

Chapter 13

Matador and the U.K.

An event of considerable importance occurred in the life of Grant MacEwan at the beginning of the 1930s. The actual event itself was to mean much in the field of animal husbandry research and had there been no side effects, it would be well worth mentioning by itself — but it is the side effects that prove of greatest importance to those interested in MacEwan's life.

It happened when the decision was made at the university by Dean Shaw to mount a vast range-breeding experiment on the Matador Ranch north of Swift Current, involving four breeds of beef cattle and eight breeds of sheep. The object of the matador project was "to carefully compare the relative merits of purebreds vs crossbreds for the production of market animals." The question was: "Is hybridization of commercial value or not?"

It was the largest and most complete experiment of its kind attempted up to that time and would take four or more years to complete, using over 1,000 breeding animals as foundation stock. By the end of the experiment, through natural increase, 3,500 to 4,000 animals would have passed through the feeding trials. Three agencies were involved: the university, the provincial department of agriculture, and the National Research Council.

This job was made to order for MacEwan, presenting as it did the opportunity to see new country, meet new people, and become familiar with livestock in a region he had not previously visited, for he was to accompany Shaw on a wide-ranging buying trip through southwestern Saskatchewan and southern Alberta to gather foundation stock for the experiment.

It can be assumd that MacEwan, working under and with Shaw, attacked the project with dispatch, earning his salary and satisfying Shaw with his knowledge and judgment of cattle, for sufficient beasts were bought in seven days on which to mount the experiment. What is of major interest is that through his journal, there is presented a graphic picture of the man in action on a broad front.

It is there to be seen in page after page of closely written notes, sometimes two and three lines of almost microscopic handwriting in one already narrow line, as if the writer had so many impressions to register that he was desperately afraid of running out of paper. No entry to that date carries such a wealth of information, revealing MacEwan's interests and powers of observation, as do the lines written about the western range land and its people on his first real trip to Alberta. (He had accompanied athletic teams to Edmonton but on such trips, he was confined by his duties as chaperone and was never able to "get his toes into the soil.") The professor moved through the country like a huge meteorological funnel, sucking up information as a tornado sucks up dust and debris in its path.

His observations display a mixture of human interest and scientific comments:

The days of the cowpuncher are not entirely a thing of the past. As one travels into the vast areas of grazing land . . . he must be impressed by the fact that much of it is ranch land first, last and always. . . . In the Cypress Hills country . . . there are to be found all the essentials of good range, namely good grass, plenty of high land, hay meadows for winter feed, protection and a climate that will permit a large amount of winter grazing. The grass in the ranch country is capable of curing on the ground and therefore furnishes excellent winter feed if the snow is not too deep.

One line in the journal reveals a characteristic thread of modesty that runs through his dealings with people, which is commendable on the one hand but which could be troublesome on the other. Grant MacEwan does not think he is different in any way from other people, save perhaps for the obvious and indisputable fact that he is much taller than average.

In his journal he wrote: "Many things are conspicuous to the outsider." He might well have written "to the observant outsider" or "to the trained observer," but it would never occur to him to set himself apart from others. It was in his nature to assume, on that and on other excursions, that whoever shared the experience with him would return with a harvest of facts and impressions, similar to his in size if not in content. They might make different use of them, they might not use them at all, but he would assume that they had seen as much and made as much of the trip as he. Where energy and physical stamina are concerned, his attitude is much the same. He is totally unaware that many of his qualities are unusual.

*   *   *

Among the things he found "conspicuous to the outsider" was the nature of Cypress Hills ranches and ranch lands, the essence of which, with a minimum of words, he captures graphically as few "outsiders" could.

"Small houses, cheaply constructed; small investment in buildings, and a substantial corral . . . land is mostly leased from the government [until 1930 from federal, now from provincial]. The lease owner pays 2¢ per acre per year, plus taxes. The lease tax is paid six months in advance (twice yearly). Leases run for terms of 21 years . . . roads of a modern type do not project far into rural districts . . . government or municipal phones are confined to the towns and immediate vicinity but barbed wire phones . . . are evidence of the ingenuity of the ranchers."

Added to such observations, his notes abound with anecdotes which he gathered through questioning and, more important, from listening to anyone who had anything to say. He set down the story of the ingenious rancher who, in a year of deep snow, tied an ox to each horse so that the horse could paw the snow away from the rich grass beneath and both could eat and manage to survive the winter; and the story of horses who emerged from a similar winter, when there had been little or no grass beneath the snow, with no hair on their tails or manes, other starving beasts having eaten it off.

Little suspecting that one day he would have a closer association with the province of Alberta, he recorded his first impressions as follows:

The country gives you the impression of vastness. Even the people, "the cow men," constitute a unique group. . . . They are by birth or adoption sons of the country, he-men, and as natural as the wide open spaces below the canopy of heaven can make. They are kind and hospitable, they are businessmen who do things in a big way. They are gamblers and the stakes are big ones. They do not count their lands by quarter sections, but by thousands of acres, and by similar figures do they count their cattle and sheep. They have all had their severe reverses and losses. . . .

In addition to Albertans and the ranchers of both the provinces as a class, he made notes on specific families and individuals and the reader, aided by the wisdom of hindsight, enjoys the privilege of seeing the seeds of future stories and books being sown. His notes include sketches on the Minor Brothers and their Lazy H and Triangle Ranch — it was John Minor who said: "Dehorn a range cow, and you knock out half her brains"; the Gilchrists and their 200,000-acre spread; the Kearns and their Hereford ranch in the Hills; Thomas Wilson and his Shady ZL Angus herd; Thomas Tinney and his horses and Galloway cattle; Fred Speers on the old Gordon, Ironside and Fares place at Crane Lake east of Piapot; the Demock Brothers whose father rode for the old "76" and had, along with Aberdeen Angus cattle, a shed that would house 2,400 sheep bedded, and who apologized for not having a bottle of whisky hanging in the well with which to welcome his visitors because "the damn boys don't drink and don't smoke and we don't keep the stuff any more"; the Martin Brothers, Bill and Watt; Jim McKenzie, Millay, Nason; Rod McLeay's Rocking P Ranch, west of High River, Alberta, with snow-capped mountains in view; and A. E. Cross of Calgary.

MacEwan had met a new breed of people on his swing through southwestern Saskatchewan and into Alberta. Somehow, someday, their story must be told.

* * *

The Matador trip was not without incident. Although it is difficult to imagine the tall professor moving about with anything but his customary affable dignity, such an occasion occurred in the southern cattle country as they were driving homeward from Alberta, Professor Shaw at the wheel.

As they sped through the treeless, rolling plains forty miles west of Swift Current, Grant found, to his intense discomfort, that "the changes of water had produced increased peristalsis in my intestinal region." On entering the town of Tompkins, the need for relief became so imperative that, at the sight of the first backhouse, he asked Shaw to drop him off and go about his business while Grant attended to his own. He sprinted across a private vegetable garden and entered the little building just in time. It was a photo finish.

Unfortunately for him, the lady of the house came out and tried the door. Grant sat quietly, basking in an aura of intense relief which rapidly turned to an embarrassed silence as she called out, "Who's in there?" She called again, and, getting no answer and possibly spiteful because of her own needs, she bolted the door from the outside and left. Grant found himself in a strange town, in a strange toilet, locked in. Somewhere in Tompkins, Shaw would be impatiently waiting to continue the journey. Grant realized the seriousness of the situation — "it was too bad, but the door had to be broken or I might have been there yet."

* * *

Two years later, the first crop of experimental calves were fed out and were to be put on the international market as the final test to compare how the meat sold with conventionally bred meats. With the United States market being virtually closed by high tariffs to Canadian meat, the British market looked attractive in the eyes of Canadian stockgrowers and it was resolved to ship them live, then sell them there at the world-famous Smithfield market. Since virtually nothing had been marketed in this manner, the economics of the movement was also to be closely studied for information of future shippers.

Grant MacEwan was to accompany the shipment and to follow the operation through auctioning, slaughtering, and marketing in the Smithfield meat market in London. While in the United Kingdom, he planned to tour parts of it — Scotland inevitably — looking at the historic scenery and livestock. He would be away over two months.

An eyewitness described how MacEwan packed for the extended trip. His crew had worked all day loading the cattle into boxcars, the last door sliding in place at eight o'clock that evening. He then took Phyllis Cline on a double date. As departure time neared, his friends drove around to the boarding house and parked outside while Grant went in to pack. "We sat there expecting to wait a long time but in fifteen minutes Grant was back, with one suitcase, to last him two and a half months!" On the trip he discovered that he had packed his bag "with things I did not need and left much of the other."

From the moment he left, MacEwan began absorbing information and observations at a tremendous rate. On board ship, he kept a log of each day's events that might well prove more informative than that of the captain of the ship. This was to continue — with increased intensity when prize British livestock loomed up — throughout the whole trip.

The experiment was a success. The cattle arrived at Birkenhead, were sold live at auction, and "attracted much favorable criticism ... the Shorthorn cross is favored, Hereford and Angus dividing second and third honors and Galloway, fourth." Meat buyers at Smithfield were later to prove equally favorably impressed and Dean Shaw was able to report a brisk sale for the duration of the experiment. (Dean Rutherford retired June, 1929, at which time Shaw was appointed dean).

*   *   *

Having completed his appointed task, Grant MacEwan turned to consider how best to fill the four weeks remaining in the United Kingdom before he was due to return to Canada. He absorbed the sights of London as a sponge absorbs water. One example, for instance, in his July 25 journal entry, shows that he was at Smithfield market at 6 in the morning, where he spent an hour; at St. Bartholomew's Church at 8; Westminster Abbey at 9; the Houses of Parliament at 9.30; Changing of the Guard at Buckingham Pallace at 10.30; Ministry of Agriculture at 11.30; 1.30, the Tower of London; 3.30, the Zoological Gardens! The entry is closed for the day with the admission that he "had a busy day in London and came out with Roy Blake [a student assistant who accompanied him on the trip from Saskatoon] to his home in Kings Langley in the evening. ..."

What is the reaction of a man who bears a Scottish name and returns to the land of his ancestors for the first time?

July 29, 1932: Bonnie Scotland ... Scotland is great. The country is one continuous picture, dotted with sheep, Ayrshires and Clydesdales. It is but little wonder that such a unique country has produced the best horses, the best cattle and the best men in the world. As I travelled from Preston to Edinburgh last night I saw the sun go to rest in the most beautiful setting that has yet come to my view. Edinburgh today. The Scotsmen and particularly the Scottish lassies make a pleasant sort of change in scenery ... visited Edinburgh Castle and the famous and truly wonderful National War Memorial and the best second hand stores in town.

Four days later, he stood in the hills of his ancestors in Inverness, overlooking Glen Urquhart letting down into Loch Ness. It was here that the Clan Grant dwelt of old, descendants of Kenneth MacAlpine, King of Scotland in the tenth century. They marched to the pipe music of "Stand Fast Craigellachie" and that was their war cry. He wrote "I stand tonight on the hills not far from Glen Urquhart from which old James Grant, son of

John Grant (Ian MacIalian) came in 1773 and landed at Pictou, Nova Scotia. It is a bonnie, gripping, wild and lovable country and surely nothing short of dire persecution would ever divorce a man from it."

In Glasgow, he wrote that "oat cakes, porridge and scones are agreeing with me much better than the English diets."

By the time the four weeks were up, MacEwan had visited at least 30 cities, attended agricultural shows and inspected herds on farms at least 30 times, had visited 28 historic sites, and conducted at least 17 interviews on farm methods, nutrition, and economics. To do so he had toured England, Scotland, Wales, Jersey and the Guernsey islands, and stopped briefly in the St. Malo district of France. All of this, crammed into one short month, was a satisfactory "holiday" for the man who proved to be no ordinary tourist.

*   *   *

Grant was due to return to Canada from Manchester to Montreal. He was actually aboard the ship and had unpacked before he received word that a desire he had expressed to agricultural agent W. A. Wilson at Canada House, London, to return via the northern Churchill route had been fulfilled. If he could get to Newcastle-on-Tyne before noon of the next day, he had a berth on the SS *Silksworth*, which was taking the Hudson Bay Route to pick up a cargo of grain.

He left the one ship "as though it were burning," reaching the dock just as the signal was given to lift the gangplank. "The officer on the dock looked at me in surprise and gasped, 'Wat the bloody 'ells the matter with you?' " When Grant explained that he had just got the chance to take the trip through Churchill, the officer said, "Bloody fool, you'll wish you 'adn't. But Blimey, if a man wants to drown in iceberg water, I wouldn't stop 'im — go right ahead!"

He reached the *Silksworth* in time to leave with her, but not without presenting the master of the ship with a problem. His vessel was not a passenger craft and there was no provision in her records to show MacEwan's presence during the passage to the northern port. To solve the dilemma, Captain Blacklock concluded that, although she had never carried one before, the *Silksworth* required the services of a purser, so the Canadian professor was described as such for the duration of the voyage. He wasn't your regular purser, however, for he insisted on paying for his cabin and his meals. During the fifteen-day voyage, he made so many notes on previous observations and on the Hudson Bay Route that he consumed every scrap of paper they could spare and ended up writing on English toilet paper, "which is thicker than Canadian."

Drama attended the man once again. Upon arrival of the *Silksworth* at the Port of Churchill, Manitoba, on August 29, 1932, T. R. Moulton and Herbert Legg, customs inspectors, issued a Daily-Non-Immigrant Report form to J. W. G. MacEwan, Canadian citizen by birth, readmitting him to the country and noting thereon, "First person to be admitted to Canada by Customs and Immigration via Churchill."

Chapter 14

Marriage

The depression hit the world in the 1930s but on the Prairies its effect was intensified by one of the worst droughts in living memory. So it was around 1935, when others saw signs of improvement, the people on the Prairies saw none, as rain refused to fall and withered crops were torn from the soil by what seemed to be a ceaseless scorching wind.

Although the economy continued slow and farm production fell, the demands on the time of MacEwan, and others like him, increased. Following his return from Britain, he registered a mild complaint in his journal that it was becoming difficult to apportion his time. Nevertheless, he was to take on one of the major commitments of his life.

* * *

By now the public had added another claim to his already long list, for although there had been a few occasions in the past on which he had been asked to speak on topics other than agriculture, they now increased markedly. It was largely due to the interesting, informative, and entertaining talks he gave on his experiences and observations while overseas. Those who heard him asked for more; those who had not, soon learned of his reputation and made demands on his already full schedule of commitments. MacEwan's reputation as a gifted and popular speaker had become permanently established.

As far as his personal life was concerned, it is a surprising fact that MacEwan went through the depression virtually untouched. The budgets of universities were at first frozen and then reduced throughout the country. Drastic measures were taken by Dr. Murray to keep his institution functioning on the reduced income; programs were canceled or at best severely restricted; building ceased altogether; salaries were at first frozen and then reduced. The heaviest blow fell on the young, single faculty members, who, in his judgment, were best able to survive on greatly reduced incomes. Some were invited to take enforced sabbatical leaves on a pittance and many did so. Some managed, not only to weather the storm, but to improve their knowledge at other institutions throughout the United States and Europe, despite a shortage of funds.

As it happened, during the nearly ten years of drought and depression, when the salaries of professors were dropping, Grant MacEwan was enjoying accelerated promotion for one reason or another. Thus, even though the salaries of the positions to which he rose had been drastically reduced, they always managed to be an increase over what he had been previously earning. He was never asked to take enforced leave, because the faculty of agriculture, short-staffed as it was, and being an essential service to the battle-weary farmers, could not spare him. Neither did it harm his position that a close relationship had developed between the president and himself.

*   *   *

While he had developed a more or less close father-son relationship with Murray, he had, at the same time, developed one of a different kind with a man more his own age — Prof. Al Ewen. Ever since the two had met and Grant had concluded that he was an interesting type, they had been drawn together, first in their work where they detected a shortage of agricultural textbooks dealing with Canadian farming and decided to do something together about it, and then in whatever spare time activities they allowed themselves. A strong bond of friendship and loyalty soon bound them together.

In some respects they formed an unlikely combination. MacEwan was still the tall, slim, and handsome man hovering about his normal weight of approximately 200 pounds, his movements rapid and purposeful. Contemporary photographs show little change in appearance from those taken during his college days save for the addition of a mustache, now a permanent fixture. He had not thickened as many men do when they leave the active life of college playing fields and take to the less active, more sedentary, life in the offices of commerce and academe.

Ewen, on the other hand, although not as tall, was a big man in every way, with thick shoulders, large hands, and the face of a pugilist (he had been a boxer in the championship class at the university in Scotland), and a nose that showed evidence of being broken at least once. His movements were slow but suggested ponderous power.

MacEwan was "dry Scot," Ewen a "whisky Scot." The difference caused little friction, save on one occasion. The two had been enjoying themselves each in his own way at a dance being held at the King George Hotel ballroom. As the evening wore on, MacEwan came to the conclusion that they had both had enough entertainment for one night and went onto the dance floor to inform Ewen, with the suggestion that the time had come

Ewen and MacEwan roughing it. The two had four-wheel-drive, tractor-tread bodies that could take them anywhere and survive (MacEwan Collection)

to leave. For the first time since they had met, MacEwan ran into the full force of the ex-boxer's straight-arm with a huge fist like the business end of a battering ram. MacEwan skidded across the floor on his back. It would be the last time he sampled the Ewen fist.

                    *   *   *

Both men enjoyed a tremendous capacity for hard work over long hours but on occasion Ewen liked a holiday — something his friend had to learn. As was customary, they were working late at their office one night toward the end of August 1931, and Ewen said that if they were going to take any sort of a holiday at all that summer, they would have to move fast, for the fall term would be soon upon them. For once, Grant agreed. They canvassed the possibilities and decided that they would float on a raft, fashioned out of salvaged telephone poles, down the South Saskatchewan River to the Forks where the North and South branches join.

Both men of action, the following afternoon they met at the riverbank, sawed poles in half, lashed them together with ropes, built a rudimentary deck with a large packing box for partial shelter, and set off with a supply of oat cakes and jam.

MacEwan aboard the raft on which he and Ewen drifted down the South Saskatchewan River   *(Foran Collection)*

At first we bedded down for the night with the idea of floating all night but there were difficulties and thereafter we tied up at nights. The adventure was great, upset once in rapids, severely sunburned, ran out of food but still great and economical. We finally abandoned the raft at the Forks ... walked to Weldon at which point we returned via train to Saskatoon.

Behind the words in this brief account, lies real action. They upset when the river turned mean near Fenton Ferry — channel narrowing, deepening and rushing between large boulders into which the raft crashed and attempted to mount, the oncoming current thrusting the stern of the craft under the surface. They were thrown into the rapids with all their belongings. Fortunately, they were able to save their lives. Some of the gear that floated, they salvaged, the rest was lost to the boiling waters.

When they walked from the Forks to Weldon, they strode into the cafe and ordered "two man-sized meals." The proprietor looked at the unshaven, sunburned pair and demanded money first. Only after the meals were paid for, would he trust them with the food. It had taken six days to drift the 100 miles and all the holiday came to was $12 each, which pleased the Scot in both men.

MacEwan and Ewen worked closely at the university and in the field. In his book *Extending the Boundaries*, dealing with scholarship and research at the University of Saskatchewan, 1909-1966, Carlyle King wrote about the well-stocked farm built up by Dean Rutherford at the university and then continued:

With these animals Professors A. M. Shaw and Grant MacEwan carried on a variety of breeding and nutrition researches which were very useful to livestock men. The experiments resulted in the compilation of numerous valuable data which attracted national attention. From 1929 to 1937 the University operated the Matador Ranch for the investigation of crossbreeding in sheep and beef cattle; the work with beef cattle especially made an outstanding contribution to the livestock industry.

When he read Dr. King's words sometime afterwards, Grant said, "It's too bad he didn't mention Al Ewen who had an equal share in this work."

*   *   *

He was a busy man with little time for dallying, but during this period another friendship was to develop. He was increasingly in demand as a public speaker as might well be expected, having added new subjects to his repertoire (including something like "the Saskatchewan River as a navigable body of water," spiked with a large measure of humor). He was called upon to judge at more cattle shows of increasing size and importance than ever before. He had also been demonstrating the "Cash Captive Bolt Humane Killer" he had purchased and brought back from Britain, the first one in Canada. (It was something like a revolver which fired a bolt propelled by a blank cartridge, killing animals instantly and humanely, without the failure and subsequent suffering that sometimes happened when using the old-fashioned ax or hammer method.) With difficulty and in time he finally succeeded in getting publicity for this new — and kinder — method of slaughter.

In addition to all of the foregoing, at Dr. Murray's invitation, the bachelor professor became Dean of Men at Qu'Appelle Hall, moved into the dean's suite and immediately began stamping the job with his own character. He formed discussion groups and conducted surveys of his charges to uncover contemporary attitudes toward such subjects as alcohol, gambling, religious belief, earning one's way through college, among others. He helped form the Saskatoon Archaeological Society and became its first president in 1935. Busy as he was, he could not forget the girl with the brown eyes he had met at the masquerade.

*   *   *

Up to the time MacEwan met Phyllis Cline, his journal shows outings with a number of young ladies but it was not long after the masquerade that her name began appearing more frequently, and eventually exclusively. Phyllis came from Churchbridge, Saskatchewan, where her father was the stationmaster. She had studied at the universities of Saskatchewan and Manitoba and eventually became "a good primary grade teacher, among the best" according to an eyewitness. From time to time, she felt the strain of teaching and, under doctor's orders, returned to Churchbridge to rest and restore her energies. She returned to her classes which, in the 1930s, was no small matter, for a class could be anywhere from thirty to forty restive youngsters. "A class of twenty-five was a mild concession," fellow teacher Esther (Wright) Sutherland testified much later. During Christmas, Easter, and the summer, she would return to Churchbridge to spend the holidays with her parents — her father liked big cars, and was an ardent motorist, so they covered the countryside. When in Saskatoon, she accompanied Grant on most of his official appearances as dean of men or animal husbandry department head.

On other occasions, they would enjoy the simple, depression forms of entertainment: teachers' dances, church affairs, walks over the nearby prairies in search of arrowheads or other relics of the past with which Phyllis may not have been as thrilled as he, the movies — Will Rogers, his favorite — sporting activities, skating. More frequently, after three or four years of friendship, Grant visited Churchbridge, where he went on outings with her parents. Once or twice Phyllis went to Melfort with Grant to meet and visit with his parents. On one occasion they motored to Waskesiu for a weekend — carefully chaperoned by Hooper Coles and his wife, good friends of both, in whose car they traveled.

Long courtships were not unusual for the time. Actually, they were forced on many young couples who hadn't the money to set up housekeeping for themselves, and had little hope of making it. There were no such restrictions on Grant and Phyllis.

The courtship had been anything but whirlwind.

As the fifth year started, Phyllis began to seriously consider her position, and the more she did so, the more she thought it wise that they come to some sort of an understanding, explicit rather than implicit. Grant wasn't the only pebble on the beach. Other young men had made it abundantly clear that, if Phyllis ever ceased going with the tall professor, they would be only too willing to take his place. One need only to look at contemporary photographs of the attractive Miss Cline, some in the newspapers as she sang here or became president of the young business-women there, to agree that there would be no shortage of eager escorts. They could not be expected to hang on forever and this was made plain to Grant in the spring of 1935.

"I became a much more attentive suitor after that," Grant recalled some years later. His journal supports his statement as it records trips to Churchbridge to spend time with the Cline family and to Melfort with Phyllis to visit the MacEwans on the farm. Finally, on June 29, 1935, "I travelled to Churchbridge by bus," and the next day, "Phyllis and I decided finally to be married about July 26." On July 8, "Phyllis Cline got her Bluebird [diamond] reg. number 70193."

*   *   *

No bachelor's party took place the night before the wedding, for the groom was fully occupied announcing the livestock parade of champions at the Saskatoon Exhibition, a performance he was to repeat time and time again at major western exhibitions. His father was with him but his mother was confined to bed in the Melfort hospital with a recurring attack of asthma.

The MacEwan/Cline wedding: (Left to right) Prof. Al Ewen, best man, the groom, the bride,
Esther Wright, maid of honor, the bride's mother, Mrs. Vernon Cline

(Foran Collection, Charmbury photo)

The entry in the MacEwan journal for the wedding day is brief and to
the point, but the date is underlined three times — the only date so dealt
with. He recorded that the day was excellent, that about fifty people
attended the ceremony, that an uncle of the bride, Dr. John L. Nicol,
performed the ceremony, and that Hon. Robert Weir, federal minister of
agriculture — a Conservative but an old friend from Melfort — attended.

It was a union of no mean consequence and was fully reported in the
Saskatoon Star-Phoenix and the *Winnipeg Free Press,* enjoying top play with
photographs in both papers. According to the *Free Press,* it was "a popular
and picturesque wedding," taking place "at the home of the bride's uncle
and aunt, Mr. and Mrs. James McLean, situated in a veritable Garden of
Eden, at the Forestry Farm," where McLean was director, "in a setting of
flowers with a background of evergreens." The university was represented
by James Clinkskill, "the venerable chairman of the board of governors."
The maid of honor was Esther Wright, who had introduced the two, and the
best man, Prof. Al Ewen.

The *Free Press* reported that the young couple (the bride wearing rose
beige with black accessories) departed by train for a honeymoon at the
Pacific Coast. It was no ordinary departure, no ordinary train trip.

As departure time approached, Ewen lost the groom. After a frantic search he found his friend in a driveway, hidden among the trees, helping a friend change a flat tire.

The trip by rail lasted about ninety miles. At Rosetown the MacEwans got off the train and spent the first night in the Rosetown Hotel. It was a memorable occasion for a number of reasons among which was the fact that, on a walk into the countryside after a stuffy train ride, Grant had the good fortune to find an Indian hammerhead.

The following day they boarded a westbound bus and took a rambling trip through Spokane, Vancouver, Victoria, Seattle (where they visited the fleet), and back to Rosetown where, once again, they boarded the train for the short return trip to Saskatoon. The nature of the trip became common gossip in university circles. The fact that the major part of the trip had been made by bus was put down to the well-known MacEwan frugality; the short train trips, from and back to Saskatoon, a concession to public opinion.

In this case, the gossips were far off the mark. As a couple, the MacEwans were totally impervious to the opinion of others about the way they lived their own lives, but despite the fact that it was not in their nature to explain themselves, Phyllis later set the record straight. The groom, she pointed out, was six feet four inches tall and always experienced great difficulty fitting into a Pullman berth even when traveling alone. He was not about to attempt the impossible now he had a wife.

*   *   *

Enjoyable though the honeymoon was, the bride had been surprised and somewhat dismayed when, with characteristic economy of time, Grant brought out the manuscript for his and Ewen's textbook and worked on it during idle moments on the trip. Looking back, he confessed that "I did more work on the manuscript during the honeymoon than I had a right to, but come hell, high water, or matrimony, I was resolved to finish it and get it off to the publisher."

The first recorded outing for the MacEwans, upon their return from the honeymoon, brings two important and persistent elements in Grant MacEwan's life together. He mentions how he and Phyllis drove to Lanigan and Govan and back and that "I secured a number of selected samples of rusted roughage for analysis," and later that "we stopped at a wind-blown field at Guernsey and found several arrow heads." No idle touring of the countryside for Grant, no matter how charming the company. Work and history would always be combined wherever possible and it would be difficult to separate vocation from avocation, so efficiently did he combine, and energetically pursue, the two.

Their first Christmas was spent with the Clines in Churchbridge. Grant surprised Phyllis with a karakul-paw fur coat and he himself received a paper case, two ties, two pairs of socks and two books — *Will Rogers* by O'Brien, *The Glencoe Massacre* by John Buchan. The following day, he returned alone to Saskatoon to work with Ewen on *Canadian Feed Unit Tables*, to fill another gap they had detected in the literature on Canadian agriculture. Ten days later, when Phyllis returned, the nutrition thesis had been completed, through working night and day.

The public seemingly ignored MacEwan's marital status; demands on his time continued unabated. If anything, they accelerated. Invitations flooded in for him to speak or judge — often both — not only in Saskatchewan, but increasingly outside the province as well. On one occasion Phyllis counted forty nights in a row during which her husband had been called away on one sort of public service or other. "Grant could never refuse an invitation, he could never say 'no.' "

*   *   *

Although at first surprised — not shocked, for she had seen him in action for five years — at the extent of the claims placed on her husband's time by the public, Phyllis had not been idle. She learned early that there would be no hope of changing Grant's habits even if she wanted to, and concluded that considerable adjustment would have to be made in her preconception of married life. Although a most feminine person, she was no "clinging vine" in the contemporary use of the term and had a mind of her own, coming from a long line of independent people on both sides of her family.

Her father's people originated in the Black Forest region of Germany, migrating to the north of England and thence in the 1700s to North America. They were "Pennsylvania Dutch" and members of the much-persecuted Society of Friends, better known as Quakers. At the outbreak of the American Revolution, they again migrated; this time to the Niagara Peninsula as United Empire Loyalists, where they became prosperous farmers and landowners. Her mother's side traced back to Huguenots by the name of Depew (the famous American lawyer, legislator, and orator, Chauncey Depew, was one of the line), who supported the British against the Americans, a relative dying while hauling supplies in the Battle of Stoney Creek during the War of 1812-14.

She had been born in Hamilton and came west with the family where her father, a Canadian Pacific Railway employee, worked at a number of centers, including Churchbridge. A precocious student, she cherished the thought of becoming an interior designer but, as there were no such courses near at hand, she spent two miserable and homesick years at the universities of Saskatchewan and Manitoba, marking time until she became eighteen and acceptable at the Manitoba College of Education. There, Phyllis Cline won her teaching certificate.

Having inherited an independent outlook along with a lively sense of humor, from both sides of her family, Phyllis MacEwan faced her position positively. She saw early that she would have to understand her husband completely, take him when he was there and make a life of her own when he was not. Others had done so successfully, why not she?

She made one early attempt to change him. "The constant energetic output worried me at the time and I did try — for his own good and at the urging of others — to get him to slow down." Needless to say her efforts were in vain save for the fact that, from time to time, Grant would grudgingly allow himself to be persuaded to see a doctor. "Prevailed upon by the good wife — but not without objection — I presented myself for medical inspection to Dr. David Baltzan. His judgment was 'physically sound,' " recalled MacEwan. What he failed to reveal was that, from time to time, the doctor added "but showing signs of fatigue." The latter, one is bound to suspect, could indicate that perhaps the physician was more in league with the wife than he was with the patient.

Apart from absences, there was little or no upset in the family, for "Grant is so well organized that he leaves nothing to chance." He would never be typical, of that Phyllis was convinced. He had never been typical in anything: farm boy, student, civil servant, university professor. At no time in the past had he fitted into a ready-made slot and it appeared he would not do so in the future. He also gave fair warning early in their married life that he did not intend gathering moss while waiting to collect a university professor's pension.

What one writer before this said about another, could well be said of MacEwan:"The mundane tasks, fears, distractions and personal concerns that occupy much of the ordinary person's energies he transcended."

Phyllis accepted his lifestyle and was prepared to live with it. The two developed their own methods of living.

Chapter 15

Campus Life, First Book

Despite drought and depression, life went on in the university community, for they had learned to cope. Indeed, some have said, looking back, that, although they had no money, life was not all that bad, they had a good time. It was to this atmosphere the newlyweds returned. They would make a home, face triumphs and disappointments in the next few years, and Grant MacEwan's interests, some of which had been rather formless, would begin to take shape and serve as indicators to the future.

He took early steps to see his wife settled in a home of her own. Upon returning from their honeymoon, they lived for one year in the upper floor of Mrs. MacCallum's private home near the college. Then a house at 313 Bottomley Avenue North, a block and a half from the university, was offered for sale. It was an attractive, two-story stucco house with a sweeping front roof line and chimney that set it apart from structures of similar class. It was five years old, the asking price was $5,500; MacEwan offered $3,500; the owner came down to $4,500; MacEwan went up to $4,000. They met at $4,240.

Phyllis applied her latent and considerable talents for interior decorating, taking infinite pains to obtain the right tone of paint for the living room, testing the patience of the long-suffering painter. She left a large expanse of wall above the fireplace to be filled in with just the right sort of art work that would require her careful consideration. It was then that Grant made his contribution to the task, hauling out and filling the vacancy with a large print of highland cattle in a Scottish glen, a wedding present from Tom Bryden, farm manager of the university farm.

However, she had free play with decorating the bedroom, which turned out to be tastefully done in white and pastel tones. A swag valance topped the windows from which gossamer curtains fell in graceful cascades tied back on either side. The rest of the room, say eyewitnesses, was decorated with a white rug and a white bed throw, creating an unusual but pleasingly feminine effect. Friends who knew them both chuckled as they attempted to imagine the six-foot-four Grant MacEwan, the agriculturist, in such surroundings.

*   *   *

In this casual day and age, it is difficult to imagine an era where entertainment was mainly done in one of two forms — the afternoon "tea" at which tea and dainty finger foods were served, or the formal sit-down dinner with a full array of dinner service, cutlery, and crystal on the dining room table where at least three courses were served. Imagine the discussion that followed an innovative dinner at the MacEwans when, with a number of guests and a large roast of beef from a prize-winning bovine at hand, they provided a supply of fresh bread, butter, pickles, and, with the host carving generous portions, each person making his own sandwich.

Formal dinners were another matter. While the MacEwans had some in their own home, they tended to discharge social debts by entertaining friends in the King George Hotel dining room from time to time. In those days the "KG" was the place to go.

*   *   *

Together they contributed other legends to the campus, as when Grant returned from a trip and presented Phyllis with two motherless skunk kittens, which were promptly christened "This 'n That." With his experience in veterinary medicine to guide him, MacEwan took them to the laboratory and rendered them odorless, enabling them to become beloved pets for a considerable time. They were given the run of the house. On one occasion, after Grant had applied olive oil to his hair to keep it in shape, Phyllis entered the living room to find her husband reading the newspaper with This or That perched on his shoulder licking the oil.

Eventually, they passed out of the picture for one reason or another, certainly not for want of care and attention, leaving a sorrowful man and a tearful woman behind. This prompted possibly the only eulogy ever composed to a male skunk:

He had become quite a part of the family unit, and while only a skunk, perhaps he could bring about as much credit and glory to his Creator as the average human of the present age. For aggressiveness, instinct, determination, olefactory capacity and understanding, he far excelled the female skunk, which will be left to hibernate alone this winter . . . we buried him under the plum tree. Attachment is a funny thing.

The MacEwans from Melfort joined the Clines from Churchbridge as their first house guests that Christmas, as Grant and Phyllis put their new home to good use. The MacEwan journal records their joy on this occasion.

On the back of a page, as if it were a memo for use the following Christmas, it also revealed a list of eight families to whom, unknown to others, MacEwan had sent groceries, sweets, clothing, toys, fruit, and nuts. It had been his habit to do so each depression Christmas and would be until it lifted — and possibly beyond.

*   *   *

To appreciate the atmosphere surrounding the newlyweds it is once again necessary to send the mind back almost fifty years and conjure up the situation on a prairie campus of the early 1930s. Most professors were dedicated men who thought almost exclusively about the instruction of their students in a search for truth (not to be confused with their own particular political predispositions), the advancement of their own discipline, and, where it proved possible, service to the community in a broad sense. They were making sacrifices to do so and consequently were held high in the esteem of the community, occupying an honored position. The public could not always understand them, and there were stories rampant about the antics of the "absent-minded professor," but this served to confirm their position in the public mind rather than to detract from it.

Sundays would find a good number of faculty and wives at church, after which followed Sunday afternoon tea. Both the faculty members and wives shared in the planning of their teas, to which other faculty husbands and wives were invited. In time it became customary for certain Sundays to become identified as the "Thompson's Tea" or the "Dean's Tea" and so on down the line. In a depressed economy, with many professors taking large cuts in pay, the teas were a practical way of entertaining a large number of friends at minimum cost. In an intellectual community, it provided full opportunity for exchange of ideas or, if one were so disposed, gossip. The latter often predominated.

As for the tea parties, there was one faculty member who made it clear in his journal what he thought of them: "A Sabbath desecrated by silly social superfluities."

There was no anonymity on the campus; the small size of the student body and of the faculty saw to that. Although outnumbered, the faculty, with the added weight of community respect for their position, were in complete and unquestioned charge. There was no doubt in anybody's mind as to why they were there, what they were striving for; nor was there any doubt about the object of the institution

The relationship of the professors to the students was clear. In the absence of their parents, the ancient principle of *in loco parentis* applied, save for a few students who had been forced to stay out of university for several years in order to earn enough money to pay the fees and board and room, and who arrived on campus often as old, if not older, than some of the junior professors. These were tacitly accepted as being able to look after themselves. If the professors were temporary parents to the students, in the eyes of a large majority the president, Dr. Murray, was granddaddy to them all.

Dr. Walter C. Murray, portrait by Ernest
G. Fosbery
   (University of Saskatchewan Archives)

The first home at 313 Bottomley Avenue
South, Saskatoon   (MacEwan Collection)

Although most of the university community took education seriously, there was nevertheless a lighter side and a full slate of extracurricular activities — social, academic, and athletic — was indulged in. In short, despite the depression, and the accompanying limitations and restrictions, these were halcyon days at the university. It is possible the like will never be seen again and the MacEwans were part of it all.

*   *   *

In October of 1935, the Conservatives under Prime Minister R. B. Bennett, suffered an overwhelming defeat at the hands of the Mackenzie King Liberal party. It was to set off a mild chain reaction on the University of Saskatchewan campus which would involve MacEwan in more ways than one.

As the new administration settled into its task in Ottawa, it began filling positions with those of its own choosing. Dean Shaw was elected to sit on the Canadian Wheat Board, leaving his chair at the College of Agriculture vacant. Dr. Murray, with an eye on his limited budget, was not in a hurry to fill it and he took on the duties of acting dean himself. However, in a short time he invited Professor MacEwan to assist him and suggested that he move into the dean's office to facilitate matters. It was from there that MacEwan operated during 1935 and part of 1936. As it worked out, Dr. Murray held the title of acting dean while MacEwan was acting dean in fact.

In the new position, but without the title, Professor MacEwan was now introduced to the higher realms of administration, which came as a complete and uncomfortable surprise. As the year opened, he surveyed his schedule of engagements, engagements that Shaw would have been carrying out if he had not been in Ottawa in his $15,000-a-year position. The calendar was filled with meetings, conferences, convention greetings, university committee meetings, and agricultural staff meetings to the extent that the wide-ranging, cattle-judging professor complained to his journal: "Jan. 14, 1935 — The next two weeks on account of conventions, meetings, conferences will not be overly pleasant. It appears now like an apprenticeship in hell." It was several months before he was able to organize the flow of administrative work to permit him the occasional trip into the field where he was happiest.

It was to be the most miserable year MacEwan put in at the university up to that time. He refused countless invitations to judge livestock in 1936. Instead, he stuck to his office and administered his college. The horseman found himself at the end of a much shorter tether than he had been accustomed to.

It was not to last. Dr. Murray himself had reached retirement age and was preparing to retire in 1937. Much remained for hi'n to do, including the filling of the agricultural dean's chair, for it would nct be wise to leave such an important task to a successor who might be out of touch with the university's traditional reverence for the college.

MacEwan found himself in an awkward position. Dr. Murray called him to his office and set the problem before him. The position must be filled. Who would be the best one to fill it? Was he familiar with the work of Dr. L. E. Kirk? There was also the new head of the School of Agriculture to appoint, requiring a man with imagination, zeal, pioneering spirit, and close association with farmers and their families. MacEwan was ideally suited to the job.

Memories are dim regarding the exact order of presentation but not on the propositions themselves. MacEwan realized he held only a master's degree (there never seemed to be time to work toward a Ph.D), while Kirk was a doctor of philosophy from Minnesota University; his research had been practical and in animal husbandry while Kirk's had been academically pure and in field crops; Kirk was a native son, had been a brilliant University of Saskatchewan student, whereas he, MacEwan, had studied at OAC. Irksome though he had found the chores of a dean to be — and it could not have escaped the notice of the shrewd and experienced, though kindly, president — MacEwan would not have been human had he not felt disappointment at not being selected, or even given the opportunity to refuse the position, the duties of which he had been fulfilling for almost two years. There it was. He knew Dr. Murray. He knew a decision had been made and it was the president's way of revealing it by seeking his advice.

However, he was to be the new director of the School of Agriculture and the manager of the university farm, for both of which Murray had said he was "ideally suited." Furthermore, the duties of acting dean had indeed been irksome and restricting. Other accomplishments would salve over any transitory feeling of disappointment to a buoyant spirit.

*   *   *

In June 1936, MacEwan and Ewen had signed a book contract with Nelson, the Toronto publisher, to have their book *The Science and Practice of Canadian Animal Husbandry* published that September. The day the MacEwans moved into their new house, Grant received the first author's copies of the book.

It was an event of some importance in the agricultural world, judging from its reception by the press. Farmer's Forum, edited by R. M. Scott, of the *Winnipeg Free Press* (Nov. 13, 1936) stated enthusiastically that at last Canadian students and farmers alike had a book that had been needed for a long time, a practical, usable, and informative one. He spotted the Western Feeding Unit developed by the authors, with the co-operation of their colleagues in the chemistry department, and said "such a presentation represents a tremendous amount of work by someone and should go far to correct wrong feeding practices of the past. It might well be worth the price of the book alone if studied and used." (For one reason or another, MacEwan says, the Western Feeding Unit Chart never really caught on in Canada. Other countries had their own and were making full use of them).

The *Saskatoon Star-Phoenix* called it "a valuable book" and commended the authors for their work. "W.J.M." also singled out the Western Feeding Unit for attention as a first. W. B. Reynolds writing in *The Ontario Milk Producer* called it "a distinct contribution to the literature of Canadian agriculture." He said it was a practical and down-to-earth publication of use to students, dairymen and stockmen alike; "the reader will be struck by the modest and practical facts set forth. So many authorities are prone to recommend rations that are too complicated and expensive, but these authors have given us rations that are within reach of all from all viewpoints. They are careful to use in feeding all of the home grains and roughages before suggesting purchase of other foods" — a perceptive reviewer who put his finger on the essence not only of the professional outlook of MacEwan and Ewen but of their Scottish propensities.

Alex MacEwan sent a letter from Melfort to the joint authors congratulating them and suggesting "now that you are started, I am going to suggest that you think about starting another on the same subject but condense it down to about one-third of the size by only dealing with the more common and practical subjects." (Ever the practical farmer, it was Alex MacEwan who said that he was afraid his son evinced a tendency to choose horses "for beauty more than for utility.")

MacEwan and Ewen had gained national attention. They were now authors as well as professors. The reviews could not have been more satisfying and it spurred the two authors onward in filling the need for other textbooks.

If MacEwan needed anything more to take his mind off the deanship — which he didn't — it was the fact that the new government in Ottawa began having recourse to his knowledge of animal husbandry and the western scene in forming fresh policies under the new agriculture minister, Hon. James G. Gardiner. Soon after the Liberals were returned to power, he was invited to Ottawa to a meeting of the Advanced Registry Swine Committee. Later he was involved in a conference of agricultural ministers. From then on his journal records attendance at agriculture meetings in Ottawa, sometimes four or five times a year, on one such mission or other of increasing importance. Seeking MacEwan's advice was to become habitual in Ottawa.

However, back on the Prairies, things were still tough, and in 1937 they got tougher, especially for the one who had been named manager of the university farm. Its very existence was threatened by the worst year of the long drought.

Chapter 16

1937 — The Worst Year

When he became manager of the university farm, along with his other duties, MacEwan inherited responsibility of no mean size. It was to test him to the limit of his ingenuity in 1937, when nature seemed determined to break the West by throwing everything it could in the way of bad weather in its direction. Even the grasshoppers, a scourge in themselves, were starving that year.

The farm spread north and east of the university buildings and covered 1,400 acres. There were barns, buildings, and livestock to care for as well as services to be provided to various departments, such as field husbandry with its experimental plots. Feed for all the animals, whether service or experimental, was raised on the farm and also on large acreages some distance from Saskatoon, either owned by the university or leased for hay and grazing purposes. This establishment, with MacEwan in charge, felt the full force of "the worst year."

He wrote, "the year has been the worst, agriculturally, in Saskatchewan history. Prices continue to be ruinous and the rainfall at a record low, the average wheat yield in the Province will stand at less than 2½ bushels per acre. Here at Saskatoon, there was no rain when rain was needed with the result that from 1,000 acres of crop we did not harvest a bushel of grain."

The only feed they recovered from their extensive holdings was Russian thistle, 200 loads of the repellent weed. Having observed livestock in the country on his travels, MacEwan had noticed that in some of the hardest hit regions, where there was nothing else, livestock munched on the prickly plant. Lacking anything else, some cattlemen were feeding it. Where

Aerial view of part of the University of Saskatchewan campus and part of the university farm of which MacEwan became manager   *(University of Saskatchewan Archives)*

there was none of the weed or ignorance of its use, livestock literally starved to death. With these observations in mind, and with nothing to harvest from the university land, MacEwan concluded, "it looks as though our research program for the year will centre around the emergency use of Russian Thistles." He attacked the problem with persistence and patience.

He had always joined in with students in their affairs and their sports, helping where he could, and now they in turn pitched in to help with the thistle research. They cut every thistle on the university farm and even went through the city, gathering what they could from vacant lots and back lanes. With thistles down their necks and in their shoes, they loaded hayracks with the thorny harvest and drew it to the university to provide MacEwan and his associates with test feed for the large herds that would become part of the experiment.

"We did everything with it," MacEwan wrote. "We pounded it, chopped it, pulverized it — even boiled it. We cut it green, we cut it late, we hammered it, we ensiled it, we mixed it but it was still unpalatable, laxative and low on feeding value. The most significant feature, however, was that the animals — mainly cattle and sheep — are eating the stuff and maintaining weight fairly well."

The professor then sought to spread the message as far and as wide — and as quickly — as possible. He broadcast the findings over the radio and

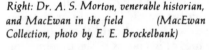

Above: John Buchan (right), Governor General of Canada, inspects the barns in company with MacEwan and others, paying special attention to animals fed on Russian thistle
(MacEwan Collection)

Right: Dr. A. S. Morton, venerable historian, and MacEwan in the field (MacEwan Collection, photo by E. E. Brockelbank)

published articles in the popular farm press; the city dailies carried feature stories on it, and he mimeographed instructions, making them available to anyone who wanted them.

Years later, William M. Wilson, a man who had worked with Grant as a student, later as a student assistant and who eventually became livestock feed specialist for Federated Co-operatives Limited, said, "we called him the Russian Thistle King — Grant saved the University herd of valuable breeding stock and the remnants of herds throughout Western Canada by his Russian Thistle project." Daily newspapers and the agricultural press were quick to editorialize on the valuable contribution the experiment had made to western agriculture at a crucial time.

* * *

In 1937, as if to make up for time lost during his term as assistant acting dean of agriculture the previous year, MacEwan resumed his judging activities. The fact that he was now an author of a book on animal husbandry added to his attractiveness and increased the number of invitations — many of them the double-barreled kind, asking him to judge during the day and speak after the banquet at night.

During the first few years at the university, he had been largely confined to small local shows and field days. In time, as his reputation and accomplishments grew, he found himself drawn toward the larger shows in the country. He would never desert the smaller ones completely, but it was inevitable that the more important pace-setting shows began claiming the bulk of his time during the spring and summers. (By this time Phyllis had come to the conclusion that her husband would never take a holiday, so if she ever wanted one, she would have to go on her own. She would travel in future, sometimes with her Churchbridge family, sometimes with friends.)

His major show assignment outside the province came from the Calgary Exhibition and Stampede, where Grant judged the Jersey cattle classes. From then on he was a familiar sight at all the major shows, his career reaching its peak in 1949, when he judged at a dozen of the majors, toured Arabian studs in southern California at the invitation of the Canadian Arabian Breeders who sought publicity and support for their breed of horses, and capped it all by judging horses at the Pacific National Exhibition in Vancouver. And twenty-five years after he had competed there as a student, he judged fat cattle at the world-renowned Toronto Royal Winter Fair.

*   *   *

It was following a horse show and ram sale in Maple Creek, Saskatchewan, that a nearly forgotten propensity returned to him, with almost disastrous results. After a long day, he caught the eastbound CPR passenger train to return home via Regina. He had not changed his habit of "sleeping raw" and he made no exception for trains. One way or another, he managed to cram his long frame into an upper berth, the only space available. As was the custom, he left the toes of his boots projecting into the green-carpeted aisle below for the porter whose nocturnal task it was to collect all footwear showing, chalk the berth number on the soles to assure safe return, carry them to the men's washroom and polish them.

The professor sank into a deep and well-deserved sleep, lulled by the muffled clickety-clack of the wheels as the steam locomotive whistled itself across the open prairie toward Regina. Some time later, he awoke with a start to find himself, stark naked, in the middle of the aisle. On one of the rare occasions of his lifetime, Grant experienced outright panic. How he got there he didn't know; how to get back he didn't know either, for he had forgotten the number of his berth. Then it occurred to him that his size twelve boots would lead him to his berth; none of the others protruding into the aisle could possibly be as big. To his dismay, he discovered that not a boot was to be seen along the green glow of the aisle — the porter was at work. He prayed that nobody would find it necessary to pay a visit to the men's washroom at one end or, more particularly, to the women's at the other end of the car. He then searched along the upper berths — surely he must have opened the curtains to get out. They were all closed.

Was he in the right car?

Only one thing remained and he was forced to do it. Dreadfully conscious of how it would look were he to be discovered naked, and peeking, in the middle of the night, he went down the aisle, and with the advantage of height, looked into each upper berth until he found a vacant one. He didn't stop to determine whether it was his or not — it was a welcome refuge. He clambered in as fast and as quietly as he could, to avoid disturbing the lady below. Only then did he become conscious of a bruise, and remember a "bump in the night," as he had fallen out of bed.

It had been years since he had last walked in his sleep.

*   *   *

Not all the incidents connected with judging proved so amusing. In a 1941 entry, the MacEwan journal states: "Judging light horses at Moose Jaw and was tossed from a horse in the first class, landing on a brittle collar bone."

What actually happened was that when he was judging the first of a long list of classes the mount from which he was officiating proved downright uncontrollable and he was thrown in the middle of the ring. He broke a collar bone in the fall. Getting to his feet, he carried on as if nothing had happened until he finished judging all the classes. Only then did he have his fractured bone attended to.

*   *   *

The late 1930s were to prove an interesting and formative stage for MacEwan. The animals from the farm were winning significant prizes at important shows and the progeny of those bred to university animals were doing so as well. Financial stress forced the president to ask him to make the farm pay for itself rather than draw on university resources, which meant a switch in emphasis to commercial, from experimental, farming. This, he and Ewen did successfully. He was elected to the Board of Directors of the Saskatoon Exhibition; His Excellency, Governor General John Buchan, visited the university and spent an interested half hour with MacEwan in his barns; he and Ewen produced their second textbook. As it turned out, there was a development that would prove to be of more fundamental significance than anything else he had done in the period. Once again, it arose with the help of a number of incidents that appeared seemingly in a cluster.

In 1938, MacEwan wrote that he was becoming more interested and more involved in western history:

> I have this year been favored with the opportunity of acting as the chauffeur of the grand old man of history, Prof. A. S. Morton. He is one of the most impractical of men but he knows the story of the early West as nobody else and it is a rare privilege to sit at his feet and listen. We have visited many sites — some confirmed, some not — of traders' posts.

Once again MacEwan's sense of humor asserted itself. He watched over the august historian with respectful amusement, for he was indeed the most impractical of men, especially on excursions out of doors. No matter what the conditions under which they went exploring, Dr. Morton always dressed as formally as he did for his lectures — tie, white shirt, silver-mounted cane, jacket and all. He was extremely hard of hearing to boot, and, immersed in his thoughts, he was in the habit of wandering off by himself into the bush in search of one old fort or another, forgetful of time and direction. When he strayed far afield, no amount of whistling or shouting would raise an answer from him and time and again his friends were forced to conduct a search. On one such occasion, Grant announced that on the next historical foray, he was going to tie a cowbell around the neck of the dignified old scholar.

Morton was not without a sense of humor himself. On an excursion in October 1941, to Fort La Corne and intermediate points to locate fort sites, they discovered the site of the post on Mosquito Point by navigating the Saskatchewan River northeast of Weldon in a leaky rowboat. Later, Dr. Morton was to state that "we were more nearly drowned in the boat than we were in the Saskatchewan River."

The early interest he had shown as a boy in the tales of pioneering in Nova Scotia and Manitoba and the notes he made during travels in the West were indications of something taking shape in his mind, but it remained for Morton to gather them together, enrich them, and give them direction. Not that MacEwan would aspire to duplicate the academic approach of the older scholar, for it wasn't his way. However, after traveling with Dr. Morton "there was no question as to what my hobby was to be."

*   *   *

The year before he began driving the historian, he had been in Regina attending an agricultural meeting and had an hour or two to kill before train time. It was then that he met Z. M. Hamilton, whom he knew as one trying to interest others in the story of the West. At Hamilton's invitation, he sat in the CBC studio while the former broadcast a popular lecture on the colorful pioneer Regina newspaperman, Nicholas Flood Davin. No doubt MacEwan turned the matter over in his mind on the journey back to Saskatoon.

The same year, J. A. Thompson, then the grand old man of the Moose Jaw Milk Producers' Association, invited him to address the group at a convention banquet with a warning to speak on any subject he chose but to say nothing about cows or dairying as, by that time, delegates would have had their fill of the subject.

As it happened, Thompson died soon after issuing the invitation, and "carrying out Mr. Thompson's last instructions to me, I talked about the history of farming in the West, and said 'nothing about cows and dairying.' " It was the first speech (1937) on record dealing with the subject for which he was to become famous. No doubt, the speaker was fully aware that the subject seemed to strike a responsive chord.

On November 10, 1937, he bought a Remington portable typewriter from Eaton's store for $38.50 and began using it.

*   *   *

The final incident of the cluster took place when, at the invitation of the CBC, he prepared and read a script over the network entitled "How Horses Came to Western Canada." The response was immediate, important, and gratifying. No sooner was the broadcast over than a telegram was on its way from Ottawa to Saskatoon: "Hearty congratulations and many thanks for your excellent address on horses in the West today." It was dated

MacEwan toured the country, avid for the stories of old-timers and characters of the West. He is seen with Two-Gun Palmer, a recluse near Dundurn, Sask., who was reputed to have associated with Jessie James. (MacEwan Collection)

December 6, 1938, and signed by Gladstone Murray, general manager of the CBC.

The program marked a turning point in what was to become one of MacEwan's major outside interests. Encouraging though the reaction was, it could hardly be said that he was propelled into an overnight rise to stardom. Things don't happen that way in Canada's low-frequency field of artistic endeavor compared with similar events in the high-frequency American culture — or, at least, they did not in the 1930s. Allowances must be made for the times when, still in their colonial-minded stage, most Canadians tended to think that any person or event worth writing about could never originate in their own country. Such pieces about western Canada were rare and only a few hardy souls persisted in presenting them, with scant reward. MacEwan had joined their slender ranks with his growing knowledge, interest, and his immense capacity for hard work.

The subjects of his after-dinner speeches also reflected his interest. He was now choosing such subjects as "Place Names," "The Romance of the Horse," "Yesterdays and Tomorrow in Agriculture." The demand for such speeches increased.

Two years later he broadcast another such program over CBC entitled "Some Homestead Memories" and sold a similar manuscript to the *Family Herald.* His interest in history was enough to spur him on but it did not go unnoticed that his income from such creative activity was increasing as well. Although not large by today's standards, it represented a respectable amount in the 1930s. Whereas he had worked gratis on programs and articles associated with his profession or, at best, sometimes collected $5 a time, the CBC paid $20 and the *Family Herald* $35 for his work.

It was in connection with his broadcast "Some Homestead Memories," that one is given a priceless view of MacEwan — not as a professor or writer gaining attention and respect from a growing public but as a son figuratively standing on the carpet before a loving but censorious mother.

If the general public was receptive to the program, Bertha MacEwan was not. The timing of it offended her strong Sabbatarian sense of propriety. In a letter to him, dated November 11, 1944, she first explained that his father had gone to a neighbor's to listen to his first program of the new season but that she had not, adding significantly — "I went to Church." Then she wrote: "Grant, I am sorry you are speaking over the air on Sunday on that subject — I don't think you asked Dr. Murray's advice. It is just a certain class that will like that on Sunday. I will stop now. I know you will think it is not my business but I trust you may see the right way."

*   *   *

The major advance that was to have far-reaching consequences came in 1942 when, after broadcasting a program entitled "Pioneer Threshing" over their network, CBC asked MacEwan to prepare a series of four programs, choosing his own subjects and title.

He had little difficulty picking a subject. MacEwan's interviews with old-timers and his research into the story of the West had taught him to admire and revere those who had originally opened it. "The frontier attracted men with imagination; fearless men; men with a longing in their souls for adventure. And certainly only those with initiative and a bit of bulldog determination remained through those testing years," he wrote of them later. The thing was that he had met many of them, had indeed sprung from pioneers like them and shared their characteristics. He decided to make the radio broadcasts into a series of thumbnail sketches about just such characters. He called it "Sodbusters."

By the time the broadcasts were finished, he had introduced Canadians, in a way never done before, to notable personalities who had dwelt in their midst in the years gone by. It was a hit with the CBC and with thousands of listeners — so much so that it almost became a program that would not die, for it was renewed in 1943 and yet again in 1944.

With additional sketches, the series was published by Thomas Nelson and Sons in 1948, under the same title. The book *Sodbusters* proved to be the first in a long line of popular western history books by Grant MacEwan.

His fascination with western Canadian history and its people was so irrepressible that it would have found an outlet in one form or another, but it is to the Canadian Broadcasting Corporation that the credit must go for discovering the West's most prolific popular historian, and giving him the audience his work deserved.

Chapter 17

The War Years

When the year 1939 opened, rumors of war abounded but there had been such rumors before and few suspected the outbreak that was to come before the year was out.

It is possible that Ewen and MacEwan took the rumors more seriously than some because, when their publisher asked the two to produce a second textbook in their field, they made somewhat of a record in producing *General Agriculture* — with the assistance of colleagues in such disciplines as chemistry, horticulture, genetics, and others — in four months! The book appeared the same year.

The demands on MacEwan's talents increased and he was, as he had been every year, faced with the problem of rationing his time. However, this did not prevent him from accepting an invitation to judge at the Kamloops Winter Fair. The show, and sale that went with it, was the first major one of the year and was viewed in beef circles as a trend-setter for prices, hence it was an attractive agricultural happening to take part in. He felt a deep affinity for the hardy ranchers of British Columbia's interior plateau and gloried in the tawny, rugged countryside. Add to this its association with the early fur trade and the fact that among ranchers there were some of the most colorful characters in the West and it's not difficult to see why this event, and one at Williams Lake several years later, would find MacEwan the livestock judge in action for a number of years.

*   *   *

He was certainly not wandering far afield in the interior of British Columbia early in May 1939, the third day, to be exact, when he made the following entry in his journal: "Phyllis to hospital at 11 a.m. Heather

Heather MacEwan and father at their Bottomley Avenue home
(MacEwan Collection)

MacEwan born at 11.45 p.m. Length 23", head 14½", hair black and lots of it. Disposition good." And, sounding forever like the animal husbandryman (and perhaps more like the superior male), he added: "Proof that a good sire pays."

The hospital experience represented all that was abhorrent to Phyllis MacEwan and, rather than spend the customary week or so recuperating there, she insisted on returning home by ambulance in a day or two. As the ambulance pulled up at the Bottomley Avenue home a small boy stood beside MacEwan watching the bearers carry the stretcher toward the house. He looked up at the tall professor with a morbid grin on his cherubic face and said, "Dead, eh!"

The following year the MacEwans had their daughter christened at the Forestry Farm, Phyllis's uncle, Dr. Nicol, officiating as he had when the parents were married four years earlier. Heather was to be their only child.

*   *   *

Grant and Phyllis MacEwan were inspecting a fur-trading site known as Isaac's Fort northeast of Melfort on September 2, 1939, when they heard that Britain had declared war against Germany.

The war would not touch Grant MacEwan as it touched others. As war fever heightened, he was to wonder where his duty lay. His colleague, Professor Ewen, with other professors, joined the Canadian Officers

Training Corps and began to take training. He was tempted but never did join. The First World War found him underage, the Second, slightly overage. He had never been a warlike person and had no desire to kill anyone. Furthermore, he well remembered the slogan with which farmers were urged to stay at their work during the First World War — "Food will win the war." It was revived during the Second World War and it had its influence on him. When Ewen joined the Saskatoon Light Infantry in June 1940 for overseas service, MacEwan was left pretty much alone to administer the animal husbandry department. He would miss this loyal, strong, and able friend and colleague. They had not always agreed, but on fundamentals they were always together and had collaborated on research, some of their projects not yet completed. For these reasons and others, MacEwan thought that his place remained at the university, contributing whatever he could to the nation's ability to feed the war machine.

His effort would remain an indirect one, but important none the less. He would work for maximum food production through livestock feeding, breeding, and production. This would be done through production committees such as: the Advanced Registry Swine Committee; the Western Society of Animal Production, of which he became president in 1942; the Prairie Farm Assistance Act Review Board (chairman); Agricultural Supply Committee, Ottawa, and others having to do with the flow of food into the national war effort. For efficient production he would also strive to break down certain superstitions livestock breeders had about the feeding of animals.

Impatient with conventional thinking MacEwan committed the most resounding error — in judgment of human reaction — of his years at Saskatchewan University in an effort to feed the war machine. The Allied Nations were desperately short of protein to feed their workers and, as Canada had a surplus of horses, he decided upon an experiment. At a livestock demonstration he had two types of sandwiches served during the lunch hour, square and triangular. After the crowd in attendance had enjoyed the meal he conducted a poll to determine which proved the most popular. Then he erred. As there appeared little choice between the two shapes of sandwiches, he disclosed the fact that the triangular sandwiches had been made with beef, the square ones with horse meat.

There were those who would never forgive him.

The position of university faculty and students who found themselves in the sciences, medicine, and food production in a country at war has been clearly set down in Prof. W. L. Morton's book *One University* (McClelland and Stewart, 1957). Dealing with Manitoba University, in words that applied to all universities in Canada, he wrote that, with the outbreak of war in 1939, "The University, as in 1913, lent itself in every way it could to the war effort. Then it had been chiefly soldiers, which were wanted; in this later war, research scientists and administrators were sought as well. . . ." He wrote that the loss of staff and students "thanks to the wise and far-seeing policy of the Federal Governments of the day, was a controlled loss designed to make the best contribution possible to the war effort. The Government held that the work of the Universities was a contribution to the war effort and should be continued with such staff and students as were essential to their work, or could be spared from national service."

*   *   *

Despite his stepped-up activity on wartime food production, MacEwan set about completing a manuscript dealing with breeds of livestock in Canada. Ever since he was a boy attending the Regina Farm Boys' Camp in 1918, he had made the acquaintance of purebred livestock at every opportunity and knew them as well as those at his age would later know the make of automobiles or aircraft, their performance and capabilities. He set himself the task of recording the breeds, their histories, and the influence of their bloodlines in Canada. This, from the depth of his background on the subject, he compiled into the book that was published by Nelsons on December 8, 1941, under the title *Breeds of Farm Livestock in Canada*. It was the first technical book dealing with his profession that he prepared and wrote by himself. From now on Canadian students of livestock would no longer have to refer to the two main American references, Plumbs and Davenport. It constituted a useful and important contribution to Canadian animal husbandry for breeders, serious farm publications, and others interested in livestock.

Although filling a large gap in Canadian agricultural publications, the response to the book was at best restrained, and, when the issue was sold out, no move was made by breeders or anyone else to keep it in print. This was a matter of disappointment to the author.

*   *   *

Neither war nor writing books could divert MacEwan's attention when it came time to buy land again, and the time had arrived. Again his eyes turned toward Alberta, which province had become part of a secret dream he had lately permitted himself. In the early 1940s he sold his White Fox farm at a good price and got rid of the weed-plagued, tenant-troubled farm at Resource, Sask.

In 1940, he and Phyllis took one trip through the Red Deer district searching for a likely place but found none. The following year, he found something to his liking at Priddis, a few miles south of Calgary, and the year after that, a spread farther south: "Having previously bought a half section at Priddis, Alberta, I today, Aug. 10th, bought a section of land . . . near Longview, Alta., from George Wambeke for $10 per acre. It has a mile of river frontage on the Highwood. But the Priddis place which I bought at $12 an acre still fulfills my dream as one offering soil, trees, scenery, water and a good climate for the writing life of which I dream." He would keep the Priddis ranch in its natural state, running a few horses on it, leasing grazing to a neighbor, the rates of which remained the same for years.

*   *   *

While his son was buying land, Alex was selling. In June 1941, the MacEwans bought their first car — a Plymouth coach, $1,357.59 plus $37

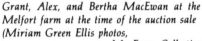

Grant, Alex, and Bertha MacEwan at the Melfort farm at the time of the auction sale (Miriam Green Ellis photos,
MacEwan Collection)

for insurance, all cash. It was on a visit to Melfort, with Phyllis and Heather accompanying him in the new car, that his father revealed to Grant his decision to sell the land they had farmed for twenty-six years. Bertha MacEwan could not shake recurring bouts of asthma and they planned moving to White Rock, B.C. where it was hoped she would get a measure of relief. What was more, it was time to retire after a lifetime of fruitful labor.

Implicit in the announcement was the suggestion that family members would have first option on the old place, which was now a model farm in the district. Alex was seventy years old, and although much of the work was now done by hired help, he still had felt the necessity of lightening his load of responsibility. Some time previously he had dispersed his fine herd of Angus cattle. Perhaps Grant would want the land?

MacEwan knew every inch of the farm but did not want it. The main reason, and a most practical one, was that while they found some, they had never been able to find a water supply sufficient for all their needs. It might be somewhere under the soil, but the MacEwans had never found it, so Grant let the land go.

The sale was a typical MacEwan sale. Alex put the restriction on it that the purchaser would have to care for his faithful old horses, allowing them to graze in green pastures for the remainder of their lives without labor, for they had well earned such retirement. He could have realized more money for the farm without the restriction, but he took less, selling it to a man he knew would keep his word. Jack Gammie, a neighbor, bought it.

The senior MacEwan departure was a sad loss to Melfort and district and to the provincial livestock industry as well. Alex and Bertha attended numerous functions held in their honor before they boarded the train to "The Coast," thus bringing to an end the MacEwan presence in that part of the country.

Chapter 18

Exhibitions, Politics, Piles

On August 12, 1942, Grant MacEwan reached his fortieth year and noted that fact briefly and simply: "Forty yrs. old. Judging at P.A. Fair."

Had he been given to reviewing his accomplishments on such an occasion, he would have found much of interest, for by ordinary standards some would say, "he had it made at forty." However, he had not nearly run his full course, and within the next three or four years, he was to see the one remaining interest, in an already broad spectrum of interests, take recognizable shape.

Professionally he had done well. He was a university department head, the director of the School of Agriculture and manager of the university farm. He was co-author of two books and sole author of another, making a notable contribution to agriculture. His popularity as a speaker was established and growing. As a livestock judge he had reached the first rank and was in demand at the top shows and sales in western Canada. He had a family of which he was justifiably proud and which fitted into his endless round of public service with a minimum of friction. He held land well situated in Alberta. He didn't owe a cent — never had for that matter — always paying cash for everything. His spiritual well being was assured, and as much as most humans, he was at peace with himself, enjoying life as it came. Nevertheless, there was more in store for the man.

MacEwan was one of the faculty members who had long since bridged the town and gown gap and he was to reach a high point in this segment of his Saskatoon activities when, in his fortieth year, he was elected president of the Saskatoon Exhibition. There were some who did not envy him the honor because much responsibility went with the job. The exhibition had seen better days.

Little Theatre group with their provincial championship trophy: (Left to right) Marguerite Latour, Phyllis MacEwan, author Helen Gordon (in front), Louise Olson, Mary Ashley
(MacEwan Collection)

Exhibitions and fairs throughout the country were hard pressed to keep their heads above water as their activities became restricted by the exigencies of a wartime economy. Among other problems, military necessity forced some to close down when their buildings were requisitioned for training purposes; the movement of equipment and livestock from fair to fair was threatened by the transport controller who placed restrictions on the shipping of freight over hard-pressed railways. Saskatoon did not escape these and other problems, among them a balance sheet that was in the red.

Soon after assuming office, MacEwan and Sid Johns, Saskatoon manager, were chosen by the Western Canadian Exhibition Association to go to Ottawa and Montreal to appeal for easement of freight restrictions as far as fairs and exhibitions were concerned. MacEwan, the spokesman, returned with only partial success, but enough to please even the most pessimistic. Exhibition material would be allowed to move by regular freight but there were to be no special trains. The easement would make possible continuation of shows that had fully expected to close down for the duration of the war.

He brought new life to the Saskatoon Exhibition as well. The following year, when Johns died, his fellow directors prevailed on MacEwan to take the title of honorary manager — unpaid, for they had little money to pay anyone — and assume executive responsibility as well as presidential for the next exhibition.

Although it previously had been a full-time job for one man, MacEwan took on the job, along with his many other tasks, running the exhibition the way he ran his own finances. They put on a good show, considering wartime conditions, and attracted large crowds. When it came time to report to the directors on the final results, their honorary manager was able to reveal a net profit of $27,000, the best in the history of the exhibition up to that time.

*   *   *

Phyllis joined her husband in the local limelight that year through the theater. One of the ways she occupied her time during Grant's absences had been to renew an interest in drama. A close friend of hers and wife of a colleague of Grant's, Mrs. Helen Gordon, had written a play, *Old Cinderella*, which she proposed directing and entering in the Provincial Drama Festival. Phyllis took a lead role, won favorable mention in the press, and the play won the festival trophy.

*   *   *

Politicians had long had their eyes on MacEwan, his recent achievements only heightening their interest in persuading him to their side.

From time to time, after his help for the Liberals in the 1926 election in Melfort, they had no doubt had him in mind. So it was in 1933 that a delegation approached him to let his name stand for the Liberal nomination in the forthcoming contest between Premier J. T. M. Anderson's Conservatives, the Liberals under J. G. Gardiner, and the newly formed farmer-labor coalition under M. J. Coldwell.

He rejected their kind offer with gratitude, his reason being that he was attempting to select "the field of endeavor to which I believe I am best suited and for the present time one which offers a generous opportunity for service to Saskatchewan agriculture." He continued that "for the present time" he would remain where he was. The last phrase was not to be forgotten by Liberal recruiters.

Ten years later, in November 1943, he dined with J. G. Gardiner, who by that time had left provincial politics in W. J. Patterson's hands and had become minister of agriculture in Mackenzie King's Liberal government in Ottawa. The second direct invitation was put to MacEwan — would he consider running for the Liberals in the city of Saskatoon constituency in the next federal election still two years away? The following month, he had a session with J. W. Estey, attorney general in the Patterson administration (later Supreme Court judge), the subject being "politics and my proposed candidacy."

*   *   *

The third offer proved to be the most surprising and wide-open offer of his political career up to that time. In January 1944, he had a discussion with Dick Bell, organizer for the newly constituted Progressive-Conservative party under the leadership of the former premier of Manitoba, as a forerunner to a meeting between John Bracken and himself the following day. Twenty years separated the two, one was in animal husbandry, the other in field husbandry, but, other than that, their careers were to prove amazingly similar. As MacEwan did later, Bracken graduated from OAC, went to an American college (Illinois) for postgraduate work, joined the faculty of agriculture at Saskatchewan, was active in practical research and

Three colleagues: J. G. Rayner, Rupert Ramsay, MacEwan
(University of Saskatchewan Archives)

extension, wrote textbooks on his subject, then left to become head of Manitoba Agriculture College where he remained until he was lured into politics!

Bracken was touring Canada to recruit candidates and to organize the former Conservative party along new lines under the recently adopted name, Progressive-Conservative. He wanted Grant MacEwan to assume the leadership of the Saskatchewan party and he wanted him badly. Discussion revealed a similarity in their views on agricultural policy and on sound, pay-as-you-go administration, partisan party politics running a poor third. The MacEwan journal reveals that on January 19, 1944: "Spent forenoon in Regina with John Bracken. The proposal is that I lead the Progressive-Conservative party in Sask."

So keen was Bracken to enlist MacEwan's aid he told him that, if the party label did not suit him, he could call it what he wanted to — perhaps "The Agrarian Party."

As always, MacEwan made the trip serve three or four purposes. Following the interview, he went on to Moose Jaw to preside over an afternoon meeting of the Saskatchewan Light Horse Society of which he was president, and then, in the evening, to speak at the Livestock Breeders' convention banquet.

Back in Saskatoon ten days later, he had a long session with H. O. Wright, former Conservative member of parliament with an abiding interest in the fortunes of his party (and father of the girl who had introduced Grant to Phyllis fourteen years previously).

Although it is significant that he studied the matter for almost two weeks, MacEwan was not persuaded. With gratitude, he turned the offer down. In so doing, he proposed the name of a colleague, Prof. Rupert Ramsay, an able and widely respected man, who accepted the leadership but who, in the end, never managed to get the party off the ground.

* * *

Political invitations did not cease. In March and April of 1944, he was bombarded with offers from Premier Patterson to cast his lot with the provincial Liberal administration. The journal noted: "Same question —

'Will you go into politics?' " The last offer came with a note of urgency, for the ninth Saskatchewan legislature had been prorogued and the province was facing a general election. Patterson even offered to swear him in on the spot as minister of natural resources and give him the Kinistino constituency in which to run. Again MacEwan was not persuaded.

In the June 14, 1944, election, Patterson's Liberals were decimated by the farmer-labor coalition, now called Co-Operative Commonwealth Federation (CCF), under their new leader, T. C. Douglas (a graduate of Brandon College). When the final count was made, the CCF won 47 seats, the Liberals 5, Active Service Voters Respresentatives 3, Progressive-Conservatives none.

Had MacEwan accepted the first direct offer to run Liberal in Melfort, he would most likely have suffered the same fate as MacFarlane, who went down to defeat before the CCF. Had he accepted the second invitation from Gardiner to run in the city of Saskatoon in the 1945 federal election, it is doubtful if his popularity could have closed the gap of 4,000 odd votes separating the Liberal hopeful, Brunskill, from the successful CCF candidate, R. R. Knight. Had he accepted John Bracken's invitation to lead the Progressive-Conservatives against Patterson and Douglas in the provincial election, it is doubtful if he would have done better than Rupert Ramsay who faced complete and utter defeat despite widespread personal esteem and a slate of capable candidates attracted by him. Finally, had he accepted Premier Patterson's offer of a nomination in Kinistino, it is also doubtful if he could have done much better than the Liberal, R. M. Paul, who ran 1,500 votes behind the winning CCF candidate, W. J. Boyle.

*   *   *

Throughout this exciting sequence of invitations and offers, Grant MacEwan remained pretty much to himself, doing things his own way. Among the many activities which he kept moving without collision, he managed to get away in April and meet Uncle John Grant in the rolling hills of his Priddis ranch. The old man had lost his wife, had tried living with his daughter Olive and her husband, Roy M. McPhail, in Winnipeg, but got fed up with idleness and — at eighty-four years of age — told Grant he wanted to build a log cabin. They strode over the MacEwan acres and finally chose a site "up high, with lots of scenery." There, Grant left Uncle John at work and happy once again.

Seven weeks later, Grant was in Alberta speaking to the Feed Manufacturers' Association (afternoon topic "Rationing Mistakes," and at an evening banquet "The Agricultural Trail Blazers") after which he hitchhiked to Priddis to see how his own old trail blazer was doing and found him chinking the almost completed cabin. He had had a little help from an Indian but had done most of the work himself!

*   *   *

In 1945, the whole country sensed change, challenge, and a new future, and the offers still kept coming in MacEwan's direction. There had

Grant's uncles with their sister Florence at Jessie Clark's North Brandon farm. Uncle Jim (left) was 86 and Uncle John, the cabin builder, 90 when the photo was taken (Nelson Collection)

been victory in Europe and it appeared only a matter of time until the Japanese would be defeated in the Pacific theater of war.

On his way from a September judging assignment in British Columbia, he had stopped over at Calgary to take a long walk over his beckoning Priddis land, something he was now doing at every opportunity, when he was spotted by an acquaintance and there and then offered the managership of the newly forming Canadian Council of Beef Producers. It was a tempting offer. Things could have been better at the university as it happened, and the council job would bring him to Alberta, possibly to his Priddis property from which he could operate. He did not dismiss the offer out of hand, and as he turned it over in his mind, others heard about it one way or another.

If Jimmy Gardiner was anything, he was persistent. Even though he was miles away in Ottawa, he continued to run the Saskatchewan Liberal party machine as his own fiefdom and he had plans for it which included the professor. Patterson had been so soundly trimmed in the last provincial election he would never be able to get up off the floor and join the fight again — he was through. The next Liberal gathering would be a leadership convention and Gardiner wanted his own man elected.

At the time there appears to have been a steadier correspondence between MacEwan and Gardiner than MacEwan's journal suggests for, soon after getting the offer from the council, he let Gardiner know he was considering a move. Gardiner replied in a letter marked "confidential" and dated Ottawa, September 25, 1945, saying in part: "You have been in my mind for many years as one who would add greatly to the strength of Liberalism in the Province of Saskatchewan, if you would associate yourself with it actively." He was sorry to learn MacEwan was considering leaving the province because "I think Liberalism in Saskatchewan is at the crossroads" — things were at a juncture where someone could take hold and do a great service. "I had sometimes thought that you might be the person to do that. I am sure that if you still have desires to enter the political field, now is the time to do it, and that we could make arrangements in Saskatchewan which would be necessary to your taking part."

In a prophetic sentence or two Gardiner then went on to say that "I know from our previous conversations that you had an idea that you might at some time become active in Alberta [politics] if you moved there" and went on to discuss the merits of such a move with little enthusiasm. He then suggested an early meeting in Ottawa when Grant was there in connection with PFRA work.

MacEwan did not accept the Calgary offer. As he recalled it, when he discussed the matter with Ken Coppock (one of the prime movers of the council proposal) he came away with the distinct feeling that Coppock, who was publisher of the *The Canadian Cattlemen*, had in mind the prospect of help from MacEwan on his journal as much as help for the Beef Council, and he did not relish the prospect of divided responsibility.

*   *   *

The meeting which Gardiner suggested earlier took place in Ottawa in May 1946. Pressure was applied to a marked degree to have MacEwan stand as provincial leader of the Saskatchewan party. Under orders from Gardiner, Walter Tucker, the Liberal member for Rosthern and the parliamentary assistant to the minister of veterans' affairs, Ian Mackenzie, invited MacEwan to lunch, doing everything he could to persuade him to accept the offer. MacEwan was unresponsive.

Tucker reported the result to Gardiner who then invited MacEwan to dine with him that same evening. The pressure was applied as only Jimmy Gardiner could apply it, but he was up against a man who knew his own mind. MacEwan again refused the offer.

It is interesting, and has a bearing on subsequent events, to know something of the background to Gardiner's persistence — and indeed, that of Mr. Tucker. Years later, Mr. Tucker revealed his reading of the situation, there being none closer to events save Gardiner. Gardiner's Liberal government entered the 1929 Saskatchewan provincial election with 57 seats, a majority of 43, and came out with only 27, Anderson forming a Conservative-Coalition administration. Gardiner had been scalded and never forgot it, putting much of the blame on anti-Roman Catholic sentiment fanned by the Ku Klux Klan. One of the strong leadership contenders in the coming party leadership convention was an able young lawyer, E. M. Culliton, a Roman Catholic. Gardiner was no bigot but he was ever the politician and he dared not tempt fate again by allowing Culliton to lead. He must find a candidate who could upset Culliton's aspirations.

MacEwan's rejection of Gardiner's offer sealed Tucker's fate. Tucker had a secure position. He usually won his Rosthern seat by majorities in the thousands; he had made a name for himself as a parliamentary assistant by piloting the Veterans' Charter (postwar rehabilitation act) through the House of Commons so ably that Prime Minister King had let him know that when his minister, Ian Mackenzie, relinquished his post (as he was known to be considering), Tucker would take his place. Mrs. Tucker loved the life in Ottawa, as did her husband and large family, and they had just acquired a new home. Despite all this, after the MacEwan refusal, Tucker accepted Gardiner's request that he return to Saskatchewan and challenge Culliton for the party leadership.

*   *   *

In a special report from Saskatoon, August 1, 1946, the *Regina Leader-Post* described last-minute preparations for the convention that would attract fifteen hundred delegates and take up most of the hotel rooms in the city. Prominently mentioned for the leadership of the party were Walter A. Tucker, MP for Rosthern, and E. M. Culliton of Gravelbourg, who had been provincial secretary in the Patterson regime.

But, the story continued, while those two were referred to, "it is believed other names are likely to be placed before the convention. . . . Prominently mentioned some time ago and known to have substantial backing is J. W. G. MacEwan, professor of animal husbandry at the University of Saskatchewan, who is known from one end of the Province to the other and who is personally acquainted with thousands of Saskatchewan's agricultural population."

MacEwan was in a quandary. It was almost certain that if he put in an appearance at the convention his "substantial backing" would press him to let his name stand. He had said "no" to Tucker and Gardiner, but would he find it possible to reject the wishes of his many friends and supporters?

As the fateful week approached, he arrived at a solution. For once in his life he would turn tail and run. Like many other active horseback riders before him, Grant MacEwan suffered from the unmentionable ailment — piles. He had been informed that they could be treated by medicine or by surgery, which he could elect at his own convenience. He picked the method and time to suit his purposes.

Telling Phyllis that he would be out of town for possibly a week, he then disappeared from sight. Actually, he didn't leave town but quietly checked into St. Paul's Hospital on the eve of the convention for a hemorrhoid operation that would confine him to bed for the duration of the political proceedings. A successful operation in more ways than one.

The ruse succeeded with politicans but not with family. At church, the Sunday immediately prior to the convention, a well-meaning friend leaned over Phyllis's pew and whispered in her ear:

"How's Grant?"

"Fine."

"Glad to hear it."

"Why do you ask?"

"Oh, I heard he was in St. Paul's Hospital."

Thinking there had been an accident, Phyllis rushed up to the hospital and found an embarrassed husband in bed. When told the nature of his ailment, she was furious at his silence on the matter. To this day it is doubtful if she learned the real reason for his lack of consideration, putting the whole thing down to her husband's well-established reluctance to admit sickness of any kind let alone give in to an ailment no matter how serious.

He had been no ordinary patient. Giving full rein to his scientific curiosity, he persuaded the doctor to arrange mirrors in such a way that, with local anesthetic only, he was able to observe the entire procedure. He later wrote an earthy but humorous essay "Base operation," which was passed from hand to hand to the amusement of many. It was in typescript only, never published.

Mr. Tucker won the leadership, but he was never able to win power.

MacEwan had avoided being drafted, but time would show that he had not succeeded in putting an end to political invitations.

Chapter 19

An Offer

The two years leading up to MacEwan's inglorious retreat from the political draft brought sad personal losses to him and to those close to him. However, life went on and there were triumphs as well. Again, with the advantage of hindsight, it almost appears as if the hand that orders such things were preparing the scene for an important change that was to come.

Even in the salubrious climate of the Pacific coast his mother, Bertha MacEwan, had continued to be plagued by ill health. As always, she was cheerful and was buoyed up by her unshakeable faith and the certainty that, although she was permitted to suffer, her loving and all-seeing Maker watched over her; His steadying hand was there to help her face her lot with serene confidence and trust. When her course was run, He would call her to her prepared place.

The call came Christmas night, 1944, at White Rock, B.C. She was up in the morning to open her parcels but weakened and took to her bed soon afterwards. A concerned Alex called the doctor. In Saskatoon, Grant received the news shortly after and recorded in his journal: "Mother passed on just before midnight Christmas day . . . she was perfectly at ease and slipped into the next world without pain and breathing freely. Just slept peacefully away, but the doctor remained, knowing that she was going." The son's private grief remains unrecorded. Little St. James Church was full of friends despite bitterly cold weather when Bertha MacEwan was buried in Melfort.

*   *   *

Alex was left alone for the first time since their marriage forty-four years earlier but he was soon to follow. A few months after his wife's funeral, he paid a visit to Ontario where he visited all his boyhood haunts and once more gloried in the vivid colors of fall found only in eastern forests. He was ailing and underwent an emergency operation at Toronto General Hospital where they discovered an inoperable growth on the colon. It was by-passed but there was little improvement. Grant rushed to his side.

Grave though the situation was, it was not without its humorous moment. Following a crowded day in Saskatoon the son flew to Toronto, arriving at the hospital at one-thirty in the morning. He sat at his father's bedside until, at four-thirty, the nurse detected obvious signs of fatigue and suggested that he slip into a vacant hospital bed nearby. He did so with gratitude, soon falling into a deep sleep until wakened by the morning shift nurse. She thrust a thermometer into his mouth, instructing him to leave it there until she returned to take it out.

Alex survived the ordeal but not for long. The MacEwan journal records that on November 14, 1945, "my father passed on to his rest today. He would be 76 at his next birthday. He was a good and sensible father." They sang the same hymns they had sung for Bertha MacEwan ten months before at St. James Church in Melfort: "Unto the Hills," "Awake my Soul," "Oh Love That Will Not Let me Go," and "Rock of Ages."

*   *   *

It was a time for dying. His aunt, Marion Grant, had died the year before Bertha, as had his old mentor, Dean Rutherford. Dr. Morton, who had set MacEwan firmly on the path of history, died early in 1945 and Grant helped carry him to the grave: "I loved the old man." Two months after the Morton funeral Grant was again a pallbearer; this time at the funeral of President Walter C. Murray: "It was the passing of one of God's gentlemen."

It was also a time for renewed life. In early September, Heather MacEwan started school. After the first half day she was home early filled with the wonder of the new experience, so much so that she phoned her father at the office. "Did you learn anything at school today?" he asked, to which the reply was, "Yes Daddy, I learned where the toilets are."

*   *   *

During this time MacEwan continued to achieve — but there were rumblings on campus.

In January 1945 the Royal Bank of Canada announced that he had been appointed a director of the bank. The news landed with a shock on campus. Faculty members had been elevated to high positions before this — Royal commissions and the like — but there was nothing academic about the directorship, indeed it had an alien ring of commercialism about which some had their doubts. It was also revealing: to qualify as a bank director, the candidate was required by statute to be the owner of a respectable number of shares in the institution!

When he went to Winnipeg to attend his first directors' meeting, characteristically and not surprisingly, he went with a number of other tasks meshed into the trip, one of which was to result in another MacEwan textbook.

He had agreed to speak to the Canadian Council of Meat Packers, who were meeting there on the same day, but had little time in which to prepare the subject of his address. The preceding night, January 25, he had been in Moose Jaw proposing the toast to the Immortal Memory of Robert Burns, had driven to Regina to catch the midnight plane for Winnipeg and his speech and meeting the next day.

During the flight the thought occurred to him that there was no satisfactory down-to-earth book on the proper feeding of farm animals and he made notes. It was from these that he spoke to the meat packers. Following the speech, he strode through the applauding audience to catch his next meeting, shaking hands with many friends as he went, when he encountered J. S. MacLean of Canada Packers. MacLean agreed that there was a great need for such a book and then, as Grant strode out of the ballroom, he called out, "You write it and I'll buy it." "It's a deal," said MacEwan.

Three months later MacEwan mailed the completed manuscript to Thomas Nelson and Sons Ltd. in Toronto. It was entitled *The Feeding of Farm Animals*. Two thousand copies were printed. They were bought by MacLean for distribution to young farmers and others, wherever Canada Packers thought they would do the most good. Recalling the incident years later, MacEwan said, "there have been better books, no doubt, but none written in a shorter time."

*   *   *

Such a stream of unbroken activity on and off the campus was bound to meet with mixed reactions among his colleagues, from admiration to downright criticism. However, by 1945 it reached the formal stage, abetted by his undertaking to manage the Saskatoon Exhibition in addition to being its president at a time when the philosophy of the university was undergoing change.

At the risk of oversimplification, with all its pitfalls, the situation can be outlined as follows. The university was switching from an outward-looking institution to an inward-looking one, not necessarily in the narrow sense of the term but in the scholastic sense. The philosophy upon which it had been built — public service to the people wherever they were in the province, no task too menial — was having less emphasis placed on it than were scholarship and pure research. The switch was from the land to the lab, so to speak. Whether this was a country-wide movement or one peculiar to the University of Saskatchewan is beside the point, but at Saskatoon it was a fact. The retirement of Dr. Murray in 1937 no doubt signaled the passing of an era in which wide-ranging coverage in the field had been completely understood and encouraged.

The evidence is clear — discussion of the professor's activities had reached the top. Submitting his annual report covering the animal husbandry department activities for the year, MacEwan, in a covering letter dated May 11, 1945, suggested to Dean Kirk that he "review carefully the substance of this report" as the dean had "drawn my attention to certain criticisms relative to assignments in agricultural work outside the university and the province." He then stated his belief that such activity was of benefit to his work and his students and, further, that "I have welcomed the opportunity for service in the broader field and have enjoyed immense encouragement." He assured the dean his managership of the exhibition was only temporary (and unpaid) and that he had promised President J. S. Thomson (Dr. Murray's successor) that 1945 would be the last exhibition he would manage. His absences from the university during the year had totaled little more than four weeks, he pointed out, and "such time is not out of line with normal holiday periods" and "I have taken no holidays from the university at any time in the past eleven years." He then asked for "specific direction" about his work program.

Although invited to do so, Dr. Kirk apparently was not about to tell this independent Highland Scot how to arrange his schedule, no matter how much he abhorred public relations. He said as much in a confidential letter to the president, May 15, 1945:

Professor MacEwan is a strong personality with very definite ideas. He is an exceptionally able man in many ways and a prodigious worker. His contacts with the live stock industry have been of great value. On the other hand he does not claim to be a research man and much prefers public relations work to teaching. I do not think he would take kindly to any restrictions on his present activity.

*   *   *

Neither did MacEwan take kindly to a movement that had sprung up after the war among his agricultural colleagues to advance their position, and he didn't win many friends for his views. Up to that time, they had been loosely bound together by an association known as the Canadian Society of Technical Agriculturists; the name, suggesting as it did that they were technicians, was wrong in their view and had to be changed. Indeed, they were professionals just as lawyers and doctors were, and as such, they argued, they needed their professional standing enshrined in legislation giving them power to govern their own members just as the College of Physicians and Surgeons governed the medical profession. They were not "technicians"; they were to be known henceforth as "agrologists." The majority agreed. A small minority did not, including Grant MacEwan.

MacEwan was never a respecter of appearances and had a full measure of the prenatal Highland self-confidence, maddening to some, that made the outer trappings of professionalism completely unnecessary to his proper functioning. Regardless of the many good arguments in favor of the new Institute (for it was certainly no one-sided debate), he felt that professional status with its attendant airs would drive a wedge between the farmer and the agrologist. Furthermore, it would make possible the exploitation of the man on the land by unscrupulous professionals, as had happened from time to time within the ranks of lawyers and doctors. While the debate raged on, it was divisive to say the least, with the supporters on occasion going to great lengths to win converts, as in the case of the blank cheque.

Upon returning to his office one day following an absence, MacEwan sorted through the pile of mail, memos, and other paper that had accumulated on his desk. Among them he found a cheque made out in the name of the Agricultural Institute of Canada (Sask. Section), the new professional organization. It was for the amount of the annual fee but had been left unsigned. The hint was clear — all it needed was the MacEwan signature and the battle would be over.

When the government of Saskatchewan passed the act and gave the agrologists the right to govern their profession, there was little left to do for those who wanted to continue in the field but to yield, which MacEwan eventually did in 1946 when he felt he could remain apart no longer, and out of a sense of duty to the profession.

The fact that thirty years afterwards the Board of Governors of the University of Saskatchewan found it necessary to appoint a committee to assess the "image" of the institution in the public mind and were alarmed to discover, among other things, that the once close relationship that had existed between the university and farmers and ranchers had been almost completely dissipated over the years, permits a delayed judgment as to the clarity of MacEwan's foresight.

This was the environment at the University of Saskatchewan following the war. The end of an era was signaled. Where once the institution had functioned with a dominant purpose, that purpose was being questioned, and for anyone as prescient and far-seeing as MacEwan, the slightest indication was enough. It would be wrong to leave a suggestion of turmoil, for there was none. The revolution was more cranial than anything else, but it did bring good men face to face on opposing sides.

Able men all, the situation was uncomfortable to say the least, and sooner or later would most likely have come to a head had not an invitation come out of the blue for MacEwan — the more welcome because of the prevailing mood at the University of Saskatchewan.

*   *   *

Without the least suspicion that he was approaching a turning point in his life, Grant MacEwan set out on a trip to Winnipeg on August 18, 1946, to attend the district convention of the Kiwanis Club. He had been elected president of the Saskatoon club and attended in that capacity, but also as a speaker on "What Every Kiwanian Should Know About Western Canada." The following day, as a complete surprise, he was elected Lieutenant-Governor of Kiwanis to represent Saskatchewan. There was yet another surprise in store for him of more far-reaching consequences.

Following his noon speech in the Canadian Pacific's stately Royal Alexandra Hotel, he received a telephone call from a person he had neither seen nor met, Dr. A. W. Trueman, the newly appointed president of the University of Manitoba. Trueman asked the professor if a meeting could be arranged between them before he returned to Saskatoon. No hint was given of the subject for discussion but MacEwan agreed to have the president to his room in the hotel the following day, turning over in his mind the possibility of another speaking engagement. The call was to change immediate plans and his entire future.

Trueman presented himself at the hotel in company with W. J. Parker, vice-chairman of the University of Manitoba's Board of Governors, whom MacEwan knew better as a farmer and a leader in the Manitoba Wheat Pool. Trueman got right to the point. The deanship of the College of Agriculture, University of Manitoba, was open and MacEwan was being invited to take the position. In the past they had experienced trouble keeping the position filled. It had been tried from inside the university a number of times in vain, and they were now looking for someone from outside with the full knowledge and agreement of present faculty who had previously filled the position. The need for someone who could take the university out into the rural areas of the province and make the people aware of the college was alluded to. In short, they needed a man with MacEwan's qualities.

Although the invitation was a complete surprise, the fact that they felt a need for change at the college was not. Almost ten years previously, MacEwan and Dr. Robert Sinclair, traveling to or from an agricultural meeting in Ottawa, had used a short stopover in Winnipeg to visit the college. He wrote in his journal of May 30, 1937: "Winnipeg, Robt. Sinclair and I went to the Agricultural College and found things in a disappointing state of repair."

They had come to the right man at the right time. There was little doubt in MacEwan's mind what his answer would be but he asked for time to consider. It was agreed that he would phone Trueman the next day with his decision.

As soon as they left, he phoned Phyllis with the news and asked her opinion. Phyllis had little hesitation and told him he could not refuse the offer, although she would have preferred more time. They would have to move fast to find a house and a school for Heather who would be entering grade two in early September. What would they do with Molasses (so named because it was "s-l-o-w"), their daughter's pony?

Grant's decision was made. His acceptance was phoned to President Trueman and he undertook to assume office as soon as it was possible to do so.

He returned to the Kiwanians and resigned the governorship after "the shortest service in history."

Moving at the customary MacEwan pace, Grant and Phyllis went house hunting three days later in Winnipeg. They bought the Ross Cavers home at 814 Somerset Avenue for $7,900 cash. He sold their Saskatoon house for $8,500 cash, double what he had paid for it.

On short notice, the MacEwans were feted by friends and organizations. Grant was recipient of at least three pen and pencil sets, a two-year-old Palomino gelding from the Exhibition Board, a tooled leather bridle from the Saskatoon Riding Club, and a number of other gifts of appreciation.

President Thomson spoke at a hastily arranged faculty dinner and described Professor MacEwan's career at the University of Saskatchewan in a few well-chosen words. After congratulating him on his appointment, the president continued:

He has brought to his work here such a diversity of gifts and experience that he is almost irreplaceable. Besides being professor of animal husbandry and head of the department and manager of the university farm, he has carried out extensive research, has been a prolific writer, and collaborated in the writing of textbooks. He seems to be able to take on more public engagements than any man at the university and has carried the name of the University of Saskatchewan from coast to coast through his activities.

An eyewitness, the late Dr. V. E. Graham (later dean of agriculture), remembered Dr. Thomson — with whom Grant had developed no more than a formal relationship — alluding to MacEwan's activities and poking good-natured fun at the situations that arose from time to time because of them, by reciting Baroness Orczy's poem from "The Scarlet Pimpernel":

We seek him here, we seek him there,
Those Frenchies seek him everywhere.
Is he in heaven? Is he in hell?
That demmed, elusive Pimpernel!

So ended eighteen years of service for the man who, in the eyes of the farmers and ranchers, had become a symbol of all that was good about the University of Saskatchewan.

Chapter 20

Dean at Manitoba

The appointment of Dean MacEwan attracted widespread attention in the press and it is from news stories and comment that a clear idea of the reasons for the appointment, the objectives of the University of Manitoba in making the appointment, the reactions of those interested in agriculture, and the philosophy of the new dean are obtained.

Saying that he was "widely known as a colorful, able educator and extension man," the *Western Producer* reported that he would replace former Dean A. V. Mitchener who was resuming his duties as head of the entomology department. According to the story, President Trueman said that the Board of Governors had determined to strengthen the faculty of agriculture, the appointment of Dean MacEwan being the first step. The plan called for: closer coordination of the university farm with teaching departments; the extension of experimental and research work; the strengthening of the faculty; expansion of work in agricultural engineering; the provision of funds to make it possible for college staff "to maintain contact with rural Manitoba."

The respected British Columbia farm journal *Country Life* in an editorial headed "Now it will be Dean MacEwan" said:

... undoubtedly the ablest and best-known judge of cattle and horses in Canada ... in great demand as a livestock judge and as a reliable authority when a particularly tough problem in breeding and raising cattle develops ... Dean MacEwan has rendered far more service to the primary producers of Canada than will ever be known or recompensed. His life is devoted to the welfare of others and he pays no attention to the sacrifices of time and energy he has to make.

The student newspaper *The Manitoban* carried a straight news report and then added: "He is now in his middle forties, but has the vitality of a much younger man. His chief love is horses, but he enjoys nothing more than talking with old stockmen and pioneers."

It remained for one of the most respected of agricultural writers, Miriam Green Ellis, western editor of the *Family Herald*, to record MacEwan's philosophy on accepting the position. She was describing a meeting of the Manitoba Agricultural Graduates Association called to welcome the new man, at which everybody who was anybody in Manitoba agriculture was present, farmers from widespread points as well, despite almost impassable roads due to a severe storm:

"The story of agricultural development in Manitoba in one man's lifetime was a story of rapid development almost beyond belief," she reported MacEwan as saying. It would be his objective to rededicate the College of Agriculture to the farm industry of the province and spread its influence "out to meet the other western provinces . . . but we must go beyond being a teaching institution. The country must be reflected in our work and that means research, so we will do a better teaching job. The opportunities for research are almost limitless."

It would be his objective to bring the college close to the farmers of the province because he believed that any department of the university that was in close touch with the farmers "would never go to sleep, the farmers wouldn't let them". He thought the college had kept pace with advancing methods "fairly well" but some of the curriculum must be reviewed and some of the courses would no doubt be due for important changes, a number of them liberalized to a certain extent. He told the gathering he was at the university because "the challenge of Manitoba appealed."

It didn't take the students long to discover that the new man was very approachable. One of the main events of the opening term was the freshman parade through the streets of Winnipeg in which the various colleges attempted to outdo one another with costumes or stunts — the new man was not to be left out. A delegation met him with an invitation to take part. He considered the possibility and it appealed to his sense of humor, for it was to be a freshman parade and who was more freshly in office than the Dean of Agriculture?

Dressed in cowboy regalia complete with chaps and ten-gallon hat, he mounted his Palomino mare, Pepita, and headed the College of Agriculture and Home Economics section of the parade. MacEwan stole the show and won the undivided attention of the newspaper cameramen. The *Winnipeg Tribune* published his picture under the heading "Ride him, Professor," reporting in the cutlines that "more than 2,000 students made up the mile-long procession" and further that "the Dean was the only faculty member in the parade." *The Manitoban* published their own picture of him, proclaiming that "Two-gun MacEwan Rides Again."

It was to become a tradition to have their dean at the head of his college in the parade whenever possible. A year or so later he even

Heather and Daddy in the 1949 Freshman
The MacEwan house at 814 Somerset Ave-   Parade, Winnipeg
nue, Winnipeg   *(MacEwan Collection)*   *(Robert Hikida photo, MacEwan Collection)*

appeared accompanied by Heather mounted on Molasses.

Working with the agricultural students, he started annual "winter fairs." They, too, were to become a tradition. However, the job was not all parades and publicity, and more serious matters were to be attended to as well. He turned his attention to them.

*   *   *

He soon realized that he had inherited "an unhappy family" in the faculty of agriculture. The Home Economics section was another matter, but there was no doubt in his mind that the morale of the agricultural staff had been badly bent over the years, if not broken. While Phyllis had been given a warm and friendly reception from a ready-made group of friends among the faculty wives, stories she heard from their viewpoint reinforced Grant's conclusion. Something would have to be done.

The first thing he did was to call a faculty meeting for the purpose of becoming acquainted with them and sounding out their attitude to change. If they could be drawn together as a group and set to work on a joint project, it would be a start. In this he was ably informed by his senior secretary, Miss Janet Usher, a diminutive, efficient career woman he was to find indispensable as a source of information about the college, the staff, and accepted procedure.

The meeting "went fine." There was open discussion during which professors appeared to welcome the rare opportunity to air their views on the nature and effectiveness of the agricultural courses. It was agreed that a committee be appointed under the chairmanship of Dr. Norman James, an able bacteriologist, its job to re-examine the whole curriculum in agriculture. They set to work immediately.

In time the curriculum committee brought in a report "which tightened the courses we were giving a bit and, at the same time made them more flexible." Among other things, flexibility was introduced in admissions to courses, making it possible for students without full formal educational requirements to be "admitted for reason." Almost as important as the conclusions, the committee work started drawing the staff together as a team.

The female side of his charge was an entirely different matter. When he turned his attention to the home economics section of the college, he found it to be in the hands of "an able and self-sufficient director, Dr. Grace Gordon Hood." The director, then close to the point of retirement, had been there for years, "had assembled a good faculty and there seemed little need for direction from an interfering male." The new dean let well enough alone, forming a cordial relationship with the director. "We got along splendidly." For many years after her retirement and subsequent removal to Indianapolis, the two were to continue a seasonable correspondence.

*   *   *

The social life of the college required different treatment but the MacEwans had something in mind despite the fact that neither of them was what could be termed socially minded. In time, they entertained at what became known as "the Dean's parties" which were held once a year and were designed to draw the staff and their families close together. There was music and dancing, games, food, and singsongs. Sometimes they were held at a downtown hall, sometimes on the campus, but they were in truth the Dean's party, for MacEwan paid for everything himself, not a cent coming out of his college budget.

Phyllis was an asset at such affairs and did much to help her husband cure whatever ailments his "unhappy family" suffered from. Often she and President Trueman, who had an excellent singing voice, would be found at the piano leading the singing, performing alone or in a duet.

*   *   *

As for Dean MacEwan's other relationships with those at the top of the administration, they were secure. The University of Manitoba at the time had two heads; the president, who was the head of all things academic and chairman of the Board of Governors; the comptroller, who was head of all things administrative and secretary of the board. The comptroller was none other than F. W. Crawford, whose father had been a neighbor of Alex MacEwan's when he had farmed north of Brandon. In addition, at one time he had served as secretary of the Aberdeen Angus Association for whom Grant had carried out an important study on a new type of animal identification while still at the University of Saskatchewan. MacEwan found him "a dynamic, diminutive fellow, not a comptroller but a dictator. Everybody hated him but respected him and nobody could ever doubt his loyalty." The two formed a close relationship.

If the dean had supporters in high places he also had opponents. A well-known journalist, H. S. Fry, an editor of the respected farm journal *Country Guide*, had recently been appointed to the Board of Governors. Having been a graduate of OAC and having held executive positions on a number of western and national agricultural organizations, it is understandable that he would tend to think of himself as being "in the position of minister of agriculture on the Manitoba University Board of Governors."

As the new dean came to conclusions and brought proposals before the Board of Governors it appeared to him that "Harold Fry opposed everything." Fry was not completely sold on MacEwan's method of "taking the University out into the province" nor the rest of the country. At one point he protested to a fellow journalist that "four hundred speeches a year" might be a laudable effort "but more publicity accrued to Grant MacEwan than to the University." MacEwan's new position was not to be all plain sailing.

*   *   *

If it was true that the Board of Governors wanted a man to take the university out into rural Manitoba, they should have been completely convinced after the first year that they had chosen the right person. Having seen Grant MacEwan in action at Saskatchewan, it would be sufficient to say that he continued to operate in Manitoba the same way, but the statistics are interesting nevertheless.

In the first twelve months with the University of Manitoba as their dean of agriculture (October 1946 to September 1947), he recorded 72 speeches in Winnipeg, 29 in cities and towns outside of Winnipeg but still in Manitoba, and 11 in centers outside of Manitoba. He judged at 12 livestock shows. When all are added up, the total shows that Dean MacEwan took the University of Manitoba out into the public 124 times at least. There were doubtless other occasions which went unrecorded for one reason or another. A surprising diversity of groups and organizations began coming into contact with the College of Agriculture through its dean, for he did not confine his public relations to agricultural groups alone. (Two years later he was to travel to Atlantic City to address the largest audience of his speaking career — five thousand Kiwanians on "*Feeds, Food and Farmers.*")

*   *   *

The speeches were a start, but no matter how numerous and widespread, they were not enough to completely bridge the gap between the College of Agriculture and the farmer on the land, and Grant MacEwan knew it. Although it had been one of the stated purposes for inviting him, he found that he had had really no appreciation of the extent of the gap. Coming from the University of Saskatchewan where recourse to the university had become habitual — often on a first name basis — among thousands of farmers with problems to solve, he was shocked at the utter lack of such contact in Manitoba and looked for other ways to span the breach.

He found another gap. There was little relationship to speak of between his college and the provincial department of agriculture. It was important that this be rectified as soon as possible. Unlike the province of Saskatchewan, extension work was in the hands of the department which, over time, had become as a wall standing between the college and the farmer. He set out to offer help and to suggest that farmers with problems which could better be dealt with by his staff might be referred directly to the college. In this way he hoped to start farmers coming his way. It would be a slow start but anything would be an improvement.

Dean MacEwan at work, supping with pioneers of North Brandon in 1948. With faces visible (left to right): Mrs. Alex McPhail (hostess), Hugh Gilmour, Dave Anderson, MacEwan, William McPhail, Dunc Forsyth, W. G. Buckley   (Elton Historical Committee Collection)

(Ironically, at about the same time as MacEwan was facing this problem in Manitoba, there was being set up in Saskatchewan a system similar to that of Manitoba wherein the department of agriculture would handle extension matters through an Agricultural Representative Service with officers in a network of districts covering the province and reporting to the department. Thus, the University of Saskatchewan would lose much of its traditional direct contact with the land — and possibly live to regret it as an institution no matter how efficacious the new system seemed — as Manitoba University had.)

An interview with the Manitoba deputy minister of agriculture, H. H. Evans, achieved little. MacEwan found him to be "difficult and apparently quite satisfied to allow the faculty to remain in an inferior position." On the other hand, he found that the head of the provincial government's Extension Department, Norman McKay, was to be helpful, having "an honest desire to give the University of Manitoba a chance to express themselves in the country." It would require perseverance but, like trying to change the course of the Queen Mary with a canoe paddle, it could be done — in time and with enough ocean.

*   *   *

With the limited funds available, a number of research projects were carried on under MacEwan's administration along fresh lines of inquiry. Among them were those in plant science and bacteriology; Dr. Mitchener

The MacEwans pose for news feature on how well-known Winnipegers look at home
(Winnipeg Tribune photo)

conducted important investigations into the effect of a new insecticide on bees and honey crops; another faculty member carried out an inquiry into selenium (the element in weeds that gives cattle the staggers).

Unwittingly, he inspired an interesting and productive research project in the high Arctic. In 1948, the fiftieth anniversary of the Trail of '98 to the Klondike gold fields, Imperial Oil Company laid on a special trip. Following a visit to Leduc Oilfields to see Wild Atlantic well No. 3 spouting 10,000 barrels of oil per day, the party headed north in a Lockheed Lodestar company aircraft flown by Gordon Latham.

The party included J. D. Bradley, George Bradley, Donald Avison, Murray Mackenzie, James Holland, Charlie Wright, Ed McQuarrie, the copilot, and Red Mason, the engineer. They visited Waterways, Fort McMurray's salt plant and tar sands; Fort Smith, Fitzgerald, Yellowknife, Hay River, Fort Simpson, Norman Wells; Port Radium, Gunbarrel Inlet on Great Bear Lake; Aklavik, Norman Wells, Whitehorse, Skagway, and Grande Prairie. They left Edmonton June 13 and returned ten days later and MacEwan's inquiring mind was never at rest during the entire time.

It was his first trip to the high northern latitudes and, as was customary, his curiosity knew no bounds. For some time, his after-dinner speeches were to be colored by the inspiration of Canada's northern riches. He described the vast treasure trapped in the tar sands; Canada's rich uranium resources and what they might mean in the future; the characters he met on the trip, among other subjects.

He discovered pockets of potential productivity all the way to the Mackenzie River and north and for some time was to be heard urging a more complete investigation of soil resources in the northwest. With twenty-two hours of sunlight a day in mid-June, it was the soil that was important, not the climate. "The rapidity of growth has to be seen to be believed." During a walk along the Mackenzie riverbank he discovered deep black loam and suggested to Murray Mackenzie, the resident Imperial Oil supervisor, that there was every prospect of growing fresh fruits and vegetables, rare and expensive but necessary foods in that part of the country.

Mackenzie was both intrigued by and doubtful of the outcome of the suggestion but agreed to plant whatever MacEwan sent him. Upon returning to the south, MacEwan sent a supply of cereal and vegetable seed, along with fruit cuttings. Mackenzie reported to MacEwan on each crop for two years. He harvested many pounds of carrots, peas, beans, and potatoes and picked good supplies of strawberries and raspberries. With tongue in cheek he reported that he got no broccoli because the long hours of sunlight forced growth at such a rate that it was found to be immature one night and gone to seed the next! "It proved something to both of us," said MacEwan.

*   *   *

However, the research projects in agriculture closer to home were to run into trouble with a change of personnel and priorities. Difficulties over the filling of a chair of medicine at the university contributed to make attractive an invitation to President Trueman from the University of New Brunswick and, three years after his arrival at Manitoba — and his hiring of a new dean of agriculture — he left, to be succeeded by President A. H. S. Gillson.

W. L. Morton's account of the situation facing MacEwan is set down in his book *One University*. He describes how the new president encouraged research in the sciences and the arts but

> . . . only in the Faculty of Agriculture was there comparative delay, a serious matter in view of the relations of that faculty with the farming industry and the ever-increasing importance of research in agriculture. The changes necessary to put research in agriculture on a sound footing were, however, simply too costly to be carried out swiftly until the university's revenues were increased. This Deans A. V. Mitchener and J. W. G. MacEwan combatted with little success.

*   *   *

The new dean formed other relationships of an informal nature at the University of Manitoba. He had known Prof. Lawson Shank for long, and when time permitted, the MacEwans were often guests at his cabin at Caddy Lake in the beautiful Whiteshell country, a comfortable drive due east from Winnipeg where Grant "charged his batteries" surrounded by natural beauty.

Dean MacEwan goes to work with two paddlers during Winnipeg Flood in May 1950
(MacEwan Collection)

He was much closer to relatives in Brandon and when the opportunity presented itself he visited them and, among other things, renewed familial ties that had long existed with his cousin Maria. It was she who aptly, and with affection, described her tall cousin's attitude to clothing as a mere expedient when she said, upon meeting him at the station, that the new dean of agriculture arrived looking for all the world as if he had obtained his clothing at a rummage sale in the church basement.

*   *   *

May 1: (1950) Red River rising ominously.
May 7: Floods threatening.
May 8: Took University offices at Broadway (avenue) because Pembina Highway cut.
May 12: Evacuated family to Saskatoon. Floods increasingly serious.
May 13: Water 30.1" above datum.

The few terse entries in the MacEwan journal described the relentless rise of Red River waters that was to become the most devastating Manitoba flood of the century. Before it subsided it had inundated six hundred square miles of land including almost a quarter of the city of Winnipeg where water rose to more than thirty feet above its normal level. When it was over and the damage totaled, the bill was estimated at $26,000,000. There was no direct loss of life but a hundred thousand people had to be evacuated in the Greater Winnipeg area alone. Dean MacEwan became involved in a number of ways.

He had more than one responsibility. First, as the head of a family, he saw to it that Phyllis and Heather were sent miles from trouble to stay with friends in Saskatoon. Then, as head of the university farm, his thoughts turned to the herds of cattle, sheep, and pigs trapped in pens and barns there.

On May 14, he managed to get to Municipal Hall where he got into a boat to be taken to the university and his animals. As luck would have it, the "dry" dean drew a couple of boatmen who apparently imagined they were in the Navy and had drawn on their rum rations before the sun was over the yardarm. They were carefree in the way they handled the boat, colliding with another as they navigated the flooded streets.* However, the vessels remained upright and the dean was delivered to the Central Office Building. From there he had to wade through water over his waist to reach the barns.

From then on, it was a laborious job of manhandling the panic-stricken animals on their way to safety: the pigs were placed in railway boxcars spotted along the university spur line; some of the cattle were also put in boxcars while others of the herd were destined for evacuation to Brandon by rail, all the protesting, bawling beasts hauled out of the flooded campus behind tractors; laboring staff, the dean included, manhandled the sheep upwards into the horse barn loft, well above highwater level.

Local cooperation was excellent, he noted later. "Disaster brings out the worst and the best in people," he wrote. "There was some looting but not much." In order to avoid as much contamination as possible, it was necessary to keep tractors running and pumping sewage through the sewers twenty-four hours a day. The dean served his shift on the "sewer gang" from three until six o'clock in the morning.

When the water subsided, leaving thousands of damaged or destroyed houses, Dean MacEwan was given additional responsibility. On May 29, Premier Campbell asked him to serve as a member of the three-man Red River Valley Board, the task of which was to serve as a flood rehabilitation committee, surveying the devastated area, appraising individual damage, and awarding compensation. His companions on the board were C. E. Joslyn of Winnipeg and Mayor W. R. Forrester of Emerson, Manitoba. The executive-secretary was a man with recent experience in flood rehabilitation, Col. D'Arcy Baldwin of Vancouver, who sat on just such a board following the Fraser Valley flood of 1948.

It was a long and laborious job, calling for aerial inspection as well as the slow and sour job of boating or sloshing through stale waters and over

---

* Those canoeists are not the ones shown in the illustration.

formerly flooded terrain in waders. It was while on such duty that Dean MacEwan experienced his first helicopter flight. "The Winnipeg flood was a major event in my life. I'd hate to go through it again but, if there had to be one, I'm glad I was there," he said in retrospect.

He was gratified to learn one lesson about politicians through his experience on the Red River Board. His group had the responsibility for initiating the distribution of many millions of dollars and deciding who was to get what, where, and how much. Throughout their deliberations, he claimed, never once did he, or, to his knowledge, any of the others on the board, experience pressure from politicians to influence their decisions or to spend money in one constituency over another.

The impression remained and he was to write about it later in his book *Poking into Politics*.

Chapter 21

Politics Again

The politicians would not let Grant MacEwan alone. He had said "no" to them a number of times before but invitations continued to come his way and one, from the city near his birthplace, was to bring a drastic change in the direction of his career.

There had been a brief flurry in such activity in the fall of 1948 at the time President Gillson had been installed. The stage was set when Premier Stuart Garson became minister of justice in Ottawa to be succeeded by Douglas Campbell as premier of Manitoba and head of its coalition administration. Four days after assuming office Campbell invited MacEwan to join his government as minister of agriculture. MacEwan begged time to consider.

In the meantime the story broke in the *Winnipeg Free Press* stating that MacEwan had accepted and would seek a seat at the Fairford constituency by-election to be held in December. Campbell issued a statement saying that it "is incorrect that Dean J. W. G. MacEwan . . . has accepted an offer." The dean confirmed the fact that he had not accepted the post and denied any intention of contesting the seat in Fairford left vacant by Mr. Garson. He also told reporters that "he is not interested in entering provincial politics." There the matter rested, save for the discussion it must have engendered among both friends and enemies in the university Board of Governors.

*　　*　　*

The year 1951 started off with good omens. The dean was presented with a watch by the Western Canada Fairs Association and was made honorary president of the Western Canadian Association of Exhibitions.

The Winnipeg Caledonian Society invited him to speak on Robert Burns. At the "Dean's Party" for the faculty in the new home economics building Hon. Jimmy Gardiner attended and, among other things, danced the Sailor's Hornpipe for the delighted and surprised crowd.

The sitting Liberal member for Brandon, L. Matthews, having died in office, politics again entered MacEwan's life. The MacEwan journal simply states that on March 17, 1951, he "visited Brandon quietly to receive invitations to take Liberal nomination for Federal By-election. Mr. G. R. Rowe, sec., Frank Taylor, Rivers, pres., Tim Bass of Cecil Hotel, sparkplug." The resolution written out by hand in ink and passed to the chairman was moved by H. O. Bell, seconded by W. A. Wood "that we invite Dean MacEwan to attend this meeting and ask him to permit his name to go before the Liberal convention on the understanding that all here present will support his nomination." It was carried unanimously.

Between that time and nomination day, April 19, he had a busy schedule at the university, speaking at various places and attending horse shows. He sought the advice of men experienced in politics. One such was Ralph Maybank, member of parliament for Winnipeg South Centre, a seasoned politician who had lost his first race but had returned to win half a dozen more. At the end of a long roadside chat about politics in general, MacEwan asked him point-blank about the forthcoming by-election and what he should do.

Maybank thought a while, then he said, "Grant, I'd pray."

Others were more confident than Mr. Maybank. Word had leaked out, no matter how "quietly" Dean MacEwan had visited Brandon, and the *Albertan* of Calgary distilled the thoughts and feelings of many friends and supporters. In an editorial published March 28, 1951, it wrote:

> The report is that J. W. Grant MacEwan . . . one of the best known and best liked agricultural men in the whole of Canada, has been invited to take the Liberal nomination in Brandon. . . . Famous as a livestock judge, an after-dinner speaker, an author, historian, traveller, as well as a teacher and agricultural scientist, he is without doubt one of the most competent men in the country, a man of unlimited capacity and good judgement. If he could be induced to enter politics he would add greatly to the reputation of the party he sided with.
>
> The story is that Rt. Hon. Jimmy Gardiner will not last much longer in cabinet and that Mr. MacEwan would take his place as minister of agriculture.

The editorial was substantially correct. In the communications Dean MacEwan had from Prime Minister Louis St. Laurent there was no direct statement that he would be agricultural minister, but implicit in all their discussions was the fact that Mr. Gardiner, twenty years Dean MacEwan's senior, would not last forever. He was in a precarious position, nothing had been put on paper and there were those who were mystified that MacEwan would place at risk his deanship toward which many strove but few achieved.

A realistic analysis of the Brandon situation was contained in the *Free Press* of March 23 written by its Ottawa correspondent, Hugh Boyd. Boyd said the reports reaching the capital about Dean MacEwan were bound to arouse interest in political circles. He would be a strong candidate "but it appears unlikely that he would take the plunge into active politics unless there were some prospects of advancement after he had been in parliament a while — always assuming his election in the first place." Boyd went on to speculate that he would be regarded as a stand-by minister of agriculture but also said that Jimmy Gardiner showed no signs of losing vigor and that, if he continued, possibly another portfolio could be found for a man of Dean MacEwan's abilities. There were others in the running, Boyd pointed out, including W. G. Weir of Portage-Neepawa, chief government whip, a farmer, and, before entering the House of Commons in 1930, prominent in farm organizations.

Phyllis MacEwan was not pleased to see her husband in politics. She reasoned that he had been either professor or dean for over twenty years and had always been respected, but in politics he would be exposed to attack and criticism such as he had never before experienced. He would take a reduction in pay as a member of parliament and would be taken away from the relatively comfortable atmosphere of the university where he was surrounded by loyal staff and admiring students. She did not relish the idea of having to move to Brandon.

Among the letters that flooded in as the news spread was one with a philosophical twist to it. We hear much about the need for high caliber candidates in politics but it's not surprising we get so few, the writer maintained, because we make it mighty miserable for public men. ". . . you will probably discover that even your noble university institution will forget its favorite platitudes about service to country when you formally enter that uncertain and thankless business of serving the nation." The writer was not only a philosopher but would prove to be a prophet.

* * *

In the meantime things were heating up back at the campus.

Later, MacEwan recalled: "At the University of Manitoba it was like stirring up a nest of bees and the Board of Governors held a special meeting to agree that if and when the nomination was confirmed the resignation of Dean Grant MacEwan would be accepted forthwith 'ipso facto.' " Not being up on his Latin, Grant asked his friend Crawford what they meant by "ipso facto." "It means you resign damn fast," came the answer from one agriculturist to another.

The governors' meeting was held on April 12, 1951, under the chairmanship of Victor Sifton with C. Gordon Smith, vice-chairman, F. W. Crawford, secretary. Present were: Dr. Gillson, Mr. Justice A. K. Dysart (chancelor), D. C. Foster, Andrew Murphy, Miss Catherine Forrest, Harold S. Fry, J. J. Trudel, and Dr. Emmet Dwyer.

Under the heading "Dean of Agriculture" the minutes state:

The Chairman raised the question of what the policy of the Board should be with respect to the position of the Dean of Agriculture, in the event that he accepts the nomination as the Liberal Standard Bearer in the forthcoming by-election at

Brandon. After full discussion of the matter, the following Resolution was passed:

That if and when the present Dean of Agriculture accepts nomination as a candidate at an election for a seat in the House of Commons in the forthcoming by-election in the constituency of Brandon, he shall immediately submit his resignation.

*   *   *

The fateful day arrived. In the face of all arguments pro and con, he decided to allow his name to stand. Grant MacEwan finally said "yes" to politics.

On nomination day in Brandon, April 19, 1951, he was chosen to carry the Liberal banner in the federal by-election. His opponent, a Conservative, was Walter Dinsdale.

He immediately wrote a letter of resignation from the university. Meeting in May, with his friend Crawford absent and K. D. McLean in his place, Murphy and Smith also absent and Miss Isobel A. Robson present among the others who had been at the previous meeting, the Board of Governors took the following action, as shown in the minutes of the meeting.:

The President presented to the Board a letter from Mr. J. W. G. MacEwan, tendering his resignation as Dean of the Faculty of Agriculture and Home Economics. The President expressed his wish that the Dean continue as Dean for the purpose of signing the certificates evidencing the degrees to be conferred upon the graduands in his Faculty for the current academic year. It was then moved, seconded and passed, that the resignation of Mr. MacEwan be accepted to take effect forthwith for all purposes except that of signing the aforesaid certificates. This acceptance is subject to the financial terms relating to this matter set forth in the Board minutes of April 12, 1951. The Board directed the Secretary to write to Dean MacEwan expressing their thanks for the service he rendered to the University.

MacEwan was shocked at the vehemence of the governors' reaction and some years later, when dealing with the subject in *Poking into Politics,* was to reveal a capacity for indignation seldom, if ever, seen in his writings. He received a letter from President Gillson telling him what a fine job he had done at the university but nowhere was there a hint that there would be a place for him if things didn't work out to his satisfaction. Dean MacEwan was left with the truth of the matter: "that with the taint of politics on my character, I could never return to the University. A father may take back a prodigal son, a the church will accept a backsliding sinner but for a proud University, a politician would be forever an outcast."

He later described with thinly disguised bitterness his actions and feelings upon leaving academic life after years of service.

I gathered books and personal files, said goodbye to colleagues and, with a certain feeling of guilt, escaped by way of a back door. Perhaps I had made a mistake; perhaps the 23 years of University work had reinforced my need for security, making me unfit to live without it. But I reminded myself that too much security may be like too much rich food. The University experience had been good but it would be invigorating to live dangerously for a while. . . . In any case I had taken the precarious plunge from high on the Ivory Tower into the polluted pool of politics.

* * *

Fortunately, not everybody followed the university's lead. A friend of the family wrote congratulating him on his courageous step, adding that in politics Grant would be strengthened by "your father's determination and your mother's faith, because you'll need them both."

As if to make amends for the harsh treatment from university authorities, friends and colleagues organized a testimonial dinner for him in the Colonial Room at the Royal Alexandra Hotel on May 16, with his old friend Walter Crawford acting as chairman. The sponsoring committee of forty-six colleagues and friends sent invitations signed by J. D. Guild, secretary, to those interested in agriculture, saying that after five years during which he "has made all of Manitoba thoroughly conscious of the importance of the University to the basic industry of this province" he had severed his connections with the university. The committee said all agricultural grads admired him for the way he had instilled in his students "the best traditions of agriculture, together with a keen sense of unity and loyalty within themselves."

The *Winnipeg Tribune* reported that 175 people attended the dinner and that they had agreed what was Manitoba's loss would be Canada's gain. Premier Campbell said that Canada was one of the few countries in the world having complete freedom in electing or rejecting government candidates "and I am pleased to see a man of his ability running for election."

Perhaps the most revealing summing up of Dean MacEwan's performance at the University of Manitoba came from a man who had served as dean himself and was in a position to know, having been associated with the campus for many years. Dr. Alfred Savage, a distinguished veterinarian, was reported as saying that "MacEwan was the best dean the agricultural college has had."

* * *

With his eye for humor and human interest undulled, the university professor-cum-politician set out to campaign wholeheartedly. His opening salvo would be over Brandon radio station CKX and the full-bellied Grant laugh erupted when he saw the advertisement in the newspaper. His picture was there as was the theme they wanted to get across to the public — "a native son of Brandon." By one of the odd quirks that happen only in the composing rooms of newspapers, a short advertisement with a big black headline was placed above the broadcast advertisement. The black headline shouted for attention — "Mr. Pile Sufferer."

The fun was to continue: as he began broadcasting his message on "Brandon traditions," the program went off the air. Phone calls flooded the switchboard asking the same question — had the other party cut the circuit?

Much as it would have helped to conjure up a case for sabotage, he had to tell the truth. It had been due to a mechanical failure in the studio itself and not the machinations of the Conservatives.

At a church service the minister took note of visitors, "especially the Liberal candidate in the forthcoming Federal by-election" and then announced his text from Luke 3:5, ". . . and the crooked shall be made straight."

"Campaigning in the country was strenuous but enjoyable," he wrote. "Usually there were two meetings a night and often they were 20 or 30 miles apart. Trying to be present at both was a little like blowing the old kerosene lamps out and trying to be in bed before it was dark. But farmer audiences proved patient and frequently accepted the late arrival of the speaker with the best of grace."

At one farmstead, a farmer was busily painting his roof when the MacEwan campaign car turned into the yard. He started down the ladder but, when Grant got out and was recognized as the tall Liberal candidate, the man returned to the roof and continued his paint job. At another farm, he found a lady in overalls forking manure in the barn. The candidate said with a smile, "Good afternoon, my name is MacEwan and I'm the fellow who is supposed to be going about kissing babies in anticipation of the by-election." The woman dropped the fork, straightened her back, wiped the sweat from "her wrinkled but kindly brow," and said, "Goody, goody, I'm the baby of our family." The candidate was not prepared for such an answer, "but she was a nice old body and I think I won her vote."

When a MacEwan acquaintance heard the story, he said: "If I know MacEwan, he'll soon discover that kissing babies is cheaper and more to his taste than buying cigars."

The story circulated that the Liberals hired the only band they could get for a MacEwan rally — the Salvation Army Band. MacEwan did his bit but when the time came for music and a cornet solo so did Walter Dinsdale, the cornet-playing member of the band.

Almost everyone was convinced it was a shoo-in for popular Grant MacEwan. The *Winnipeg Free Press* editorialized in its April 21 issue congratulating Brandon Liberals on their choice and expressing some surprise that the dean would leave the security of a comfortable and congenial academic chair for the "onerous responsibilities and somewhat dubious rewards of public service." It then alluded to previous attempts made to involve MacEwan in politics and concluded with confidence: "now that he has finally decided on the political plunge, there is every indication that he will go far in Canadian public life."

The *Calgary Albertan* went farther in its editorial page of April 23: "He is resigning his university position, a safe enough move since his election to Parliament can be taken for granted. Mr. MacEwan will without doubt be one of the strongest men in all the Liberal ranks at Ottawa including both front and back benches."

However, one seasoned politician looked at the Brandon campaign with foreboding. Walter Tucker said nothing to his friend and fellow Liberal but he told his wife that Manitobans were clannish and still regarded the dean as a Saskatchewan man — an outsider parachuted in — and that they might well resent the implicit suggestion that one of their own was not good enough to send to Ottawa.

With all the optimistic comment and the fact that the Brandon seat had been taken handily by a Liberal in the last general election, the MacEwans can be pardoned for being somewhat overconfident. They didn't say much but certain actions revealed the nature of their feelings on the matter, one especially. As the campaign ground on, Phyllis wrote to her long-time friend, Esther Sutherland, who now lived in Ottawa, asking her to send the primary French textbook then in use in the capital city schools so that she could coach Heather. She wanted her daughter to be at no disadvantage at her new school in Ottawa in the fall of 1951.

* * *

The thunderbolt hit the MacEwans on June 25, 1951, election day in Brandon. Grant wrote later that his friends thought he was winning, everybody thought he was winning. "The man in the street said we were winning. But those little people who go into booths to mark ballots on election day — the mighty men and women of Democracy — had other ideas and I was defeated." Dinsdale polled 11,124 votes, MacEwan 8,371.

The crowd in the committee room dwindled until only a few of the faithful remained. They constituted a quiet group, there being nothing for which to cheer. The friends tried to say something comforting but it was no easier than finding cheerful remarks for the bereaved at a graveside. A dozen loyal supporters ate what they could of the food ordered for a hundred. I visited my opponent's committee room and extended congratulations and went to bed, wondering what defeated candidates who sacrifice their jobs do to make a living.

There were explanations for the defeat of such a popular, widely known candidate, most of them boiling down to the unpopularity of Mr. Gardiner's grain marketing policy. The *Albertan* hoped he would stay in politics and said in the next general election two years hence he could pretty well pick any seat he wanted, outside of Alberta, and win "provided he stood on his own feet and not on Mr. Gardiner's." The newspaper also alluded to the fact that the successful candidate had campaigned "in a church uniform," but MacEwan would have none of that. He said it had been "a fair political fight" and a "wheat marketing protest vote."

Most commentators overlooked Walter Dinsdale, whose family had been in public service in Brandon for years and who was known by every man, woman, and child in the district. His father had been councilor and mayor of Brandon and member of the legislative assembly for eleven years before he died in office. Dinsdale was a native son, too, who didn't move away. He had started work with the CPR and was a card-carrying union member in a railway town — a member of the Salvation Army Band to boot. In the Second World War, he won the Distinguished Flying Cross for operations with 410 Night Fighter Squadron, RCAF. He, too, was now in the academic world as director of public relations and social services at Brandon College. A hard man to beat even for a seasoned politician.

Grant MacEwan had experienced reverses before but the defeat in Brandon constituted by far the most severe one to that time and possibly in his entire lifetime. He now left Brandon in defeat, as his father had thirty-six years before. It offered little consolation that five by-elections had been held that day and the Liberals lost them all. He had lost a seat everybody said he was winning. His loss of prestige would be great in the public eye; he was now neither MP, dean or even professor and, what was more, he was a man without a base. To a good many men approaching fifty years of age such disaster would be enough to write finis to a career. A colleague back at Saskatchewan University, Dr. J. W. T. Spinks (later university president) said he suffered a severe loss of prestige and recalled that people were watching to see how he would emerge from the drastic drop in full public view — if indeed he could.

Chapter 22

Wandering after Defeat

Following the Brandon debacle, MacEwan, who was now plain Mr. MacEwan, was destined to spend exactly a year wandering in the wilderness before he reached anything that would resemble a new direction in his career.

For one brief interlude, there appeared to be an ideal solution. The political campaign had occupied him fully and he had had little time to keep in touch with things relating to agriculture in western Canada over a period of many weeks; consequently, he was not aware that something important was afoot at the Calgary Exhibition and Stampede office. What was actually brewing was a confrontation between the directors of the exhibition and their managing director, H. Charles Yule, over a matter of policy. Yule was overruled and he resigned.

When MacEwan got the news, he didn't have to review his qualifications long before making an approach to the Calgary directors. Who had more impressive background to apply for the job than Grant MacEwan, who had taken over the Saskatoon Exhibition and lifted it out of the red in two years; who had written a book on Western Canadian Exhibitions and Fairs; who had judged livestock at all the most important shows in the country?

He made a discreet inquiry, asking if an application for the managership would be in order. He was told that it would not. A commitment had been made to another person earlier. In September 1951 it was announced that Maurice Hartnett, one-time deputy minister of agriculture for Saskatchewan, had been hired for the job; Maurice Hartnett, with whom Grant had traveled far and wide throughout the West, judging and lecturing in the early period of both their careers, had arrived first. Had the job been open to MacEwan it would have suited him to a tee, and no doubt would have steered him into an entirely different path than the one he was to take.

*   *   *

On a trip through Saskatoon, MacEwan called on an old friend, A. P. "Pat" Waldron, editor of the widely circulated agricultural weekly newspaper the *Western Producer*, as he had done many times before. W. J. Bradley, the executive editor, was also well known to him, as they had for years traveled to livestock shows and sales, Grant to judge, Bill Bradley to report, often sharing cars and hotel rooms. The columns in the newspaper had carried MacEwan's writings on animal husbandry many times in the past. It was a social meeting of old friends, but a question of importance arose.

When Mr. Waldron discovered Grant MacEwan had no definite plans for the future, he offered him a job. The newspaper had been without an agricultural editor for months — would Grant take the job? There ensued a discussion of the possibilities, MacEwan revealing that he might take up residence on land he owned at Priddis, do a little farming and continue to write, and move around the country to livestock shows, sales, and other agricultural events of importance. He also let Waldron know that the editorship interested him. Could he possibly manage to fill the position and still spend part of his time in Alberta?

Waldron revealed that he had always had in mind the possibility of his newspaper's agricultural staff having on it a man who was a practicing farmer as well as a journalist. It would be of great advantage to the newspaper, keeping it current in the matters of farm costs and returns. He would have preferred to have the farmland owned by his editor somewhat closer than Priddis but, as a person couldn't expect to have a completely ideal situation, the offer still stood. Would MacEwan be willing to give it a try?

In the *Western Producer* issue of February 14, 1952, there appeared a boxed, two-column story, with his photograph, announcing the new arrangement in the form of a note from Grant MacEwan, saying in part:

> The *Western Producer* has a new hired man. I'm it. Whether it is a long or short period, the prospect of the associations and responsibilities seem most attractive. Any one sitting in an agricultural editor's chair must be conscious of the opportunities as well as the responsibilities that go with prescribing a fair share of the agricultural reading for 160,000 subscribers and a bigger number of readers. It represents a much bigger audience than I have ever had the pleasure of facing and there is an attractive challenge about it.

The newspaper had hired a hard worker. According to Bradley the association was a good one despite the unusual nature of the arrangements. MacEwan was a slow typist who "could think much faster than he could operate the machine," the executive editor recalled, but who was prepared to devote long hours to his writings, and, time and time again, returned to his office to work well after midnight turning out a story to his own satisfaction, only to report at regular working hours the following day to perform other duties. He went about his work "coattails flying," said Bradley.

However, the association between MacEwan and the newspaper was to be one of short duration. Two weeks after he joined the staff, he covered a major story which would be the indirect reason for his leaving. The headline was, "Foot and Mouth Disease Hits Livestock in Southern Sask."

The story described the disease and its aftermath. Livestock prices had been sliding downward for some time, markets were sluggish at best and, when the United States closed its borders to Canadian cloven-hoofed animals because of the disease, they deteriorated with alarming rapidity.

By the spring of 1952, with the continuing downward trend and the chaos following the outbreak of the disease, the producers wanted something done and they made their demands known to their main commodity organization, the Council of Canadian Beef Producers (Western Section), located at 28 Michael Building, Calgary. Their president, D. J. McKinnon, was convinced that what they needed was a full-scale public relations campaign and a product promotion program for the beef and cattle industry in Canada.

With this in mind, the president and the secretary-treasurer, Kenneth Coppock, both touched on the subject with Grant MacEwan as he traveled here and there to agricultural meetings throughout the west as agricultural editor. It culminated in a meeting of the three in the Beef Council office April 17, 1952, when a verbal proposal was put before MacEwan for consideration. McKinnon wrote MacEwan on April 22, reviewing what they had discussed.

They invited him to join them in Calgary as General Manager of the Council of Canadian Beef Producers (Western Section) to conduct the type of campaign the producers felt they needed. For this they would give him a guaranteed annual budget of $15,000 minimum. Out of that sum he was to provide secretarial staff, rent, travel, publicity, and other office expenses. Apart from the budget, he would be paid a salary of $6,500 per year, plus $500 for moving expenses provided he was with them at the end of the first year. As producer support increased, so also would the money available for the position.

Grant would have full freedom to continue with his livestock judging and other similar interests, as the council would look upon such activities as being in line of duty. If it proved that the program was not being "successfully prosecuted [by MacEwan] or supported" (by producers), neither party would be considered bound to a three-year contract.

They wanted MacEwan as soon as possible because they thought that an announcement of the fact that Grant MacEwan had joined them "would serve the purpose of injecting in the industry new hope at a time when Foot and Mouth disease, embargoes, lower market prices have tended to undermine the faith in the future of the industry."

After a week in which he discussed the move to Calgary with Phyllis in Winnipeg and with his editor in Saskatoon, Grant wrote from his Winnipeg home that he would accept their offer, and would try to join the council staff by July 15, 1952 — a few weeks before his fiftieth birthday.

The real estate market in Winnipeg had leveled off but Grant MacEwan sold the house at 814 Sommerset Avenue for just about what he had paid for it, and the MacEwans set out in the car for their new home town, Calgary. It was this move which prompted Wesley Gordon Nelson, husband of Grant's cousin Maria, to say that "the defeat at Brandon was the best thing that ever happened to Grant . . . it sent him back to the province where he had really always belonged."

Chapter 23

To Calgary

When MacEwan set out for Calgary, he thought he was returning to the service of agriculture; he also thought he would partially capture the long-standing dream of writing in the beautiful Priddis hills by Fish Creek. Neither came to pass. He was to set an entirely new course, one that he could not foresee.

Their arrival in Calgary was timed to coincide with the Calgary Stampede. It also coincided with the poliomyelitis epidemic which swept the Prairies in the summer of 1952. They put up in the Palliser Hotel, an unusual extravagance for MacEwan and one that suggested he wanted the initial impression of their new home town to be as pleasant as possible for Phyllis and Heather. But it wasn't.

The weather was hot, the city virtually closed to public gatherings — swimming pools, theaters — due to the epidemic. A hotel room, no matter how luxurious, was no place for an active, athletic girl of thirteen, nor for her parents. The cabin at Priddis beckoned.

It had not been used for some time and was in need of cleaning and certain repairs, but the wide-open spaces were much to be preferred over confined quarters in the city. In short order, matters were set right, provisions brought in, and the MacEwans set up housekeeping in the dream world.

Their arrival in Calgary was a stark contrast to other arrivals they had made during their married life. Returning to Saskatoon after the honeymoon, they had entered community life with an already well-established and broad circle of friends and a full round of faculty social events from which to select. Similarly in Winnipeg, the new dean had been plunged into

The dream cabin and the view at Priddis, Alta.   (R. H. Macdonald photos)

the duties of office without pause, his wife had been taken over by a warm and welcoming group of faculty wives with a ready-made schedule of social commitments to fulfill. However, when they arrived in Calgary, they did so as private citizens who must make their own way.

Idyllic though their surroundings were, reality soon pressed in on them. Leaving the cabin for the city one night early in their stay, their car became hopelessly bogged down in what proved to be more of a running spring than a rustic road and they were forced to settle in for an uncomfortable sleep in the car. However, as dawn broke they heard the sound of a motor approaching. It turned out to be Bob Renner, the son of neighbors, Mr. and Mrs. Tom Renner, who ran a fine farm close to the MacEwan land. Mrs. Renner had spotted the car and sent her son to pull them out with a tractor.

With the car standing on firm ground once again, Bob said, "Mother says breakfast is ready at the house as soon as you can get up there." Phyllis recalled that she had never tasted a better breakfast and would treasure the memory of this real western hospitality for the rest of her life.

Soon prospects brightened and, as her husband went about familiarizing himself with his duties at the Beef Council office and fulfilling livestock judging commitments throughout the country, Phyllis went house hunting and eventually found an attractive, moderately styled bungalow in a neat neighborhood close to a school at 502 25th Avenue Northwest. In time, she discovered two girlhood friends of hers from Saskatoon now living in Calgary — Lorna and Enid Stevenson, (now Mrs. Hugh Robertson and Mrs. Enid Cameron) — and they were to resume their former close

friendship. Mrs. Coppock, the wife of the Beef Council secretary, was also of great help at the start of their life in the new city.

In his dream cabin at long last, Grant MacEwan wrote not a word.

*   *   *

Calgary was enjoying a period of expansion when the MacEwans arrived in late June, 1952. Five years before it had been a pleasant but relatively quiet prairie city of 100,000 population, known more for beer, its proximity to the mountains, and its annual exhibition and stampede, than anything else. The Imperial Oil Company's discovery of the Leduc oil field in 1947 changed all that and Calgary became an oil capital for hundreds of petrochemical-related firms, enjoying a greatly accelerated growth in size and economy. In 1952, the city's population was 140,000 and growing.

The Beef Producers Council's new general manager had no trouble fitting into the position. He either knew most of the cattlemen personally or, if he did not, then he knew more about their cattle and pedigrees than the owners did themselves. His relationship with Kenneth Coppock was one of long-standing, for Coppock was editor and publisher of *The Canadian Cattlemen* which had printed many MacEwan articles in the past. Grant had allowed his name to appear on the masthead of the monthly journal as associate editor (unpaid), for whatever authority an animal husbandry professor's name would suggest.

Now his contributions to *The Cattlemen* increased to three items per issue. He wrote a column for young cattlemen, he conducted a search of old western newspapers and published quotations under the title "Gleaned from Pioneering Pages," and he usually wrote an article on animal husbandry or something along similar lines. This he continued until December 1953 when ownership of the journal was transferred to the United Grain Growers and F. M. Jacobs became editor. The names Coppock and MacEwan disappeared from the masthead and MacEwan contributions ceased to appear in its pages. From that time on and for the next thirteen years, MacEwan transferred his interest to the *Farm and Ranch Review*. One journal editor said of MacEwan that he had become "the main feature writer, tailoring his contributions to suit the paper and succeeded in raising the tone of the paper through his serious articles that did not talk down to the farmer."

Whereas the new man had little trouble starting to work, those who had hired him had more in bringing their plan to fruition. The initial budget was to have been a starter only, the success of the plan depending upon agreement among cattlemen to permit a check-off amounting to a few cents per head sold and this was to be contributed to a beef promotion fund. On paper the plan looked promising and, had it worked, there would have been ample money to mount an advertising and promotion campaign on a scale larger than anything seen up to that time. For their own reasons, beef producers did not support the proposal.

The Beef Producers Council and anybody working for it had two built-in problems to contend with. They had to deal with their members, notorious as a breed of rugged individualists, the last to be regimented in any way. They also had to act within an industry traditionally subject to boom and bust cycles that could be traced back as far as accurate figures had been kept. The idea of a public relations campaign came at the end of a downward trend which, once the foot and mouth disease was cleared up, began to show signs of rounding out and climbing toward a new high point. This, more than anything else, would modify the urgency behind the council's plan and the likelihood of support from its members, no matter who made the appeal or how effectively it was presented.

Possibly because he sensed a lack of enthusiasm among the producers themselves, and although he gave it a good try, the job failed to capture the MacEwan imagination completely. Within two or three years he had decided to gradually ease out of Beef Council work.

*   *   *

If the Beef Council job was not occupying all his energy, time, and interest, the unforeseen would. He had already begun to make his mark in his new home town, taking an active part in the Chamber of Commerce Agricultural Bureau and its education committee. His efforts did not escape notice.

Grant had been in Calgary barely fourteen months when a committee from the Civic Government Association paid him a visit, asking him to stand as an aldermanic candidate in the forthcoming civic elections.

"I'm not yet well enough known to successfully contest for a place on City Council," he replied, still somewhat gun-shy after the Brandon debacle. Brushing his protest aside, one of them said: "MacEwan, you had better run now; if people knew you better they probably wouldn't vote for you. This is your chance."

Eventually he agreed to let his name stand and plunged into the 1953

civic campaign. He demonstrated interest and knowledge in education and
other matters, but much of his presentation to the public had to do with city
finances and the need for care and caution in forthcoming expansion, lest
spending outstrip what citizens could afford to pay in taxes. He quoted the
famous character, Bob Edwards, editor of the *Calgary Eye Opener*, on the
wisdom of electing the "tightwads" and letting the "free spenders" go.

The *Calgary Herald* commented favorably on his candidacy, saying
that there were three outstanding candidates in the election — Grant
MacEwan, Arthur R. Smith, and Mel Shannon — who would provide
within council "a hard core of above average ability which will stand the
city in good stead."

When the ballots were counted, Smith was elected on the first ballot
with around 7,000 votes, MacEwan on the second count with 5,000, and
Shannon on the eleventh with about 4,000. So began a term that would be
active, filled with public occasions and appearances and attention from the
news media. It was a beginning that would lead him along the same path
much farther than he could imagine.

*   *   *

Civic politics stood in marked contrast to the more or less protected
life of a former professor and dean. Alderman MacEwan quickly discovered
the fact of election seemed to suggest to the public that each of the
successful candidates had presented himself to public scrutiny and
examination. No longer were they ordinary citizens enjoying a right to a
certain degree of privacy. It was open season and he no longer was one of
the protected species.

The comment of one of the local newspapers, however, suggests that
the twelve aldermen and mayor were acceptable — at the beginning at any
rate. "The voters of the city are to be congratulated on making what is, on
the whole, the wisest selection of public officials that they have made for
many years," it editorialized.

Grant MacEwan found himself with a mixed lot, he later revealed in
Poking into Politics. Some had previous experience in public administration,
others had none. Some would score high in intelligence, others low. Some
were carried away by the need to make lengthy speeches on anything and
everything, others "had the good sense to keep quiet until an expression of
opinion would have benefit." With their vices and virtues these were the
men chosen by a democratic community to speak and act in behalf of all the
residents of Calgary.

The shrewd eye of the writer combined with the synoptic vision of the
journalist came into play, and the impact of this new experience was
captured by the MacEwan pen while still fresh and recognizable and before
it became commonplace and blended with the ordinary round of events in
everyday civic life. Speaking for the new alderman, he wrote:

At once he was the object of scheming individuals and avaricious pressure
groups seeking more parks and playgrounds, zoning concessions, the sale of
property to the city at twice its value, higher grants to favorite organizations, and, of

course, lower taxes. Not always reasonable in their requests, the petitioners wanted better streets with less traffic on them, more industry but fewer smoke stacks to pollute city air, better transit service but lower fares, improved garbage disposal but no sanitary land fills within miles — in other words, more of every convenience as long as others paid for it.

If the new alderman refuses to support the petitions, he is a political phony and is told the voters will not forget his failures at next election. He will find that trying to please everybody who reports voting for him will be quite impossible. He might as well accept the fact that he will be criticized and the editor who wrote generously about him when he was elected will be ready to ridicule him severely on slight pretext.

Winning criticism will be easier than winning praise. The alderman failing to attend all meetings will be scored for carelessness; if he attends avidly to every call, he is "a climber who is out to become mayor." If he accepts all invitations to parties and receptions, he must be a "booze-hound" and if he fails to attend he's "a kill-joy." If he votes against spending, he's a "tightwad"; if he supports big spending he's the reason for high taxes. If he supports salary increases for aldermen, he's "money-hungry" and if he votes against them, he's "putting on a show." As an alderman, he is closer to the people, closer to their wallets, closer to their problems and whims than he would be as Member of the Legislature or House of Commons and can expect to be the first to feel the whiplash of immoderate public displeasure.

As an elected member of local government, he becomes, immediately, a favorite subject for the popular press and radio pastime of hazing or baiting — not unlike the once-popular entertainment of bearbaiting. But instead of chaining a bear to a post and releasing a pack of savage hounds to torture the captive animal and entertain the cheering spectators, the modern version consists of turning a pack of press and radio commentators against a captive alderman or mayor to bait, confuse and inflict mental torture for public pleasure. It brings cheers when the elected man is made to squirm under the clever attack. As a "whipping boy" he can try to defend himself against the attackers whose only purpose is to make news but he is not likely to triumph.

He is the man in the middle when there is divided opinion and it is up to him to consider the demands of all the affected groups, remembering that he is the one who will be held responsible for success or failure in the outcome. The noisy prattle of those who indulge in propaganda will be quickly forgotten but the man whose council vote determined the outcome will not be forgotten.

Life is a strange mixture of black and white and nowhere will a person encounter more striking extremes of joys and sorrows, thrills and disappointments, bouquets and brickbats, than in public service at civil level. Backbenchers in the House of Commons may suffer from monotony but in city politics where small annoyances appear like major problems to individuals concerned and most citizens have telephones, there is no chance of boredom. Calgary's council, from its initial meeting in Clarke's Saloon, could never lay claim to tranquility.

Local government is also the best possible stepping-stone for the individual planning to run for a seat in Legislature or House of Commons. Many politicians with familiar names were aldermen before becoming Members.

The writer might well have added that one of those with familiar names to enter the legislature from a seat in city council was the author himself.

Chapter 24

Party Leader

By the spring of 1955, Alderman MacEwan was "gradually easing out of the Council of Beef Producers. . . . the Council was not developing as expected and I was not very enthusiastic about the work anyway."

His main activities were still city hall work and his writing. To facilitate each, he secured an office in the McLean Block (since demolished), fitted it with secondhand furniture, and decorated the walls with prints of the Old West by Charlie Russell — one entitled "The Last of Five Thousand" hung over his desk. Operating from there, he made himself accessible to the public in the office, took the occasional assignment, wrote for a number of journals, and prepared manuscripts for forthcoming books.

One assignment he accepted was an unusual one for him. Early in April of 1955 he received a request from the Royalite Oil Company Limited asking him to make a survey of the prospects for the fertilizer market in the state of Washington in view of Royalite's interest in building a fertilizer plant in the northwestern United States. MacEwan agreed to accept the job, spending a good part of two weeks researching for the study, traveling through the state and writing the report.

The results were threefold. The report, written in 1955, proved to be a far-seeing one presaging by years the coming of a period in agriculture when the massive use of fertilizer would require mountains of the material not only in the northwestern states but also in western Canada.

The study also resulted in possibly the smallest expense account ever submitted in the history of both the consulting business and the huge petrochemical industry. The four days of travel through the state cost

MacEwan a grand total of $54.40. Sample: April 7 — Hotel, Spokane . . . $5.00, bus fare Spokane to Pullman . . . $2.15, taxi to State College . . . $1.00, bus fare Pullman to Walla Walla . . . $4.15, three meals during the day . . . $3.75!

The MacEwan caution with cost was exceeded only by Royalite's cautious response, possibly establishing a mark for penury that should be, if it has not already been, entered in Guinness' Book of Records. Royalite wrote the former dean of agriculture a letter of appreciation stating that, as "negotiations are proceeding between parties other than ourselves," they would be holding off on a fertilizer plan, but when they resumed planning, they would call upon him for further consultation. Meanwhile, the letter went on to say, Royalite appreciated his efforts very much.

Two days later a letter arrived at the MacEwan office signed by the secretary-treasurer of Royalite. It contained added words of appreciation and a cheque for $103.40 — $53.40 covering expenses and "honorarium of $50.00 for services performed for our company."

*   *   *

As Grant MacEwan later wrote, city council often provided a launching pad for those wishing to serve in higher levels of government. That was the case with him when, at the urging of a good-sized delegation of Liberals, he agreed to allow his name to stand at a forthcoming convention called to nominate candidates to contest Calgary seats in the June 29, 1955, provincial election.

The rally was termed "the most rousing [Liberal] rally in Calgary in many years." Four hundred gathered in the Al Azhar Temple where Grant MacEwan was nominated by fellow alderman Mel Shannon. Together with the other candidates, he made a short speech, condemning the Social Credit government and Premier Ernest C. Manning for smothering democracy and permitting the level of education to fall alarmingly. Alderman MacEwan was among those nominated to contest the six-seat constituency of Calgary.

According to the *Calgary Herald* the provincial campaign proved to be one of the most aggressive in twenty years. Alderman MacEwan was in the thick of the fight.

When the votes were counted the first time through, MacEwan was in eighth place for six seats. The man who topped the polls in the civic election, Alderman Arthur Smith, won for the Conservative party on first count. It took twelve counts to elect a Liberal, Hugh John MacDonald, who, like Smith, was a long-time Calgary resident. This was followed by the election of two Social Credit candidates, Fred Colborne and Mrs. Rose Wilkinson. Finally, in what proved to be the longest election count in the city's history — twenty-six hours — Grant MacEwan was elected on the twenty-first count! The final seat went to another Social Crediter, Arthur J. Dixon. MacEwan had won his first political elective office as a member of a political party.

Having decided to continue to hold his seat on city council while serving in the legislative assembly, MacEwan was criticized along with others in a similar situation. A *Herald* reader, Frank T. Taylor of Calgary, set out his views on the matter. "Surely," he wrote to the editor, "in a city of 178,000 we can find enough capable men and women without having to load all the work and honors onto a few aldermen." Alderman MacEwan reasoned that there was precedent for holding both seats. In Calgary these included Rose Wilkinson, who was returned as a Social Credit member and was holding her council seat, and Paul Brecken, the Conservative candidate, who was defeated but who had intended holding his if elected. MacEwan's mind was unchanged — he would hold both seats while he remained an ordinary member of the legislative assembly.

*   *   *

The Alberta general election of 1955 no doubt was wearing to candidates such as Grant MacEwan who had to watch the count grind slowly onward, but when the results were finally made known, there was encouragement for the Liberal cause and to the party leader, J. Harper Prowse. Born in Taber, Alberta, Prowse was first elected as a servicemen's representative while overseas, was elected party leader in 1947, and had been working diligently to bring the Liberals, who had been out of office since 1921, back to power. With all votes counted, standings in the 61-seat house (with previous standings in brackets) were: Social Credit 37 (52), Liberals 15 (4), Conservatives 3 (1), CCF 2 (2) and 4 others. Although Premier Manning won a substantial victory, the Liberals had increased their strength in the house at the expense of his Social Credit party.

Early in the first session of the thirteenth legislature, Grant MacEwan not only attracted attention with his maiden speech but revealed subjects and topics that would be among his main interests during legislative sessions. He was critical of plans for Alberta's golden jubilee, maintaining that there should be much more to the celebration than fireworks, parades, and speeches about the past. He urged upon the government measures that would be of lasting benefit: the planting of trees in a province that was becoming alarmingly denuded; a study of population trends that would facilitate sound planning of future schools and roads; the conducting of surveys on soil erosion, wildlife, and provincial coal resources; an assessment and improvement of museums.

He was critical of the manner in which the provincial government had settled veterans on land in northern Alberta, claiming that the land upon which they were expected to farm and extract their living was submarginal and the "most deplorable land-use spectacle I have encountered."

Following the first few days of the opening session, one cabinet minister told the press that he was "impressed by the rookie crop" of new members in the house.

*   *   *

Once again MacEwan, the writer, found himself in a position to observe from the inside one of the country's important institutions. In *Poking into Politics*, he said later:

MacEwan judging Arabians at Chilliwack, B.C., 1956

(*Maynard photo, MacEwan Collection*)

Having retained my seat on the Calgary Council, I was able to serve in the double capacity of City Alderman and Member of the Legislature. In that dual role, it was possible to compare fairly the weights of work loads at the two levels of government. That Provincial Cabinet Ministers worked hard, just as hard as Members of the Federal Government, there could be no doubt. But it was easy to conclude that sitting as a backbencher on either Government or Opposition side was appreciably less onerous than serving on a Council within easy calling range of every citizen in a big population of city constituents. For the relatively short period when the Provincial Legislature was in session, work could be steady and tedious. Elected Members had a moral duty to attend all or nearly all daily sessions. In other hours, there was research and preparation for debates and speeches and the study of endless Bills which seemed to be written to bring the greatest possible confusion to weary readers.

Those years in the Legislature brought me back to party warfare, from which it had been possible to escape while confining one's self to City Council. Provincial politics had no fewer animosities than federal.

* * *

The man who, as an academic, had moved among his fellow citizens in an atmosphere of admiration and respect, soon found it otherwise as a party politician. Shortly after being elected to the legislature, he was returning from a meeting in Grande Prairie when he was forced to leave a stalled car and hitch a ride with a farmer hauling a load of pigs in his truck to Edmonton. "What's your name and what do you do?" the farmer asked. "MacEwan's the name and I sit as a Liberal on the Opposition side of the Legislature," was the answer. The man slumped in his seat and the truck slowed down. "MacEwan? I never heard of you but if I had known you were a Liberal, the only place you'd get in this truck would be back there with the other swine." It proved to be no joke, the remainer of the trip being made in utter silence.

* * *

Despite the fact that he was commuting between Calgary and Edmonton and sitting on two legislative bodies, Grant MacEwan continued to carry a heavy program of research, writing, judging, and other outside activities. He had become a director of the Toronto Royal Winter Fair in 1954; in 1956 he was elected president of the Calgary Men's Canadian Club and later vice-president of the national organization, the Association of Canadian Clubs. He had resigned his directorship of the Royal Bank upon entering politics but became a director of Cockshutt Farm Equipment Ltd. In 1957, his book on Calgary's famous character, Bob Edwards, was published by The Institute of Applied Arts under the title *Eyeopener Bob* and the year after, the *Western Producer* published his book of Western character sketches entitled *Fifty Mighty Men*. The two proved to be best sellers and are still being bought by the hundreds each year.

More importantly, they marked clearly and distinctly his entry into the field as a writer of popular western history books. Up to now, all his books had either been related to agriculture or, as in the case of the book *Sodbusters*, had been an offshoot of his radio broadcasts. He was now a serious writer of books for general consumption and would continue to be, but in no ordinary way, for he began producing more Western Canadiana than any writer heretofore.

In 1957, he again ran in Calgary civic elections, but this time he did not have to wait an interminable length of time to discover his fate. The citizens had seen him in action as an alderman and as an MLA and obviously felt that he could carry both responsibilities, for they sent him back to city council at the top of the polls.

* * *

At this stage of his life, being a member of the legislature agreed with him. He wrote, "those years proved again that politics is like jail: once in, it is not easy to get out."

What he was referring to was the fact that when Prowse resigned from the leadership of the Liberal party "to take a breather from politics," Grant MacEwan and a number of others in the party were eyeing the position.

It would prove to be an interesting battle, attracting widespread attention both within the party and outside of it. Following the announcement of Mr. Prowse's resignation, there was much speculation about the leadership. Interest heightened each time a hopeful candidate declared himself for the nomination at the forthcoming convention to be held October 31-November 1, 1958, in Edmonton.

At the appointed time, crowding into the Macdonald Hotel for the nominations were 898 delegates, close to 100 alternates, and about 200 guests. A group of enthusiastic supporters sought to draft the chief magistrate of Edmonton, but Mayor Hawrelak declined their invitation. In the end there remained three contenders: Ralph Walker, a thirty-four-year-old rancher-oilman from Raymond, Alberta; Richard Hall, fifty-one, for Athabasca; and Grant MacEwan, fifty-six, freshman MLA from Calgary.

If there was tension on a large scale in the convention hall, there was a small but tense drama being acted out behind the scenes in the proverbial "smoke-filled room" somewhere in the hotel. Harper Prowse was angry. There had always been tension between the federal Liberals and the provincial Liberals which, at times, amounted almost to open warfare between Mr. Prowse and the man who went from Edmonton to Ottawa to become minister of mines and technical surveys, Hon. George Prudham. The federal Liberals held the purse strings to party funds. Prowse had invested not only his energy and dynamic leadership in the party's provincial fate but had spent a good deal of his own money as well. Although this sort of information seldom reaches the public in Canada, it was accepted in journalistic circles at the time that "Harper was mad, he was in debt to the tune of $15,000 [which was much more in 1958 than it is in 1979] and he wanted something for it — in writing and on paper!" If he didn't get what he wanted, he threatened to walk right out into the convention hall and throw his hat into the leadership ring for re-election, upsetting things completely and, at the same time, exposing a family squabble to full public view.

While this was going on, Grant MacEwan and his fellow candidates were circulating as much as possible and greeting delegates from far and near. It was not a difficult job, for MacEwan knew many of them, certainly a good number of the rural delegates who had seen him judge livestock and had heard him commenting at fairs and exhibitions as an agriculturist.

Whatever took place behind the scenes, Harper Prowse did not make an appearance, allowing the election to proceed as planned with three candidates standing. Grant MacEwan won the party leadership on the second ballot, 314 to 200, over Ralph Walker and was faced with the task, described in the *Edmonton Journal*, "to break Social Credit's 23-year stranglehold on Alberta Politics."

Opposition Leader MacEwan speaks at a special ceremony in the Alberta legislature with Premier Manning (extreme right) and others in attendance (*MacEwan Collection*)

In his victory speech, Liberal Leader MacEwan said it was time for a change. Premier Manning and the Social Credit party had "been in the driver's seat for too long and the people are looking for a new driver." Social Credit was "making U-turns all over the place, and we're not sure where it is going." He was critical of Manning's oil and gas dividend policy or lack of policy; he wanted homes for the aged; a major hospital in Calgary; and changes in the law that would permit farmers to use tax-free purple gasoline. He accused the government of being more concerned with the well-being of the oil industry, than with the welfare of the farmers.

* * *

The party leadership brought changes into Grant MacEwan's life. No longer was he the backbencher with a relatively light load. He was a frontbencher and leader of his party to boot. He had the able member from Calgary, H. J. MacDonald, to turn to for advice. MacDonald had been leader, in fact if not in name, for a good part of the twelfth legislature, while Prowse went back to school to get his law degree. There were a number of other members of long standing to support him. He wrote:

Before the end of the term, I was the Leader of Her Majesty's Loyal Opposition and Leader of the Alberta Liberals. At once I was inundated with messages, some extending good wishes, some offering advice, some hinting that the senders would make excellent Senators or Deputy Ministers. Newspapers reacted favorably but there were exceptions. A news release from Edmonton said: "A lean and lanky westerner, Grant MacEwan, has been elected to leadership in the Liberal Party." When the story appeared in one weekly paper whose editor had strong Conservative leanings, it read: "A mean and cranky westerner. . . .' The editor called it typographical error.

The new responsibilities made me realize at once how good and able were the people with whom I was surrounded. No doubt the Leader on the Government side could say the same about elected representatives with high principles, whether the public chose to recognize it or not.

His maiden speech as leader came as the prelude to moving a motion to amend the speech from the throne. Opposition Leader MacEwan criticized the government for having no long-range plan and for having failed to solve basic financial problems facing municipal governments throughout the province. Premier Manning's administration was bringing instability to the province, it was arrogant and no respecter of the people. They were remiss in not providing for flood control of the Bow River, in not controlling increases in gas rates to the consumers, and in their lack of long-range land-use programs. With reference to a five-year plan proposed by the premier, Opposition Leader MacEwan stated that his party had never quarreled with most of the points in the program advanced by the Social Credit government. "The fact is the Liberals proposed most of the items and stood to record their votes for them just as all Social Crediters stood to oppose most of them." He castigated the premier for revealing his plans in a public address rather than in the legislature where such policy matters belonged.

The speech was really the new leader's opening salvo in the coming Alberta general election due sometime in 1959.

*   *   *

On May 9, 1959, the Alberta legislature was dissolved, nominations were held on June 4 and voting on June 18, giving the new leader little time to marshal his forces for his first election as party head. A political scientist, Gordon A. Anton, dealing with the situation in an unpublished thesis (University of Calgary, 1972), wrote, "older members of the Alberta Liberal Party were resigning much to the disappointment of the leader Grant MacEwan." Five MLAs did not stand for re-election (including Prowse) and in well over half the sixty-five constituencies new candidates had to be found. In many cases, local constituency organizations had matters well in hand; in others, however, the leader's help was sought and MacEwan traveled from one end of the province to the other and crisscrossed back again recruiting talent, encouraging party workers, and lambasting the government in public speeches.

While it was arduous work, he seemed to thrive on it. As usual, the writer's eye was open for the unusual or the humorous, for which he didn't have long to wait. At the first constituency meeting held to persuade good people to stand as candidates, he soon discovered a fact of political life: most women dislike the idea of their husband being in politics.

He was successful in lining up candidates to the extent that three prominent citizens in the constituency said they would stand for nomination provided Grant could obtain their wives' approval. He telephoned one of the wives and the answer was an emphatic "no." He approached the second wife in the midst of a well-attended reception. He tiptoed up to the woman and meekly whispered in her ear, for privacy's sake, the question, "Would you approve?" The answer came immediately and so loud and clear that everyone at the reception turned to view the tall leader bent toward the ear of the lady in question. "No — certainly not!" she said, casting a horrified look at MacEwan, leaving everyone at the reception to speculate as to what sort of a proposition their new leader had made to the lady!

The third wife said neither yes nor no and so MacEwan suggested that the prospective candidate take it as a sign of approval. The reaction was once again negative: "I wouldn't dare accept without her acquiescence," replied the man, "I may have a duty to the Liberal Party but, damn it, I don't have to sleep with the party!"

If he had difficulty recruiting men, his job appeared easier when it came to persuading women to stand as candidates. In the 1955 election, Prowse had one woman candidate running for the party. In 1959, Grant MacEwan had no less than five.

*   *   *

Unfortunately, his efforts bore no fruit. Of the campaign he wrote, "we worked to win, knocked on doors, travelled far, kissed babies and made speeches, but lost in the gamble. Circumstances were strongly against us, which is the loser's alibi, always. It was another landslide victory for the party which had been in power."

Indeed it was. It was a disastrous defeat for the Alberta Liberal party which was all but annihilated. Of the 15 seats the Liberals had held they lost 14; the previous election's popular vote of 31 percent in their favor shrank to 14 percent. The Social Credit Party increased their seats from 37 in a 61-seat house to 61 in a 65-seat house, their popular vote increasing 10 points to 56 percent. Like the Liberals, the Conservatives elected only 1 but, riding on the coattails of the then prime minister, they increased their share of the popular vote from 9 percent to 24 percent largely due, so political observers concluded, to Diefenbaker-mania. The only consolation the figures held for the defeated Liberal leader was that he had managed to increase support for the Liberals in rural ridings to 48 percent from 17 percent in the 1955 election. As a party leader who lost his own seat, he was not alone, for W. J. C. Kirby, Conservative leader, and Floyd A. Johnson, CCF/NDP leader, lost theirs as well.

When Grant MacEwan wrote that "circumstances worked strongly against us," it was a characteristic understatement. Many politicians would have more than likely launched a diatribe against the governing party for throwing out the principle of proportional representation for the election. Had it continued to use proportional representation, the results would have been different. That is not to say Premier Manning's administration would have been unseated, but it is to say the opposition and other parties would no doubt have won a few more seats. The *Edmonton Journal* commented the day after the election: "the results show that the governing party knew what it was doing when it threw out the proportional representation system of voting" and went on to speculate that, in Edmonton alone, at least three and possibly more candidates from other parties would have been elected under proportional representation instead of the nine elected on the government side.

Had no changes been made in the system of voting, MacEwan's followers would not have suffered such devastation at the polls, but the leader would have suffered defeat nevertheless. The Social Credit candidate in Calgary-North constituency, Mrs. Rose Wilkinson, was elected by a clear majority. The figures were: Rose Wilkinson, SC, 6,655, James Macdonald, PC, 3,385, Grant MacEwan, Lib., 2,429, and A. J. E. Liesemer, CCF, 374.

The result was the end of party politics as far as MacEwan was concerned. It constituted a defeat much more extensive and far-reaching than the one in Brandon eight years earlier, for the party had tumbled with him. He resigned the leadership of the Liberal party in 1960, and once again in his life, at fifty-eight years, faced an uncertain future — with equanimity.

One thing was certain — Grant MacEwan was no party politician. Close observers in the Alberta Press Gallery agreed the man lacked "the killer instinct" seemingly so necessary in modern politics. He had never been an out-and-out party man, although he had been a Liberal all his life. The fact that, in the past, he had seriously considered an offer from another party testifies to his openmindedness where party labels were concerned. Indeed, in the Alberta legislature, it was known that from time to time MacEwan, as party leader, invited a member from another minority party to sit in with his caucus if he cared to, the other member seemed so lonely. This is not the mark of the hard-driving, ambitious, ego-feeding leader who claws his way to the top of the heap. It can be taken for granted that when MacEwan resigned as leader he did so with a sense of relief and turned to other things more suited to his nature.

Would he finally build his retreat in the Priddis hills and, as he had dreamed, finish out his days putting on paper the countless stories he had stored away in his files?

Chapter 25

Civic Politics Again

In October of 1959, three months after his defeat in provincial politics, former Alderman MacEwan again threw his hat into the civic election ring as a candidate for alderman. He topped the polls. "The people who voted against me in the provincial election now supported me with the biggest aldermanic vote in the city. It was not easy to understand. Next time I saw Peter Dawson [respected and long-time speaker of the Alberta legislative assembly], he agreed: 'Voters are never easy to understand.' "

In the early 1960s the MacEwan reputation as alderman and as writer grew steadily. Those who watched him operate in city hall called him the "pay-as-you-go Alderman" who spoke only when necessary and then on the side of cautious and careful administration of the people's money. Depending upon whether it was an admirer or the opposite speaking, he became known as "frugal" or as a downright "tight alderman."

With the publishing of *Eyeopener Bob* in 1957, *Fifty Mighty Men* in 1958, *Calgary Cavalcade* in 1959, *John Ware's Cow Country* in 1960, and *Blazing the Old Cattle Trails* in 1962, he became recognized as an author, an indefatigable book-a-year writer who was becoming indispensable to the unfolding story of western development.

There were other facets to the journalistic segment of his interests. In 1957, he began building an audience with a regular radio series called "Cominco Commentary," sponsored by Consolidated Mining and Smelting Company of Canada Ltd. The same year, he was invited to write for the *Calgary Herald*, starting a regular column in the newspaper's magazine section.

The editor soon found he had engaged an innovative columnist when the new man suggested that his column deal with conservation and say so in its title. However, the editor demurred as the word —even the subject — was almost entirely new to the public at that time and, he maintained, the columnist, being a pioneer in the field, might be looked upon as eccentric. They called the column "Our Natural Heritage." Twenty years later, the newspaper column was still appearing regularly although simply under the heading "Grant MacEwan", "conservation" and "environment" having become familiar words, due to efforts of MacEwan and others like him.

In 1963, he began writing another column entitled "The Western Farm Scene" for the *Western Weekly Supplement,* a weekend section carried in over fifty local independent weekly newspapers in the four western provinces and the Northwest Territories. MacEwan had become a columnist with a readership the size of which not many journalists in the entire country could claim.

*   *   *

He thrived on his life in Calgary and enjoyed his work as alderman. In contemporary photographs — and for the first time since boyhood — his face was rounder, more filled out than the customary leanness up to that time. Life was to become more interesting all the time.

In the federal general election of 1963, the Diefenbaker Cconservative administration was put out and the Pearson Liberal administration brought in. With it went the city's mayor, Harry W. Hays, who ran as a Liberal and was elected in Calgary-South. Five aldermen eyed the empty chief magistrate's chair jealously and the jockeying for position began, council splitting into several factions.

Grant MacEwan was not attached to any of the factions and did not seem ambitious for the mayoralty. Possibly this worked in his favor, as such a person, if elected by his fellow aldermen to finish out Hays' term, would not be likely to stand again for the office in the next civic election. Council voted in secret and then appeared in open session where a motion was made that Alderman MacEwan be named mayor of Calgary to fill the remainder of the term. The motion was carried unanimously.

It was unanimous with the daily newspapers too. Next day both praised the decision. The *Calgary Herald* said that in council he had conducted himself with dignity and moderation, and that council had made a wise decision. The *Albertan,* under a heading "All's Well," said that "council made an eminently satisfactory choice".

*   *   *

Calgary soon discovered that it had an unusual mayor. There was at his disposal a big black Chrysler Saratoga and a police constable driver to chauffeur him as he went about his business. MacEwan scarcely used it.

Herald columnist Johnny Hopkins wrote:

. . . the mayor never made any secret of the fact that he was a Scot, with all the thrifty attributes that his race is believed to adhere to. And using the city car for functions, however official, wasn't something that he really enjoyed. In fact, it's on record that the mayor himself never asked for the use of the car. He'd use his own, he'd take a taxi and, on occasion he found the CTS [Calgary Transportation System] quite suitable for his travelling needs. This is not to say that his charming wife held to the same rigid views. There would be times when she felt that the mayor should arrive in some vehicle befitting the rank — especially if the MacEwan's personal car happened to be dirty at the time. Then the wheels would be set in motion whereby the car would arrive for the mayor's use, without his knowledge — the mayor's secretary, Kay Wood, would take it upon herself to see that when circumstances demanded it, the mayor arrived in an official vehicle rather than, as did happen . . . on foot.

Hopkins went on to say that more often than not the mayor was to be seen striding through Calgary's streets in time for an appointment at one office, hotel, or other in a gait that "carried him around the downtown section of the city as though he were being chased by demons."

Again, it is possible to see the mayor's job from the inside through the eye of a trained and practiced observer. He related how, on comparing jobs, members of parliament who had been aldermen or mayors, stated unequivocally that city council work was by far the more difficult job. MPs could get away from their constituents from time to time but civic servants must live surrounded by them and accessible to them. But, wrote Mayor MacEwan, it was a mixture of good and bad:

Any man entering public life should have been prepared to take the bitter with the sweet. For 85 percent of the time, the person occupying the Mayor's chair would find the duties both enjoyable and satisfying; for the remaining 15 percent of the time, he might wish one of his tormentors had the job. He could be pardoned for trying now and then to get away from the telephone, away from interviews, away from the thousands of employees who believe their salaries are too small, away from the committee meetings which make him think that Hell can be no worse than a committee meeting unbroken through eternity.

What he did not record was the fact that, upon becoming mayor, he immediately took steps to divest himself of all party political connections, the better to represent all of the people of Calgary. This he made known not only to the party but to anybody who would listen. In recalling the move, he did so with an air of relief and confided the fact that he had not been comfortable as an out-and-out partisan, having found the constraints put on able men by the party caucus system — any party caucus — often to be detrimental to the search for true solutions to problems facing the people. "If I ever ran again I'm afraid it would have to be as an independent," he said.

*   *   *

Earlier it was said that Calgarians found their new man to be an unusual mayor and they delighted in hearing the latest evidence to the fact. In order to get the job done to his satisfaction, it was his habit to stride to work arriving at eight o'clock in the morning or earlier. Occasionally (if he felt he needed exercise), Mayor MacEwan could be seen running. On one occasion, this proved embarrassing to two rookie police constables who were not familiar with the appearance of their city fathers. Seeing a tall, suspicious character carrying a stuffed old brief case running at a fast clip through early morning gloom, they pulled their patrol car up beside him and questioned him. Where was he going? To work. Where did he work? At City Hall. A flashlight shone in his face for a moment and then two embarrassed constables apologized to their mayor and offered to drive him the rest of the way.

On another occasion, he accompanied the Board of Trade on a good-will tour of northern Alberta during which, as mayor, he was the speaker for which naturally there would be no fee. Upon entering the hall where the banquet was being held, he was stopped at the door by an officious person who demanded that he pay a five-dollar entrance fee. MacEwan had never in his life spent five dollars without knowing why, so he asked the reason for such a high-priced dinner. The ticket taker answered: "The dinner really costs only a buck — the other four is for some son-of-a-bitch from Calgary who is going to give a talk afterwards." Grant paid the five and walked in shaking his head but later got his four dollars' worth when, as he spoke, he addressed some of his words to a red-faced ticket taker.

There were different kinds of mayors running the cities of the country, he discovered. In *Poking Into Politics*, he wrote:

To have filled the position of Mayor satisfactorily, arising early enough to get all the essential work done and remaining at night to discharge all social demands, an incumbent needed the constitution of a superman. There have been mayors who accepted all the social calls and had no time for city business, just as there were those who saved the taxpayers many thousands of dollars by attending to business and had little time for public appearances. People raised on pioneer Canadian farms recognized three kinds of equine mares, brood mares, show mares and work mares. But there was no reason why a show mare could not do a reasonable amount of heavy work. The best mare on the farm was the reliable worker which when washed and dressed in show harness, could enter the ring and present an impressive performance.

There is little doubt to which category "mare" MacEwan belonged. He had a letter to prove it. With the "Grant" scratched out and "Mr" written above it, the letter read: "To Mr Mckewan: Yow are The *greatest* Mayor I know of in this world." It was "sighned" by wee David John Downing, and promptly became one of the most prized mementos in the MacEwan collection.

*   *   *

Often the work in council was heavy and it was to become heavier soon after Mayor MacEwan took office. It was an era of great change in city planning. It was also an era of expansion in the West when communities looked ahead to unprecedented growth and began planning for it. Included in the change were the railways, around which communities had built for seventy-five years. Now, the trains having become less important as carriers of passengers, planners in some of the larger cities were discussing the possibility of removing them from the center of town, relocating them on the periphery, and turning the land thus freed into commercial property of high value.

Before he left to become minister of agriculture in Ottawa, H. W. Hays, together with representatives of the Canadian Pacific Railway, had signed a list of "headings" under which the two parties agreed on broad principles as to how such a withdrawal of the railway from the center of Calgary was to be undertaken. As is usually the case when the stakes run into the millions of dollars — the estimate was $35,000,000 — feelings ran high and charges and countercharges were heard in city council as positions were taken. With a civic election approaching, aldermen eyeing re-election, or even the mayor's seat, postured for the benefit of the citizens. Debate became bitter at times and the mayor found himself faced with charges that he was favoring now one side, now the other. Some came close to charging that the mayor was dishonest, placing him in a position entirely new and strange to Grant MacEwan.

At the second last council meeting before the October 16, 1963, election the *Calgary Albertan* reported that one alderman termed the skirmish "disgusting," another said it was "something less than ranting and raving."

Not being one to back out and leave a difficult question unresolved, MacEwan decided to run for the office of mayor after all, much to the dismay of one or two aldermen who had thought he had no ambitions for the job. A political associate of MacEwan's, Nick Taylor, had conducted a casual poll of a few hundred citizens and found support for MacEwan to be encouraging.

On nomination day, it appeared that two people would be major contenders: the sitting mayor serving out Hays' term, and Art Smith who had topped the polls the first time MacEwan had run against him, who had run for a seat in the provincial house and later the House of Commons and had never been defeated. As the campaign began, MacEwan's manager, Bruce Watson, sat down with Grant and Carl Nickle and assessed the chances of success. Watson said later: "We were the loneliest people in the world."

In its September 21, 1963, issue *The Financial Post* said that when Harry Hays stepped down some Calgarians began referring to Smith as "the mayor-in-waiting." They were sure that the man who had topped Calgary polls before and who had never lost an election would be a shoo-in when October 16 elections rolled around.

As time wore on they were not so sure; the newspaper said the cause of the change in attitude "is the quiet, but sudden, emergence as a political force of Grant MacEwan, a scholarly, bird-watching agriculturist-turned-writer who, though experienced in municipal and provincial politics, has not in the past impressed people as a man with big political ambitions."

The newspaper sized the two candidates up like prize fighters about to enter the ring. MacEwan's advantages were: he was the incumbent; he was, similar to Hays, a man of the soil, "a homespun individual who conveys the impression of being as practical as a plowed furrow and as honest as the day is long"; he was concerned for the taxpayer, a cautious spender and a "pay-as-you-go advocate," sometimes referred to as "Mr. Economy."

On the other hand, Smith was no weak contender. He had never lost an election and had been campaigning weeks before MacEwan even announced his intention to run. Neither was Smith a spendthrift in the eyes of the voters, having the reputation as an advocate of more efficiency in city hall and fat-trimming of some programs.

The newspaper described the two contenders thus:

Smith is as boisterous as MacEwan is quiet and as personable and aggressive as MacEwan is shy and retiring. He is a forceful and entertaining speaker and a master debater. An elegant dresser, he has the youthful polish that appeals to the whitecollar crowd. MacEwan, on the other hand, is a slow, deliberate speaker — a man who obviously prefers quiet discussion to sharp debate. He is an austere dresser. His strength, if past political performance is any criterion, lies with the old voters, particularly those with rural background.

A further glimpse of MacEwan in action came from Peter Thurling, writing in the *Albertan*.

He's tall, a little stiff and maybe pokey. He often stands at city council with both hands in his pockets and his elbows sticking out. Or he might lean forward across his desk with elbow down and hand cupping the back of his ear so he can hear. An alderman for nine years, he has been counted more and more as a conservative and steadying force. Not that he isn't sometimes cantankerous for he often votes against the rest.

This, then, was the line-up for the big fight in Calgary. It was to be a battle royal. The MacEwan campaign manager who once felt lonely was soon swamped with volunteers to help in the campaign — but few were placing bets.

Both Grant and Phyllis MacEwan entered the campaign with foreboding. Possibly they had other defeats in mind when they decided "to be philosophical in defeat."

When the votes were counted, MacEwan started out ahead and never looked back. *Herald* columnist Johnny Hopkins wrote next day: "Rationalize it any way you wish, but this mayorality race had to be an upset." In the end MacEwan had a 13,000-vote majority over Smith which astounded even the most optimistic MacEwan-for-Mayor committee members — Bruce Watson, John C. Ayer, Mel Shannon, Carl Nickle, Hardy Salter, Nick

MacEwan victory smiles at Calgary mayoralty election, October 1963
(Michael Burn photo, MacEwan Collection)

Taylor — who earlier had set down predictions that gave him majorities of from 500 to 5,000.

Grant MacEwan gave credit to the many hundreds of workers who had helped him. Carl Nickle credited the hard work of chairman Bruce Watson and manager John Ayer who had organized and promoted his campaign. Watson said they had worked for a likable man and that "the public knew he was a man that could be depended upon." Phyllis MacEwan, who at first opposed the decision to run because it would once again leave them so little time together, said "now, of course, I'm proud of him and so glad that he decided to run."

Next day, the *Albertan* said that, in the two candidates, the voters had to choose between dynamic leadership and somewhat cautious solidity and the people "plumped for solidity in decisive fashion." The *Calgary Herald* said: "Calgary citizens can expect from Mayor MacEwan a display of most sincere and honest efforts on behalf of the city." It then went on to say: "Now that his position has been confirmed, it will call for more decisive qualities of leadership than he has sometimes displayed," no doubt referring to the fact that MacEwan, as a chairman of meetings, tended to be too democratic, allowing speakers to go on much too long in the opinion of other aldermen and some of the public — but not in the opinion of the one who held the floor.

Heather as the Mayor's lady (top) at Faculty Women's Club ball, Palliser Hotel, Calgary. Piper William Hosie is followed by Dr. C. E. and Mrs. Challice, President H. S. Armstrong and Mrs. Armstrong   *(Calgary Herald photo, MacEwan Collection)*

The MacEwan administration was to last another two years, and, although with characteristic modesty he would spread the credit to many of those who also deserved it, he was able to make solid contributions to the city he had grown to love since first settling there in 1952. He had captured much of the cow town's spirit and in a re-issue of his book *Calgary Cavalcade* he wrote:

No city enjoyed more loyalty from its people. Boasting was not unknown among its citizens but there was reason. They were proud of their ranchland heritage; proud of associations with the North West Mounted Police; proud of pioneer personalities like Commissioner James Macleod of the Mounted Police, Sam Livingstone who was the sole resident at the confluence when the police arrived, Pat Burns the builder of industry, Senator James Lougheed with the visions of city greatness, Bob Edwards of *Calgary Eyeopener* fame, Paddy Nolan the great orator, and R. B. Bennett who became Prime Minister. Those citizens talked affectionately about chinook winds clothed in lovely Indian legends and blowing warmth from the Pacific, about their city's proximity to mountain playgrounds, about their football team which in 1971 won the Grey Cup for the second time, about their Stampede, St. George's Island Zoo, parks, planetarium, libraries, university, cultural facilities, and so on.

He went on to say that as Calgary's population multiplied (approximately 150,000 when first elected alderman in 1953, to 311,000 in 1965, his last year as mayor), the city was still careful to see that, with all its expansion and building, a certain "Calgary distinctiveness" was not neglected. Heritage Park was a shining example, "an entirely new concept" dedicated to many familiar institutions of the pioneer era, Mayor MacEwan said when he opened it by driving the last spike in a one-mile railroad carrying a steam locomotive, July 1, 1964. He was instrumental in attracting a multi-million dollar fertilizer industrial complex to the city, no doubt reinforced by background information he himself gathered as a $50-consultant earlier.

His ability to drive hard bargains saved Calgary money when the federal government War Assets Corporation put former military property up for sale at $1,250,000. Mayor MacEwan, accompanied by Chief City Commissioner John Steel, headed for Ottawa to negotiate. When they returned they had bought Lincoln Park at $750,000.

The much-debated city center redevelopment plan came to nought for a number of reasons. Despite city taxes it would yield, estimated at approaching $90,000,000, the city would none the less still have to contribute many millions and citizens began to take a second look at the proposal. A surge of interest in the environment at the time brought into question the wisdom and desirability of moving the rail lines from the city center to the south bank of the Bow River, somewhat neglected up to that time but with great potential for beauty. Critics of the MacEwan administration looked upon the failure to accept the CPR plan as a great mistake, but the mayor had other ideas and firmly believed it was the right decision. In *Poking into Politics* he described the situation:

When Calgary Council negotiated over more than a year for the removal of railway tracks from the centre of the city, the pressures from without reached monumental propotions. One organized group contended that the council was moving too slowly in concluding an agreement with the railway company; another proclaimed just as loudly that plans were being made with dangerous speed. An organization of businessmen displayed an eagerness to secure the scheme with no apparent regard for the cost to the city and city taxpayers, while another citizens' body was just as strongly opposed to various aspects of the redevelopment plan in the only form acceptable to the company. Newspaper interest indulged in unprecedented propaganda to popularize the scheme but in spite of all, public resistance stiffened and feeling ran high. There were unworthy performances on the part of some individuals and writers, but they were forgotten; only the way the

The mayor continues to judge. He is seen at Abbotsford, B.C., with Barbara Tussey of Abbotsford, and Les Robson of Haney   *(MacEwan Collection)*

aldermen voted was remembered. But those elected people, after long and objective study, moved to abandon the scheme as being too costly. The aldermanic decision was ridiculed by a few, applauded by many but, in any case, it was the carefully considered judgement of those elected officials who knew they would have to live with their recorded votes and were anxious to be right.

MacEwan told Inger Voitk of the *Albertan*, "Calgary could never have afforded, in money or otherwise, to fall in with the plan." He felt that an adequate discussion and airing of views had been permitted, "for it was an important matter and had to be given serious consideration." Public opinion became so clearly detectable that the matter was not even put to a plebiscite. (Some years later CPR began a somewhat reduced but more evolutionary development on its own — not lifting the railway tracks and relocating them but erecting buildings over the railway tracks on its own.)

*   *   *

MacEwan had served out the remaining term of Harry Hays and when his own elected term came to an end he had had enough. As he wrote:

> My years in office of Mayor were rewarding and wonderful in many ways but I reached the point where my feeling was like that of the man with 14 children: he would not take a million dollars for any one of his youngsters and wouldn't give two cents for another.

He put down the mayor's gavel for the last time on October 7, 1965, amidst praise from all quarters, including aldermen who at times had been in conflict with him over weighty matters. Alderman Roy Farran said that as opposed to the idea of a strong man at city hall he had "been a true democrat . . . fair, unbiased and honest" despite tremendous pressure put on him during his term of office. Alderman Ernie Starr said it had been a pleasure serving under MacEwan. "You've bent over backwards to be fair."

In the *Calgary Herald*, Johnny Hopkins wrote in his column that Grant MacEwan had made up his own mind to step down, that there had been no concerted movement to have him leave — "quite the contrary had he chosen to run again, it's not unlikely that he would have won easily — quite possibly by acclamation." He wrote that when MacEwan critics were asked to substantiate their stand they usually ended up lamely stating that "he's too nice a guy."

Grant told an interviewer that he was still a young fellow who should move on to some other challenge. "It's good for the man and good for the job," he said. Another newspaperman, who had been around public figures long enough to become disenchanted, said of Mayor MacEwan that he was "one of the few men of whom I stand in awe."

Already, a growing number of citizens began to suggest he would be a good man to send to Edmonton to fill the chair being vacated by J. Percy Page who was finishing his term as lieutenant-governor of Alberta.

Chapter 26

To Edmonton

In October of 1965, released from the shackles of administrative responsibility, MacEwan turned to his writing. It would prove to be the beginning of his most fruitful period as he put the finishing touches on a manuscript dealing with conservation, later published as *Entrusted to My Care*, and worked up a file of notes he had made along the way into another manuscript that would appear as *Poking into Politics*. The former was published by Western Producer Prairie Books and the latter by the Institute of Applied Arts in 1966. It was the first time two MacEwan books were published in a single year — but it would not be the last.

Grant MacEwan was contented with life and busy at his own work. There was no shortage of ideas which were all tucked away in files he had begun, a good number of them ready to become books that would fill gaps in western Canada's memory. His family life was now more active than it had been for years as Heather, now with a place of her own, lived nearby. A striking, tall brunette with a smile that would be the envy of a model, she was a teacher and the wife of Max Foran, who was himself an educator involved in the adminstration of the Calgary school system.

In true MacEwan fashion, Heather had met her husand in no ordinary way. During summer holidays and usually accompanied by fellow teacher Audrey Cowan, Heather had circled the globe following her hobby of deep-sea diving. In the process she had gathered a large collection of sea shells that were displayed in a museum, appeared in a movie, and attracted national attention. On a prolonged stay in Australia, she and her companion, running low on funds, were forced to return to teaching briefly to recharge their travel treasury. It was in a school at Sydney that Heather met an athletic, bespectacled deputy headmaster by the name of Max Foran who later followed her back to Calgary where they were married.

The MacEwans enjoyed a relationship especially attuned to their circumstances. As Heather often said, her father really needed at least two women to keep up to him as he went about his wide-ranging public duties — and even then they would find it difficult to attend everything. Phyllis agreed and, as Heather matured into a young woman as attractive and personable as her mother, mother and daughter divided social appearances with Grant be he alderman, mayor, author, or speaker on those occasions a partner seemed appropriate.

On the other hand, if Heather was called on to help her father, she did not hesitate to call on him and it was on such an occasion that the next chapter in the MacEwan saga was to open. The scene was the public school where Heather was a teacher; the time, a few days before Christmas 1965; the action took place one morning when the father had been invited to speak to the class on conservation, which he did. Word spread through the school that there was a famous author in attendance and, as additional classes joined Heather's, the lecture turned into one on early days in Calgary, then into another, and so on.

He was speaking on the history of the West when he was called away to the phone. As Walter Nagel reported in the *Calgary Herald*:

... there was characteristic warmth and simplicity ... in Grant MacEwan's reaction to an announcement he will become Alberta's next lieutenant-governor. "I am very happy that I can share my pride with you boys and girls first of all," he told 150 excited youngsters at William Reid Elementary school in southwest Calgary, where he had been speaking when word of the appointment came from Ottawa. ... Thumbs hooked in his tweed jacket pockets — a pose that has almost become his trademark ... he told the students that his appointment will probably require moving to Edmonton but ... "I will still be living in Alberta and Calgary will remain part of my province. In this bonnie province — this wonderful province — this appointment makes me very, very proud."

He then took Heather and the other teachers across the street to a small coffee shop where he treated them to a "celebration lunch" of hamburgers or whatever else the menu offered.

The reporter continued:

Mr. MacEwan will have a chauffeur-driven limousine provided for his exclusive use in January when he takes office as the Queen's representative. But Monday he will still be the man Calgarians know best, as he left the school on foot — at his usual arm-swinging pace — for a bus stop eight blocks away on Elbow drive and a transit ride the rest of the way home.

The newspaper reported that Grant MacEwan would receive an annual salary of $18,000 plus travel and entertainment expense allowance of $15,000, plus $4,000 from the province to maintain a vice-regal residence,

Grant with children   *(MacEwan Collection)*

an automobile, chauffeur, and office. (These were the starting figures that increased considerably over the years of his service.)

*   *   *

The city was jubilant at the news. The MacEwan phone rang steadily with messages from hundreds of friends and acquaintances. The newspapers spoke for the general public. The *Albertan* said that the fact that the news was greeted so enthusiastically in the city was no surprise:

> Mr. MacEwan is a man of considerable stature in this province, and although he has been active in public life at both the provincial and municipal levels, we doubt that he has any enemies. Most importantly, he can be counted upon to perform the duties of his new office with dignity and distinction.

The *Calgary Herald* ended its editorial by taking a shot at the provincial government for not having a permanent and official residence, saying that now was the time to get one. It is possible the newspaper was revealing an unspoken fear that the former mayor of the city, noted for his frugality, might provide himself with something — sensible, of course — but somewhat more modest than the burgeoning province should have in the way of vice-regal living quarters. However, it first stated that he was "a true son of the West" and the appointment was fitting recognition of the respect so many of his fellow citizens had for him. It traced his many careers, saying that "in the process he has become one of Canada's most popular regional historians and opened the eyes of thousands of modern readers to the excitement and adventure inherent in the story of the growth of the Prairie provinces. . . . In all these varied tasks, Mr. MacEwan has performed with an engaging wit, a keen dedication and a notable lack of pretension. These are the qualities which one expects in a lieutenant-governor. A good choice has been made."

It is doubtful if the *Calgary Herald* expected the new lieutenant-governor to go as far as he did, for Hon. Grant MacEwan was to become one like no other, and it began to be noticeable to Albertans almost immediately. He wrote in his journal:

A few days ago, I was appointed to a high office in my province, a post to which I shall try to bring respect and honor. Already I have had advice about how I must conduct myself. Some of that gratuitous counselling is good, some I shall not be taking. Publicly I will promise to "be loyal and bear true allegiance." Privately, I promise myself to be myself — in other words, to act naturally. It is sad to see a man trying to reshape his personality to fit some new and higher role. Most people have charm but they can lose it easily when they try to revise it.

Residence in Edmonton will be a requirement of office and Calgary friends will offer sympathy. I'm sure that life in the northern city will be pleasant but one pitfall I must avoid at all cost; I must not allow myself to become the "Lieutenant-governor of Edmonton." If the office is worth while, it should be taken to the country, to Peace River, to Medicine Hat and to Lloydminster.

Soon after his appointment, he told John Stanley of *The Edmontonian* that he would continue writing while serving as lieutenant-governor because:

. . . there is so much history of this part of Canada yet to be chronicled. "I see so much that calls for attention and while I may have to change my routine — perhaps even the character of my writing will undergo a change because of this new chapter in my life, I will keep on writing. I believe the new position will help me . . . Lord Tweedsmuir produced some of his best books while Governor General of Canada. Perhaps I can emulate him in my own way. Perhaps I can encourage other Albertans to write about their province. I don't think there is any better way to encourage writing than in doing it yourself."

*   *   *

Grant MacEwan's first day in office was an indication of things to come. He was sworn in January 6, 1966, at three o'clock in the afternoon.

The Chief Justice, S. B. Smith of the Alberta Supreme Court, conducted the swearing-in ceremony: Premier Manning was there as were his cabinet ministers and retiring lieutenant-governor, Dr. J. Percy Page, in the Lieutenant-Governor's chambers in the legislative building.

MacEwan is sworn in as Lieutenant-Governor of Alberta, January 6, 1966, with Chief Justice Smith officiating and Premier Manning (right) and former Lieutenant-Governor J. Percy Page witnessing the ceremony

(Alberta Government photo)

The *Edmonton Journal* reported that MacEwan at six feet four inches tall looked like everyone's idea of the typical Westerner and "exhibited typical western informality at the brief ceremony."

"This is just like getting married," he remarked as he stepped before the desk, flanked by the premier and Dr. Page, "but we accept things as they are."

After the ceremony His Honor and the First Lady went house hunting and found one at 13845 MacKinnon Ravine. "My wife bought the house. I bought the ravine. I had no idea how lovely the view was," he said.

When one lieutenant-governor succeeds another it is often merely a matter of adjustments to the sleeves, pantcuffs, and waist of the gold-braided official Windsor uniform, and, with plumed hat, white gloves, and sword, the new governor is ready to function officially. Such was not the case when MacEwan appeared in Edmonton with his six-foot-four frame to be covered with formal wear. The uniform — he had to pay $800 plus tax for it much to his dismay — was not ready by the time the new session of the legislature was to open, forcing him to wear formal morning coat and tall silk hat.

As had come to be expected, his plans for the position proved to be no empty resolve, and MacEwan took the vice-regal presence into all corners

The MacEwans chat with Premier Manning at a reception. Mrs. MacEwan wears the wide-brimmed type of hat that became her hallmark   *(Alberta Government photo)*

of the province, often traveling under the most rigorous of conditions. Andrew Snaddon, editor of the *Edmonton Journal* wrote, "as lieutenant-governor he has averaged 35,000 miles a year along Alberta's four-lane highways and dusty district dirt roads, going to functions in metropolitan hotel ballrooms and draughty [community] halls, plus thousands more miles in the air and along railroad tracks."

No sooner was he installed in office than he began to establish his own routine. Word spread, his actions became the bases for legend, and quite unconsciously he added to the legend by acting naturally. As always he rose early in the mornings to run a mile or two, then breakfast on porridge after which he agreed to be driven to the legislative buildings, enter the doors of the vice-regal suite at eight o'clock, ready for the day's work.

The first day the chauffeur opened the rear door for His Honor. Said Grant MacEwan: "Nothing doing, you don't get me in the back seat." He explained that in the front seat he was less conspicuous and found it more congenial. He also requested that the customary flag markers be removed from the front fenders save on the most formal of occasions, for the same reason. He told one reporter that "when the warm spring days come I guess I'll just hoof it."

The Queen's representative and First Lady dance at a military ball in 1966, with a portrait of Her Majesty overlooking the scene   (*MacEwan Collection*)

St. John's *Edmonton Report* wrote: "In a way the vice-regal office in the Canadian provinces is a dream appointment. A man can do with it just about what he pleases. So long as the lieutenant-governor fulfills the few mandatory functions — reading the speech from the throne, assenting to bills, signing various documents — and so long as he stays out of political controversy the incumbent can do nothing or everything, depending on his wont. Grant MacEwan's wont was to do everything."

Chauffeur Henry Weber waits for the governor   *(MacEwan Collection)*

As he had resolved at the beginning, he didn't change his personality nor did he lose his sense of humor. In her column "Under the Dome," Lynne Cove of the *Edmonton Journal* wrote on March 9, 1966:

The pomp and ceremony of the lieutenant-governor's position hasn't scared the "devil" out of Grant MacEwan.

Alberta's new lieutenant-governor proved that when he made a brief appearance in the Legislature Tuesday to give royal assent to a bill amending the Alberta Municipal Financing Corporation Act.

In he came, wearing a hat as tradition demands, (that's about the only time he does wear a hat).

The staid, sober image one normally attaches to the Queen's representative doesn't quite fit the former Calgarian. And he obviously doesn't worry about it.

Neither do the members of the Legislature.

When the formalities were complete and the lieutenant-governor was being escorted back out of the chamber, some of the members couldn't help but smile at the picture presented by the normally informal official involved in a very correct procedure.

He must have appreciated it, too.

As he passed the last two rows of backbenchers, his old self got the better of him and he admonished: "Stop grinning."

The twinkle in his eye spelled "joke" and it brought the House down.

*　　*　　*

The cynic might suspect that such incidents were carried off or even created for effect had they always taken place in the full glare of publicity, but such was not the case. As often as not His Honor, in being himself, was even more entertaining off camera, so to speak, than he was on.

Henry Weber, the chauffeur, was often the solitary eyewitness to what the ordinary person would label eccentricity — for instance, the time Henry and His Honor left Calgary and headed for Edmonton after a late engagement in the southern city. A few miles out on the highway MacEwan asked Henry to turn down a side road and then stop at a particularly attractive spot whose beauty stood out in the full of the moon. MacEwan pulled two sleeping bags from the trunk of the limousine and, arranging them carefully on the soft grass, he prepared to bed for the night. He expressed the hope that Henry would not mind, explaining that it was a wonderful night and most likely, with his crowded schedule in mind, the last opportunity of the year to sleep out under the stars. He didn't want to miss it.

On another occasion Henry was driving him to work one winter's day through a blizzard and snow-choked streets. They came upon two teenagers trying to push a minibus out of the ditch. Grant asked Henry to stop, got out and pushed with them. When the vehicle was finally on high ground, the two young men looked up at the tall stranger only to discover that he was none other than their own lieutenant-governor who had given them a helping hand.

Incidents occurred that tickled his sense of humor and he frequently returned from official engagements to recount jokes on himself. Mr. Snaddon wrote about one occasion that involved the lieutenant-governor's well-known sweet tooth (his definition of a good dessert: "if it tastes as good the third time round as it did the first, it's a good one" — pecan pie is his favorite one). He attended a banquet at a skating club where he addressed junior members and their fathers on the importance of health and fitness. One young man had been watching His Honor closely throughout the meal and finally, in a high-pitched voice that carried well, he was heard to protest to his father: "Boy! he had three helpings and he's not even a member of the club!"

His lifetime habit of treating clothing as a mere expedient caught up with him one day in the streets of Edmonton. A breathless man overtook him and asked: "Are you the new lieutenant-governor?" "I am, the name's MacEwan," replied Grant extending his hand in his wide lateral sweep to shake. "My God," said the man, "I thought you'd be dressed in better clothes!"

The mystified Edmontonians had seen nothing like the man Calgarians saw at one posh evening affair not long afterwards. The lieutenant-governor had an engagement in Calgary and, to get the most out of the expense of traveling from Edmonton, he accepted another. The first was to attend an evening reception and dinner at which he was to speak, the second was to join a group on a walking tour of the Glenmore dam site. As the walking tour was first on the agenda His Honor set out from Edmonton in the limousine wearing rubber boots, for the dam site was, at the time, notorious for its mud. He made the tour and then returned to the hotel to change for dinner. To his dismay, he discovered his dress shoes had been left behind. Henry's shoes were too small, all other shoes were too small. The stores were closed.

That night His Honor appeared at the dinner suitably dressed from head down to where the rubber boots began.

*   *   *

As MacEwan ranged about Alberta seeking out the most remote communities into which to carry the exuberant vice-regal presence in his own inimitable manner, he was usually alone. Back in the city Phyllis, as first lady, patronized certain cultural activities that would not necessarily attract Grant's attention. Where protocol demanded the appearance of the lieutenant-governor and his lady, Phyllis would accompany him but as she was plagued by a tricky back which often made it painful to stand for long periods in reception lines, Heather Foran sometimes appeared in her place. Both striking and charming women, whether accompanied by the mother or daughter, MacEwan was assured of regal company and the prairie rose province of most fitting representation.

There had been nothing in the MacEwan family life to compare with most families' "three-week holiday." From time to time there were weekend excursions to the cabin at Battle Lake, the Priddis ranch, and, latterly, to "Westward Ho," the term they used for the cabin built near Sundre, Alberta — and straight north from the hamlet, Westward Ho. In fact, Phyllis maintains that she and her husband have been on only two real holidays in their lifetime. The first was the honeymoon, the second —thirty-one years later — arose indirectly from his appointment in 1966.

In that year the government of the State of Israel invited the lieutenant-governor and his wife to tour the country, and the invitation was readily accepted. They spent a number of weeks touring the fledgling nation, seeing, and enjoying, nearly all of it unhampered by the necessity of judging livestock here or there. It constituted a memorable journey altogether. While they were in that quarter of the globe, they also visited Athens, Rome, Madrid, and London and were glad that they did.

However, although Phyllis was to visit a number of continents in company with Mrs. Enid Stevenson Cameron or Mrs. Esther Wright Sutherland, Grant's chief travel was in western Canada, which he loved. "I suspect that an insight into Canadian history and local history has helped to make Fort Chipewyan or Fort la Corne or Lloydminster more intriguing to me than to the person who did not know the background." His only regret was that he did not visit the Western Isles of Scotland. "If I were going to

MacEwan at home with Nature   (*Edmonton Journal photo*)

cross the Atlantic tomorrow it would not be to see London again; it might be to see the Outer Isles and Hebrides. I'm sorry that I missed Skye and Mull and Lewis but that is just sentiment," he said years later.

His travels in the West left a trail of legend where his choice of accommodation was concerned. Wherever he went he asked for the simplest, most spartan rooms available. Once when he was to speak in Saskatoon at the opening of a new building the one in charge of arrangements informed him by letter that a suite in the Bessborough Hotel awaited him. An immediate reply from His Honor left no doubt that what he wanted was simple accommodation, preferably in the King George Hotel which was handier to the scene of the ceremonies — it was also only a block away from the Saskatoon Public Library where, as it turned out, he spent most of his spare time carrying out research. A call was put in to the reservations department of the King George, where they knew him. "Oh, yes, that's for Mr. MacEwan — he'll just want a nice single room," was the answer. "Perhaps you've got a room down by the furnace, where he'll really be comfortable," came the reply. (However, he did accept a basket of fruit.)

Much later, he set his views down:

I have been disturbed by the skyrocketing of travelling accommodation and the tendency of so many Canadians when away from home and on expense

"Chic" and "Billie" Miller of Olds, Alta.   *(Miller Collection)*

accounts to demand much more than they are accustomed to. I am inclined to blame luxury accommodation for at least a part of our inflation problem and, anyway, we have allowed our standard of living goals to soar to the point that they threaten us. It is strange that throughout history, the extremely high standards of living have been followed by a fall. Ours is coming. In the meantime I am making a feeble protest by staying at the YMCA.

*   *   *

The new governor obviously took pleasure in his public duties and his appearances were so numerous the public might be excused for thinking that he was always on show. Such was not the case, for, whenever it was possible, MacEwan slipped from public view and took to the countryside. The wilder and more remote it was, the better it suited him, for it was there he restored his soul. Much of the time he tramped alone through the foothills of Alberta, a tall man in a big country, having arranged with Henry his chauffeur to drop him and pick him up, sometimes a day or two later, at an appointed place and time.

It has been said earlier that MacEwan was a loner, which seems paradoxical in the light of the hundreds of people he knew personally or the thousands who knew him as lieutenant-governor, judge, or speaker, but it is a fact. As has been shown, he simply moved too fast and crowded too many lives into one to allow himself the pleasures of relaxed companionship most citizens enjoy. Close friendships demand time. However, he was not always alone.

Art and Carmen Moore with Grant in the Red River valley near Dorothy, Alta.
(Henry Weber photo, Moore Collection)

Early in his Edmonton sojourn he struck up a jogging acquaintance with Mrs. Marion Hyde, a forty-five-year-old neighbor. "Our jogging hour [near the scenic Edmonton ravines] is 6:30 a.m. and she is the best possible jogging companion — eager, fit and silent." Mrs. Hyde was "punctual, cheerful in the early hours and she has the good sense to refrain from conversation when we jog." (It was in Edmonton he was to disprove the widely held theory among joggers that below a certain temperature one should not run for fear of freezing the lungs. "Ran all winter, sometimes at forty below — never froze a lung."

Other outdoor relationships developed when he formed friendships with two couples who were to become what could be called "intimates" in a way few others were. The association was not of high frequency, for the opportunities to meet with them were scarce as public commitments flooded in to the vice-regal office without letup, but from time to time, Grant MacEwan communed with nature in the company of Mr. and Mrs. W. F. Miller ("Chic" and Lillian "Billie") a well-known Arabian horse breeder and businessman of Olds, Alberta, and Arthur and Carmen Moore of Calgary.

It is obvious how Grant would come to know Chic Miller, the horseman, and his wife, who were roughly in the same age group as he, but not so obvious how he could come to know the Moores, a much younger couple. MacEwan first met Carmen Moore at the Hudson's Bay Company bookstore where she worked when Grant appeared frequently at autographing parties introducing his new books. Knowledgeable about literature and an ardent supporter of Western Canadiana, she later opened her own bookstore and sold hundreds of MacEwan titles. Perhaps her best recommendation for friendship in MacEwan's eyes was the fact that her father kept a respectable herd of Aberdeen Angus cattle on his farm near Alsask and, in addition, a fine string of Percheron horses which he stubbornly refused to replace with a tractor, using horsepower to do his work up to the day he quit farming in 1946. Arthur Moore, a real estate agent, handled a number of the MacEwan transactions over the years.

This diverse group had one thing in common — they worshiped the outdoors, and gloried in testing their ability to survive arduous excursions into untouched and rugged country with as few modern conveniences as possible.

With MacEwan, the Millers and the Moores found their solitude in two different ways. MacEwan enjoyed them both. When he joined the Millers, it was for treks into rising foothill country on foot or horseback, leading packhorses. With the Moores it was usually an excursion into country inaccessible to the automobile, involving hiking with backpacks until they reached a navigable river (on one occasion at least, the Red Deer River) where they would build a raft, using whatever material nature provided, and drift with the current for several days. On such voyages they uttered few words lest they startle wildlife and lose priceless views of birds and beasts unaware that humans were present.

Chic Miller wrote of Grant MacEwan:

We have spent much time together in the woods just studying nature, and during those days I have learned a great deal about life and values just by quiet association with him. If I had children I would try to have them exposed to . . . Grant MacEwan with the firm belief that they would receive more valuable education in a given time, just being with him, than in any other manner I could think of.

The Moores relate an amusing anecdote arising from one of their trips. The three had been out over a hot Labor Day weekend drifting on the Red Deer River, having previously arranged with Henry to be picked up at a small town downstream a number of miles. Grant was a sight to see — sunburned nose peeling, a couple of days' growth of beard, dressed in stained khaki trousers and an old torn shirt. The Moores looked no better. Little wonder that the townspeople, failing to recognize their lieutenant-governor, were uneasy and suspicious of the strangers who seemed to be loitering about town with no purpose. It must have occurred to some to inform the nearest detachment of the Royal Canadian Mounted Police in case they turned out to be Bonny and Clyde characters. Then, the big black limousine drove up, out sprang Henry, with a smart salute, to hand them into their seats. Off they went with the memory of a weekend in the wilds of Alberta to carry them through the sound and clutter of the city until the next Tom Sawyer holiday, leaving a puzzled community in their wake.

Rafting on the Red Deer River

(Moore Collection)

Observing MacEwan at close hand, Chic Miller came to the conclusion that Grant's well-publicized fondness for the beaver is partially due to similarities in temperament.

They are both early risers and hard workers. They both definitely believe in good planning and preparation for the future. They both have the power and the ability to harm their fellow beings, but never use it. On the other hand they are both stubborn enough to stand up for what they think is right or achieve what they set out to do. . . .

One thing is certain — intimates though they are, the Millers and the Moores see a Grant MacEwan who is no different from the person the public sees when he is in full view. They may see him for longer and at closer range than most people, apart from family, but that is the only difference, for it is not in his nature to dissemble. There is not a hypocritical bone in his body. As has been said of another, it can be truthfully said of Grant MacEwan — his private personality is his public personality.

Beyond that, one can sense a very private domain to which there is no admittance, an impenetrable reserve beyond the friendly face, the dancing eyes, and the boisterous Grant laugh.

Chapter 27

More MacEwan Parties

Upon being informed of the nature of social functions held under previous governors, His Honor and the First Lady decided to change things somewhat. It had been the habit at various stages for the lieutenant-governor to hold a reception for the members of the legislature and for his wife to hold a tea for members' wives. There was also the quite natural tendency for the various political parties to have their own functions from time to time. Why not have them all together in a good old-fashioned party, possibly with a theme, the MacEwans asked themselves.

So began what could well turn out to be the most informal series of vice-regal functions in the history of the British Commonwealth — the MacEwan parties, an enlarged version of the "Dean's Parties" they had held at the University of Manitoba. In place of the formal white invitations printed on large expensive cards and stating that "His Honor the Lieutenant-Governor and Mrs. MacEwan request . . ." and so on in Royal Script type, MLAs and their wives received from the MacEwans folded mimeographed sheets with a sketch by Heather on the cover and, on the inside, a message such as, "We hope you'll remember the day of our party/We'll be waiting for you with a welcome that's hearty./You know it's informal — Western too;/The time is seven — we'll be looking for you." It was signed, simply, "Phyllis MacEwan and Grant MacEwan," the address was Mayfair Club, date March 8, and a reply was requested only from those who would not find it possible to attend. There was a postscript: "Don't be unprepared if there are some contests for whistlers, nail pounders and tellers of tall tales."

MacEwan invitation drawn by Heather Foran   *(Patricia Halligan Collection)*

The fare at the party was as simple and original as the invitations. In those days, if you wanted to throw a party and needed room for a big crowd, the Mayfair country club was one of the most suitable places to have it in. The person contacted for arrangements about matters such as food, flowers, and service was Kathy Boyan (later Mrs. Kathy Nelson of the Edmonton Club), who lost her last name as custom and customers began calling her simply "Kathy of Mayfair." Looking back on the MacEwan regime, she remembered the vice-regal informals with affection.

In "Kathy of Mayfair's" view, Phyllis MacEwan, with whom she dealt, was no social butterfly but she did love to put on simple and good parties, usually with a theme, at which everyone was made to feel at home and at which most people would meet and mix and none would leave without making many new acquaintances. Dancing was planned with frequent partner switches as mixers — Phyllis helping the master of ceremonies with the dances, games, and singsongs.

"When they were together at the parties they were two of the most beautiful people, as a pair. Mrs. MacEwan would come high-keyed before the reception, wanting everything just so," Kathy of Mayfair recalled years later. The special touches added by the Mayfair staff never went unnoticed by Phyllis and, following the parties, she would make a point of telling each of them how thrilled she had been and thanking them for their extra efforts

— Tony's flower arrangements, the kitchen staff's preparations, the girls waiting on tables. Said Kathy, "she was a wonderful, warm and vibrant hostess and all the staff loved her."

The MacEwan parties were noted for another reason — no liquor was served. To quench the thirst there was always a "nice bowl of fruit punch." Elsewhere in the club guests might find a regular bar open if they really needed a stronger drink and were willing to pay for it themselves. Few felt it necessary because "the receptions were always the way Mr. and Mrs. MacEwan wanted them: relaxed, homey and lots of fun, just as if the guests were in their own home."

The food was extraordinary too, and it always suited the theme: roundup time, Thanksgiving, the rodeo. "They served the meal plain, but good, and in quantity. Sometimes they had stew, farm-style vegetables with fresh hot buns and usually pie with ice cream for dessert, other times it would be stew and brown beans with fresh hot brown bread." MacEwan, by this time having been converted by his own line of reasoning and belief to vegetarianism, would pass up the stew and Kathy would have prepared for him a special fruit salad with melon, cantaloupe, grapes, bananas, apples, oranges, peaches with ice cream. "He had a sweet tooth and loved dessert."

MacEwan also loved porridge and he devised his own type of entertainment centered around that ancient and honored dish. Whenever Phyllis left on one of her trips to foreign lands in company with a woman friend — "if Phyllis were here she would want to pretty everything up" — he would hold what he called one of his morning "porridge parties." Sometimes as many as thirty or more attended, feasting on large bowls of the host's own concoction washed down with orange juice. Always the porridge was served with brown sugar and ice cream. He continued to experiment with the mixture and, in 1970, arrived at one which he recorded: four parts ground wheat, one part soybean grits, a pinch of salt, one handful of raisins, handful of sunflower seed and "with sugar, buttermilk and ice cream on the cooked product, it is food fit for the gods." As he says, "like morning prayer, everybody needs a good plate of porridge to start the day."

*   *   *

Soon after becoming the first Canadian Governor General in 1952, the Right Honorable Vincent Massey on one occasion was explaining his position: what he could do, what he could not, what he could say, what he must not. He stated that no longer could he make statements of a political nature, nor become embroiled in party politics. Whenever he spoke, said His Excellency, he had to confine himself to "governor-generalities."

The same principle applies to lieutenant-governors of the provinces and Hon. Grant MacEwan had little difficulty living up to it — but there were times when some people thought he had stepped over the line. One such occasion arose when he was called upon in 1969 to attend the opening of a special project financed by a group of St. John's College students at

Genesee on the North Saskatchewan River. In order to raise funds, they had trapped animals and sold the furs.

The lieutenant-governor praised them for their efforts and for their enterprise but he did not stop there. Having congratulated them on their industry, he then went on to speak in strong terms about the savagery of killing animals with steel traps.

"I don't like your steel traps for animals," said the lieutenant-governor. "I wish you would leave my fur and feather friends alone."

The bishop was incensed by the latter part of the message and, one way and another, revealed his feelings on the matter. Grant MacEwan made amends as graciously as possible under the circumstances, but left nobody in doubt as to his abhorrence of any and all inhumane treatment of animals.

When he was to leave office, he stepped over the line once again with a few words in the legislature asking the members to look after his office and not to be wooed by the philosophy of "change for the sake of change." The royal concept was a good and useful one and should be treasured by Canadians as an old institution that had proved its worth. The vice-regal chair, being above politics, had a balancing effect in government and was valuable because of that alone. Change must be approached cautiously and done in such a manner that the best of the past was conserved, said MacEwan to applause from both sides of the House.

The message to the legislators came straight from the heart, for in 1970 he had written:

As Canadians acquire more goods, more luxuries, the cry for change becomes louder and louder.

If I thought the demand for change was born in understanding, I'd be for it with more enthusiasm. But I fear that the demand comes from frustrations born in the disillusionment of easy living. Wealth and luxury do not yield happiness and the discovery produces anger.

If changes can be made by enlightened and benevolent people, I am very much in favor of them. There is no progress without change. Let's re-examine economics, politics, religion, educational methods and so on, do it the way old Socrates would re-examine them and discard anything which is found to be phony. But for God's sake let us not throw the good things overboard. Let us not fail to safeguard the best of the past because, in spite of what anybody may say to the contrary, there was much good in the past. There were the old ideals, respect for honest work, resourcefulness, thrift and human fibre. Let's "prove all things, hold fast to that which is good."

*   *   *

He had continued to write his column in the *Calgary Herald* while serving as lieutenant-governor and on November 1, 1968, wrote one entitled "Peanut Welfare." His old friend Chic Miller clipped it because, although it dealt with squirrels, he felt it was really a parable illustrating the human

On May 1, 1966, the University of Alberta awarded MacEwan his first honorary doctor's
degree   (University of Alberta Photographic Service)

condition and also a fundamental MacEwan political statement. In part,
MacEwan wrote:

> I am worried about the red squirrel which spends much of his time in my
> spruce trees. He appears to be in the best of health and the best of spirits, but he is
> not as active as he was in the spring. If the saucy fellow has become sophisticated
> and soft during these summer months, I may have to assume much of the blame.
>
> The point is that he has had so much welfare in the form of peanut butter
> during these months that he may have forgotten about that "rainy day" or wintry
> day for which squirrels normally provide. I hope I am wrong in my fear that this
> impudent fellow has failed to make the reasonable provisions for his own security
> during that winter period when he will be confined to a hole in the tree. If he has not
> done something for his own protection and survival, the winter will be a grim one in
> spite of all the good eating during the peanut butter season.
>
> It was fun catering to the squirrel's tastes and seeing him returning at about
> the same time every day. Early in the spring, his desire for peanut butter was in the
> nature of a gentle hint. By midsummer, he was asking boldly for his rations and in
> the autumn he was demanding the handouts as though they were a matter of right
> rather than benevolence.

On one other occasion he stepped over the "governor-generality" line
when he felt impelled to do so. In the last days of his term he spoke to
Indians of the Enock Band and treaded the narrow line between insult and
inspiration. His message was simple and candid but he felt that, if there was

Honorary chieftainship ceremony at the Blood Indian Reserve with Chief Stephen Fox, Sr.,
inducting the Lieutenant-Governor   *(Lethbridge Herald photo)*

any power in his office at all, he would use it one last time to help those he
respected. "Beat the booze," he pleaded with them. "Face and come to grips
with it. It's your number one enemy." Don't look to the government to ban
liquor, he told his friends. What they needed was a self-generated
movement against the thing that had always put them down, he said.

Had it been any other lieutenant-governor but Grant MacEwan,
Honorary Chief Aka-tah-si (Owns Many Horses) of the Blood Indians and
Chief Walking Moose of the Sagatawas, the plea might have caused a
national incident. However, those who listened to his counsel knew it came
from the heart of a brother and accepted it in the spirit in which it was offered.

*   *   *

After the initial shock of finding herself working for a boss who came
to the office an hour before opening time. Miss Patricia Halligan found the
work interesting and enjoyable and her relationship with her superior
something she could never have anticipated. She was with the lieutenant-
governor as his secretary for the last years of his tenure.

His early hours took some getting used to, but in a short time she
realized that there was no criticism of her arrival at regular hours implied,

and that it was Dr. MacEwan's preference and lifetime habit to arrive early. Often she would enter her office, separated from the vice-regal office by a reception and sitting room, to find His Honor seated at her desk, going through the mail. A discussion of the various requests and invitations would follow and in a short time decisions were made, instructions on each letter set out, and that part of the day's work was done.

MacEwan laid down few rules about accepting engagements, the governing principle being to accept all of them if possible. He had a delicate sense where the dividing line between social niceties and social pretensions were concerned. Soon his secretary developed a similar sense and was able, without referral, to detect and reject, as tactfully as possible, invitations from those who sought His Honor's presence for no other reason than to reflect glory on themselves and impress others. Much the same treatment was accorded purely commercial occasions.

On the other hand, as people learned of the genial affability of their lieutenant-governor, it was out of the question to accept all invitations from the hundreds that poured in, no matter how sincere or worth while the community or organization involved. It had long become apparent that the MacEwan regime would not be confined to purely formal governmental functions and this provided him with a rough rule of his own. It might well have appeared to the outsider that in the MacEwan head was a map of Alberta with every kind of community, from the smallest to the largest, marked on it; into this he stuck imaginary pins to mark those places he had visited. It seemed that he had set himself a challenge to seek out the most remote center and the least likely to attract notice from the outside world, and appear there.

Other criteria guided him. There were geographical regions he had to cover — the grassland country, irrigation districts, parklands, the northern boreal forests, the foothills, and the mountain communities. He was careful to visit Albertans of all ethnic origins: the British, German, Ukrainian, Scandinavian, French, and all the others including his brother Indians.

Thus it was that Lieutenant-Governor MacEwan set about making certain that during his regime he became anything but "the lieutenant-governor of Edmonton."

Throughout it all, the governor's office was a pleasant place to work. MacEwan usually kept a jar of either cookies or candies (usually bridge mix) on the corner of his desk to satisfy his own sweet tooth or that of members of the staff or the legislature when they came to his office. When visitors called, the vice-regal suite rang frequently with the full-throated Grant laugh.

*   *   *

Outside the office the relationship between the lieutenant-governor and "Miss Pat," as he called his secretary, remained on the same good terms but with a difference. She wasn't just working for Grant MacEwan (Dr. MacEwan, she always called him), for very early she and Phyllis MacEwan discovered a common interest in collecting Canadiana. Phyllis referred to it as "a disease for which there is no inoculation" and they soon were attending auctions together, joined, when time permitted, by Grant, who was a collector himself. Miss Pat ran to Canadian glass, as did Phyllis, Grant to furniture, but none of them could resist a good buy in any category.

On one occasion, the three were at an auction when a maple sideboard was put up for sale. Miss Pat thought it would be ideal for her suite and began bidding but, for one reason or another dropped out and the piece sold for fifty dollars. She had second thoughts and revealed her regret at having stopped bidding to Phyllis at her side.

A day or so later the lieutenant-governor came into her office and said, "I spent some of your money last night." He then explained that the same sideboard appeared on the block at another auction he had attended. He remembered overhearing her remark to Phyllis and bought it at sixty dollars. She needn't take it if she had changed her mind, he reassured her, but Miss Pat was delighted. That afternoon His Honor and Henry saw that it was safely installed in the Halligan suite.

* * *

On only one occasion did Miss Pat approach the personal in her relationship with Dr. MacEwan. It was during a bus strike when Henry had picked her up in the governor's limousine, afterwards calling at the vice-regal residence for His Honor, who emerged dressed in Buchanan tartan kilt, MacEwan tartan tie. It was one of the few times he was to wear the kilt and did so on this occasion because it had been presented to him by a Highland Regiment to which he was to pay a visit that same day. To her horror, Miss Pat saw that he had added to the color combination a pale blue shirt. She protested, saying a plain white shirt would look much better. Somewhat taken aback, Dr. MacEwan returned to the residence to change. Out he came shortly, this time wearing a pink shirt!

Once again, Miss Pat stepped across the boundary of propriety and an argument between her and MacEwan ensued over the choice of shirts. Finally, she appealed to Henry for support. The chauffeur sagely replied "No, no — I'm keeping out of this."

However, Miss Pat persisted, and finally the lieutenant-governor exclaimed, "Thunderation woman!" and stomped off to the house once again. This time he emerged wearing a plain white shirt, pleasing to his secretary's eye. To this day she suspects Dr. MacEwan has a touch of color blindness. It is possible she is right where clothing is concerned, but one thing is certain — the MacEwan eye never had any trouble distinguishing such shades of color as bay, sorrel, Palomino, red roan, or blue roan!

Whatever her thoughts before, Miss Halligan soon discovered that lieutenant-governors were needed and had a place in affairs. At least that was the case with Grant MacEwan and she hasn't experienced anything since to change her mind.

Time after time she would receive calls on the telephone from a chairman of a group in a distant corner of the province asking for a speaker. "We've had all of the politicians . . . we don't want any more of them . . .

MacEwan in Highland dress *(Photo Copywrited, MacEwan Collection)*

send us the lieutenant-governor. . . ." The premiers appreciated them too, "It gets them off the hook," she said.

From what she had seen, "lieutenant-governors certainly earn their pay," said Miss Pat. * * *

One day, after several public appearances and interviews, MacEwan tarried at his office to clear up a few things. He ended working far into the night.

Someone stood at the door. He looked up. It was the cleaning woman, with her pail, brushes, and brooms. Grant knew her well and all her history, having chatted with her on previous occasions such as this.

MacEwan at a Banff walkathon   (Jamie Sanborn photo, MacEwan Collection)

She didn't look well and wasn't her old cheery self. Upon pressing her with the fact, he discovered that indeed she had been feeling ill since starting work but could not rest until she had finished the last office, that of the lieutenant-governor.

MacEwan took the brooms, pail, and mops from her, set them down, and ushered her out and into the black limousine that was waiting to take the lieutenant-governor to his residence, sending her off home with Henry at the wheel. He then returned and finished cleaning the last office himself.

*   *   *

From mopping floors to meeting royalty might appear to be a big step to some, but not to Grant MacEwan. As Her Majesty's representative for Alberta, he was to meet Queen Elizabeth on great occasions.

In 1967, the Centennial of Confederation, governors and their wives were guests at a dinner aboard the Royal Yacht *Britannia* at Kingston, Ontario. "It was a nice affair and ran into several hours." One exchange of that evening occurred when Phyllis recounted an experience at the waterfront earlier in the day. She and Grant were walking along the shore when an American pulled up in a houseboat, and, mistaking the formal Windsor uniform for that of a policeman, inquired as to where he should tie up. Without setting him right, Grant immediately directed him to steer clear of the crowded area and moor his craft further downstream. The man remarked on how friendly the Canadian police were, thanked him, and sailed onward.

Prince Phillip laughed boisterously at the account and said, "If you had told that American that you were Lieutenant-Governor of Alberta he'd probably have replied 'Ho, ho, ho, I'm Father Christmas.' "

The Queen and her representative again met in Calgary in July 1973 at the Stampede. At a state dinner MacEwan sat beside Her Majesty. "Her Majesty is not one to make comments but is tireless in asking questions," he said. "Our conversational exchanges consisted of her questions and my replies as well as I could make them — mostly about Alberta."

*   *   *

It was about 1967 during Centennial Celebrations that "walkathons" were becoming popular as a method of raising money for one good cause or another and they were to become almost a trademark of the MacEwan regime as lieutenant-governor of Alberta.

He first walked with Mayor Vince Dantzer in the Centennial March and that seemed to start it all. From then on, he was given little peace if there was money to raise for charity.

One of the earliest beneficiaries was Oxfam's "Miles for Millions" campaign to have people gather as many sponsors as they could at so much per mile and then hike over a twenty-five-mile route through the city. There were nine check points along the way where hikers had their entry sheets stamped by officials as verification that each had got that far at least and could, with justice, charge their sponsors whatever mileage rate had been agreed upon — all to go to the starving people of the world.

Linda Curtis of the *Calgary Albertan* (June 6, 1967) wrote an account of the walk:

The weather couldn't have been worse. Rain, cold and wind combined to make it a bone-chilling endurance test for the 25,000 optimistic starters.

We saw Lieutenant-Governor Grant MacEwan hiking along, his plastic raincoat stretched over the shoulders of two or three young schoolgirls. With his free hand he was kept busy holding onto his straw cowboy hat that had been presented to him by representatives of The Bay . . . one of the sponsors.

They were a bedraggled looking bunch, stretched out over the course that was marked by Oxfam signs. Reminded me of a bunch of weary refugees in flight.

Early in the afternoon the rain eased off but the cold wind persisted. Only the hardy had survived the gruelling weather.

It was about this time we were cruising the course and again came across Grant MacEwan . . . still going strong.

I joined him about five or six miles from the finish.

He still was clutching his straw hat and the four school girls who had latched onto him at the start were still with him.

But he was in much better condition than any of them. The vice-regal shoes were well worn down at the heel, but the stride was as long and strong as ever.

He was telling me that he likes to get up about four o'clock in the morning and walk through the ravine near his home.

"Walking is the finest exercise in the world," he said. "Everybody should get out and use their legs. I'd like to see trails all over the country where families could walk. If I could choose my companions I'd take along a geologist, an archeologist and an ornithologist. Then what interesting conversations we could have!"

"These girls have stayed right with me and I wouldn't want to leave them now," he explained as we stopped for one of them to re-arrange her blisters.

"By gosh, I've been putting up with this bit of gravel in my shoe long enough," he declared a little further on. "I'm going to dump it out."

So he sat down on a bench, took off his shoe, shook it and put it back on. The gravel was still there. He shook the shoe again.

"Say, that's not gravel at all. I've got a blister!" he cried in astonishment.

But we pushed on.

Some of the girls were wearing running shoes without any socks. Their feet were killing them. A big toe was poking through one girl's shoe.

Several walkers had taken their shoes off and were tramping along in their bare feet or socks.

When we hit Jasper Avenue, out came combs. The girls were more concerned about appearances than they were about their sore feet.

We were constantly being honked at as motorists recognized the tall, spare figure of the lieutenant-governor.

"Nice going, sir!"

"Keep it up. You're doing great!"

"You're a wonderful inspiration!"

At the finish line we were welcomed like a victorious army as we trudged up the driveway. Mr. MacEwan's hand was pumped by everyone and a radio announcer grabbed him for an interview.

I doubt if we have ever had a more popular figure in the vice-regal office. He has a common touch and can converse with kings and cab drivers with equal ease.

Of the 25,000 who began the walk, over 8,000 finished. But none finished in finer fettle than Grant MacEwan.

*   *   *

Not only did the idea of walkathons catch on and sweep through hundreds of communities in the province but the possibility of having the lieutenant-governor present to open them caught on too. Soon invitations to open walks began arriving with regularity in the lieutenant-governor's mail. He accepted as many as he could but not in the ordinary way. Up to that time no community committee would have expected the Queen's representative to do anything more than make an appearance, say a few encouraging words, declare the event open, shake hands all around and be off. They would have counted themselves lucky had he done only that much.

When Grant MacEwan "opened" such events he not only shook hands and inspired with suitable words, he walked the distance with the entrants and every time without fail reached the finishing line, usually

MacEwan's 1000-mile boots are bronzed and a new pair presented in their place at a Calgary Miles for Millions reception, November, 1970   *(MacEwan Collection)*

before the rest of the pack. Soon he was walking distances from twenty to thirty-five miles. He was sixty-five years old when the fad started, and it lasted over the years to the point where they lost count (at over a thousand miles) of the miles His Honor had hiked for charity. Knowing her man, Phyllis tried going behind his back to take some of the pressure off. She phoned officials of various charitable groups, explaining that her husband would never say no to an invitation, would never settle for a token walk of a mile or so, and that he was not getting any younger. Hadn't he done his part, and could they not now invite somebody else? she asked.

Not only would he never say no, he would go out of his way to accept. This happened in 1968 when he was invited to head the Miles for Millions March on a day he was to leave Edmonton for an evening engagement. He asked when the march was scheduld to start and was told eight o'clock in the morning. "Could I go out and start earlier?" he asked. "If I started at six o'clock could there be someone there to check me out?" It was arranged. He didn't miss the march. Starting out two hours earlier than all the others, he completed the twenty-five miles and was on his way with Henry at the wheel for a three-hour drive to Drumheller, arriving in good time — and good shape — to deliver his address.

Phyllis's pleas were made in vain, for when the public has found an idol they are not only generous with their praise, they are also completely selfish in their demands. Invitations continued to arrive until, to Phyllis's

Grant MacEwan greets Hutterite friends from the Standoff Colony, July 1973
(MacEwan Collection)

relief if not to that of her husband, other methods of raising funds came into vogue displacing the walkathons.

In a final and fitting gesture of appreciation, someone thought the worn shoes that had walked hundreds of miles and helped raise thousands of dollars for charity should be bronzed, and saved for posterity. They are to be seen today at the Mill Woods campus of Grant MacEwan College, Edmonton, in a display of MacEwan memorabilia.

*   *   *

As he had in most things, the lieutenant-governor early developed highly individual and efficient techniques in the performance of his duties. When he rode in the official limousine with Henry Weber, it was usually up front. The relationship was friendly and enjoyable — never "chummy," for neither would have wanted it that way — and made pleasant the many miles they traveled together. Even when he had work to do, he sat up front with Henry, reading and making notes as they sped along the highway. On occasion, when the trip was long and the engagements heavy, he would steal a catnap at Henry's side, to awaken refreshed, amazing Henry with his resilience.

The relationship affected Weber's life. Living close to this tireless man with limitless energy, Henry, years younger than Grant, began to think in terms of his own fitness. Soon he had stopped smoking, was taking off weight and, from time to time, helped the governor with his more strenuous projects.

Upon arrival, MacEwan usually emerged from the car coatless and bareheaded (save for the few strictly formal occasions when headgear was prescribed) with hand outstretched, a smile and a few hearty words. It did not matter what the weather was, even at forty below zero, MacEwan would leave his topcoat in the car, for he had found early in the game that, having carried out all the formalities to the point of leaving, it often took an extra five to ten minutes for the coat to be produced and the lieutenant-governor helped into it with all the ensuing additional conversation, thus reducing the amount of time available to spend at the next engagement on the list.

MacEwan moved across Alberta like that natural force, the Chinook wind, warm and always welcome but seldom at rest. Wherever he went to speak, he was greeted with openness and warmth as his rural and other audiences sensed that here was a man who had put his hand to the plow and had labored alongside them. He returned their affection measure for measure as he strode among them, usually in a community hall or a school gymnasium. As he went, his shrewd blue eyes missed nothing, for his interest in people was profound — he always maintained that when traveling on bus or train, if one selected "the toughest looking man or the prettiest woman to sit beside," it would prove a most interesting trip.

"When Grant MacEwan talks to you he doesn't sort of look around to see who else is there." That, coming from an eyewitness, is all that need be said in explanation of the manner in which MacEwan captivated most of those he met, with his total attention no matter for how brief a moment, coupled with a warmth, humor, charm, and kindliness that are fundamental to his nature. At the same time, he held himself aloof from intimacies and familiarities, retaining a dignity befitting the Queen's representative, yet coupled with an affability befitting a Westerner.

When he spoke as lieutenant-governor, he was never pedagogic, he never lectured. Rather, his tone was the same as that which had captivated students over the years — one part of an informal discussion — putting his audiences at their ease. However, when dealing with a subject close to his heart, the pitch of his voice rose higher and his delivery became staccato, like the hoofbeats of a cantering pony on the sunbaked prairie turf. More often than not, the subject was western history.

Chapter 28

Retirement?

During Grant MacEwan's commission as lieutenant-governor of Alberta an old grudge between the federal and the provincial government seemed to be settled. It was generally assumed that the zeal, energy, and stamina he displayed in office had something to do with the decision of the provincial government to let bygones be bygones and provide a home for the federally appointed representative of the Queen.

The story was that in May 1938, when Premier William Aberhart's Social Credit government presented the then lieutenant-governor, John Campbell Bowen, with a number of controversial bills for his signature he refused to sign, thus withholding royal assent. Some of the bills went to the Supreme Court of Canada where they were declared unconstitutional. In the meantime, an angry premier evicted the governor from Government House, a stately, three-storied, sandstone structure, over which the provincial government had control. From that year until 1967, lieutenant-governors of Alberta were without an official residence.

Former Premier Ernest C. Manning, now Senator Manning, who was close to the scene at the time, places a different construction on the closing of Government House. "The former very elaborate Government House was closed by the Government in 1938 as an economy measure during the Great Depression. With the substantial improvements which occurred in the Province's economy, the Government felt it appropriate to re-establish a Government House." The move, says Senator Manning, was in no way connected with the fact that it happened to be Grant MacEwan who was in office at the time of restoration.

Government House, 58 St. George's Crescent, Edmonton   *(Alberta Government photo)*

However, it was a fact that a Calgary newspaper decried the absence of a governor's residence and stated bluntly that if Edmonton would not provide one, Calgary would.

For whatever reason, toward the end of the first MacEwan year, the Alberta government purchased a rambling, roomy, single-storied residence at 58 St. George's Crescent as the official residence. It was refurbished and the MacEwans moved into it in 1967. It was not long before they began to impress their individual stamp on the vice-regal quarters. There was as much room in the basement as there was on the main floor, a large part of it eventually becoming known as the Canadian room as it became the repository for collector's items they both picked up at the countless antique auctions they visited.

The day the government revealed the decision to provide a residence was the day the MacEwans closed the deal on the home they bought, on Summit Drive near MacKinnon Ravine, in Edmonton. They spent a year in it whilst renovations were being made on Government House, then sold it. "I made a dollar."

*   *   *

Just about the time workmen were putting the finishing touches on the residence in Edmonton, His Honor was in Calgary carrying out an official duty when his past caught up with him and a secret he had kept for over thirty-five years was published in a newspaper for thousands of eyes to read.

As it happened, the *Calgary Herald* sent staff writer Eric Erickson to interview MacEwan at the Palliser Hotel. When he returned to the newsroom, he sat down and started his story thus: "The second last time I saw Lieutenant-Governor Grant MacEwan, I was about four years old and he towered over me, about three times my height. At that time he was talking to my mother in the yard of the log cabin in which I was born. . . ."

It turned out that the cabin was on the first land Grant MacEwan ever owned. (He was then a young university professor at Saskatoon.) Situated in the White Fox district, it abutted land Erickson's father was homesteading. It was 1929 and the Ericksons were hard pressed. With Grant's permission, they moved into the cabin on his land and there they lived free of charge until the family found its feet and were able to move onto their own land and into a newly built cabin.

With this accidental disclosure of one instance of private generosity in mind, one is bound to wonder how many more lie buried in MacEwan's past.

*   *   *

Honors descended upon MacEwan like golden poplar leaves on a warm fall day. He was awarded Canada's highest honor, the Order of Canada in 1975; Edmonton named a community college after him as did the University of Calgary a student center; a conservation award was set up in his name; there were many more. He first received from the University of Alberta, what he had never had time to get after he won his master's degree forty-one years before — a doctor's degree. Later, degrees were conferred on him by the universities of Brandon, Guelph, and Saskatchewan. In October 1967, the University of Calgary awarded him the degree and also asked him to deliver the convocation address, which he did in his usual manner.

After complaining that the doctor's gown he was wearing had no pockets in which to put his hands but admiring the three-cornered John Knox hat, saying that "it would have filled my Presbyterian mother with admiration," and telling them that "after a man gets too old to set a bad example, he begins to give good advice," he delivered a conservationist's plea to the graduates. In the glare of space-age wonders, man must never lose sight of two things, he said: the old-fashioned values of the past — vigor, thrift, self-reliance, resourcefulness — upon which the individual and the nations of the world still stood or fell, and man's staying in touch with the community of nature "upon which the future of our race may depend."

When the newly installed Dr. MacEwan stood before them, lean as an arrowhead, tall as a lodgepole, and tough as a sinewy pine, it is unlikely that a single person in the auditorium realized what they were hearing when he spoke that day in Calgary. In fact, they were being honored with a convocation address that had taken well over twenty years to prepare. The words "and man's staying in touch with the community of nature upon which the future of our race may depend" were not written overnight. MacEwan had always been a man with strongly held beliefs. He was also one of intellectual honesty, which caused him to subject such beliefs to periodic examination. Some of them did not escape alteration as he followed the truth wherever it led him.

His mother, Bertha MacEwan, had passed on to him her solid and uncompromisingly fundamentalist faith, which he had accepted without question in his early years. However, around 1934, there is clear evidence in his journal that his restless mind was at work, and uneasy with his church. At the same time, he was drawn to the quiet countryside where he could sense the divinity in nature.

"Feb. 11, 1934: This morning I had more than average difficulty remaining awake in church. I came out of a doze with a jolt to see Rev. Orton's finger at arm's length pointed at me and the Rev. gent looking right at me. I felt his challenge but don't know yet just what it was." In a couple of weeks there was another entry, contrasting the words of a hymn with the ritualistic presentation of a solo. He had read in the hymnary, "Strong Son of God immortal love, Whom we that have not seen Thy face, By faith, faith alone embrace, Believing what we cannot prove," then listened to the solo. "Perhaps the solo was very fine . . . I don't know, but to me the verses of the hymn and the solo contrasted sharply. The former had depth and meaning and reality, the latter . . . echoed meaninglessly." There were other entries in similar vein. Strange words for MacEwan the good churchman.

That summer he and Ewen spent a rugged holiday packing into Candle Lake, then a virtual wilderness. "One cannot help but love the wild unoccupied country. . . . I have thought so often today of the hymn *Peace Perfect Peace* (in this dark world of sin). It all contrasts so obviously with the environment we labor in day by day. It is good for one's soul to get away . . . [to where] peace like a river surroundeth my soul."

There is little doubt that MacEwan was held to the church as much by the presence of his old Guelph friend and minister, Jim Mackenzie, as well as by innate kindliness and reluctance to cause pain to him or to his fellow elders or to the congregation by an open break. By the time he left to take up the deanship at the University of Manitoba in 1946, he later revealed, he had separated from the church in mind if not in body.

In Winnipeg, he failed to renew membership in the United Church or any other, although it was not for want of searching. He ranged about religiously, attending services at churches of all denominations, including Greek Catholic, Orthodox, Anglican, Roman Catholic, even the Synagogue, but to no avail. He had lost all interest in the trappings of religion, and, what was more, he was repelled by the bitterness and division that sectarian rivalry often gave rise to.

MacEwan had lost his church but he had not lost his God. Neither had he lost trust in prayer, which would always be essential to his spiritual nourishment. A new faith was in the making. It took years to forge; what began around 1934 took recognizable shape about 1956 through his own quest and from meeting others who had faced similar quandaries. One such was Walking Buffalo, chief of the Stoney Indian tribe, also known as George McLean, adopted son of Methodist missionary Rev. John McLean. Soon after arriving in Calgary, MacEwan met and sat with him in his teepee at the Calgary Stampede. "When I sat at his feet, I had the feeling that one of the ancient philosophers had come back to life."

The lieutenant-governor put it all in his book entitled *Tatanga Mani* (Walking Buffalo's Stoney name), published by M. G. Hurtig Limited, Edmonton, in 1969. As his belief took shape he applied it honestly to all his actions and it was at this time he became a vegetarian, to be in harmony with nature and to keep faith with his fellow living creatures under God — a space-age step for a man who had spent a good part of his life instructing in the proper raising of livestock for slaughter. Also, a measure of the struggle he had undergone silently since 1934.

His new belief cost him money as well as inconvenience but he has held to it without faltering. Chic Miller speaks with authority when he says that a petroleum company offered MacEwan $10,000 for permission to drill on his land, plus a generous royalty on any oil they discovered, only to be told that such activity would disturb his fellow living creatures and for that reason no permission would be issued.

Grant MacEwan set his creed down:

I believe instinctively in a God for whom I am prepared to search.

I believe it is an offence against the God of Nature for me to accept any hand-me-down, man-defined religion or creed without the test of reason. I believe no man dead or alive knows more or knew more about God than I can know by searching.

I believe that the God of Nature must be without prejudice, with exactly the same concern for all His children, and that the human invokes no more, no less, of fatherly love than the beaver or sparrow.

I believe I am an integral part of the environment and, as a good subject, I must establish an enduring relationship with my surroundings. My dependence upon the land is fundamental.

I believe destructive waste and greedy exploitation are sins.

I believe the biggest challenge is in being a helper rather than a destroyer of the treasures in Nature's storehouse, a conserver, a husbandman and partner in caring for the Vineyard.

I accept, with apologies to Albert Schweitzer, "a Reverence For Life" and all that is of the Great Spirit's creation.

I believe morality is not complete until the individual holds all of the Great Spirit's creatures in brotherhood and has compassion for all. A fundamental concept of Good consists of working to preserve all creatures with feeling and the will to live.

I am prepared to stand before my Maker, the Ruler of the entire Universe, with no other plea than that I have tried to leave things in His Vineyard better than I found them.

So spoke MacEwan, the Caretaker in the Great House. The habit of prayer that he learned at his mother's knee never left him but his attitude to it is not the orthodox one. Early in 1971 he wrote:

This was the day of the Premier's Prayer Breakfast. Prayer means much to me but I don't want to leave my praying to somebody else, don't want anybody else to leave his praying to me, don't want my praying to become a public performance. Heretofore, I managed to avoid the Prayer Breakfast. This year I was invited to give the Prayer For The Province and I declined, then yielded with the understanding that my supplication would be my own, be honest more than orthodox and might win disapproval from the Baptists.

Well, I carried out my part, apologized to God for purporting to speak for 300 people present, each of whom should be praying from his own heart. Prayer should be intensely personal; it should be in the spirit of complete honesty; it should entail less talking and more listening; it should be from the heart more than from tongue or the written page — all of which rules out the rehearsed public oratory and eliminates the banquet hall and church assembly as the best place for it. The bedside is a better place but I would nominate the woods or river valley as first choice, anywhere offering solitude and silence. I'm sure God must get tired of human oratory, especially when it is prepared for human ears more than for Him.

Grant MacEwan is a man of so many parts it is difficult to say which of his contributions will be judged most important by history. Certainly, his naturalistic religion, founded on reverence for God, humanity, his fellow creatures, and the environment, will be among the leading contenders. Two generations before it was the popular thing to do, MacEwan's mind had turned to the idea of conservation, inspired by his father who believed "that Nature's Gentleman could be identified as the person whose motivating purpose was to leave things better than he found them" and by Hon. W. R. Motherwell, then federal minister of agriulture, who urged him to use his voice and pen for the "protection of Canada's soil, grass, water, trees, and other resources." He accepted these as a sacred duty.

It is impossible to estimate the hundreds of thousands of words MacEwan has written, spoken, and broadcast on the subject. In 1966, he published the book *Entrusted to My Care* which, in setting out his belief, spoke with alarm at man's extravagance and greed in the use of limited resources. Mankind had no right to exploit the environment at the expense of other creatures, he said.

The Lieutenant-Governor in the Calgary Stampede Parade, July 13, 1970
(Duffoto Process Co. Ltd. photo, MacEwan Collection)

If man is really deserving of a place above his fellow creatures on earth, he should display superiority in more than predation and exploit: the man who sings psalms on Sunday and robs future generations by thoughtlessly depleting stocks of resources on Monday is not a good citizen. . . . It is time for a new dedication to stewardship of the earth and its riches, a new emphasis upon the responsibilities of good guardianship.

It was a book before its time, sold slowly for a MacEwan book, and was allowed to go out of print.

The bystander who termed MacEwan "our modern Moses" with the "best conscience in today's sick society" might well have been anticipating history's judgment. Perhaps future researchers will turn to MacEwan's newspaper columns, in which he has exhorted mankind weekly in a thousand and more ways to guard the land and creatures upon it, to judge the writer and give him place among the immortals.

In MacEwan's faith, under God, conservation is religion and religion, conservation.

* * *

In the spring of 1966, the Historical Society of Alberta honored him "for the most outstanding contribution to Alberta history." Another honor which particularly touched him came from across the border. In the United States a nonprofit educational organization dedicated to the advancement of local and regional history throughout their country and Canada, the American Association for State and Local History, made a survey of the works produced and, meeting in Atlanta, Georgia, chose Grant MacEwan for the 1966 "award of merit." The citation stated that it was for "exceptional contributions to the field of western and agricultural history through books, lectures and articles."

* * *

It is little wonder that when the normal end to a five-year term neared, many Albertans began to fret lest they lose this extraordinary man, this dynamo they had for a lieutenant-governor. The *Calgary Herald* spoke for thousands when it said in an editorial that appeared on June 20, 1970:

Alberta is extremely fortunate in the high-calibre type of man it has serving in the office of lieutenant-governor. . . . The Alberta government will be doing the province a good turn if it urges Mr. MacEwan to accept a renewal of his appointment and stay on for another term. . . . He carries a sense of contagious enthusiasm about with him wherever he goes. His knowledge of the Prairie region and its people goes deep, as does his unabashed affection for them. . . . In short, he makes an ideal lieutenant-governor, and we hope the government will insist upon him staying on.

There was rejoicing when it was announced that he was to begin, at sixty-eight years, another term. After saying what a hard-working governor he had been, that he was "in tune with the Alberta temperament combining a western informality and friendliness with due regard for his serious responsibilities," the *Edmonton Journal* said, "it is good to know that his cheerful presence will continue to grace our official occasions. We wish him well in his extended term of office."

* * *

On his seventieth birthday he was carrying out his duties thinking that with luck the occasion would pass without remark. He was driven in a hackney-drawn carriage to open the Canadian Derby in Edmonton. He entered the royal box and stepped forward to receive the Royal Salute. There was an awkward pause. Then, as one, the crowd of 18,000 rose to its feet and sang "Happy Birthday." "It was one of those moments when I laughed but could easily have cried," he confided to his notes later.

Max Foran and daughters Fiona (left) and Lynwyn   *(Foran Collection)*

It was around this time that MacEwan took a severe drop in his asking price for land he had bought on Battle Lake west of Wetaskiwin. He had bought it some time before and had left it untouched, unspoiled, adding nothing save a simple cabin to which he escaped from time to time. Such land was in great demand and, he concluded, with his Priddis ranch and other property in mind, should be put up for sale. On the advice of his real estate agent, Arthur Moore, an asking price of $150,000 was put on it. Moore was dealing for MacEwan and felt he had a sale. When MacEwan learned that the potential buyer was the 4-H Clubs of Alberta, he told Moore he wanted them to have it. The deal was made at around $100,000.

*   *   *

What would his second term hold? What would their lieutenant-governor do next? Would he ease off a little, as would be expected of a sixty-eight-year-old person who has done a good job?

In his first term, he had brought out five new books, including a western history, *West to the Sea* (later called *A Short History of Western Canada*), in collaboration with his son-in-law, Maxwell Foran, then a school principal. He had walked hundreds of miles in cities, towns, and villages all over Alberta in walkathons. He had delivered hundreds of speeches, and he had done much more. Was there anything else?

The log cabin that MacEwan built overlooking the Little Red Deer River. Called "Amisk Haven," it is near Sundre, Alta.   *(R. H. Macdonald photo)*

Indeed there was.

He was to serve another three and one-half years in office and during that time would continue writing, walking, and speaking. Despite Phyllis MacEwan's behind-the-scenes efforts to the contrary, he continued to walk for charity whenever and wherever he could. An expert with the pocketknife, he produced exceptional works whittling figures out of native wood, most notably hundreds of beaver-chewed logs upon which he fashioned the form of Canada's national symbol — the busy, industrious, and resourceful beaver with which he had a deep and abiding affinity. They became known as "MacEwan's beaver logs" and are now collector's items. Seldom has a work of art suited the artist more.

He then launched on a task that would be most ambitious for a man half his age. He searched for the right unspoiled location and, with the help of Chic Miller, he located a quarter section of land on the Little Red River near Sundre, Alberta, and bought it.

There he would build a log cabin with his own hands, using only the materials provided by nature. It would be like ones that pioneer homesteaders had built at about the turn of the century. He would furnish it just as they had furnished theirs and he would collect implements they had used, farm it the way they had farmed.

Although he made little of it and mentioned less, the story eventually came out. The log cabin appealed to everything in Grant's disposition; it was honest architecture, making use of that which God had provided, performing its function admirably, efficiently, and economically with no fuss and no frills. He told a Canadian Press interviewer: "It's not very handsome, not very square and not very level but log houses were never supposed to be level or square."

As always, with an eye to history, it was his plan to leave it to the community as an example of the homesteads that dotted the western parklands when he was born at the turn of the century.

He confided that the urge to build came as a primordial drive to complete the circle and return to the farm where he had started. There he would "live at peace with the soil and trees and water and beavers and listen to Nature's voice. I want the farm to pay for groceries and taxes and beyond that I will take my dividends in the satisfaction I expect from kinship with nature."

He finished building the cabin with only minor and sporadic assistance from friends and chance visitors. While he and the family traveled to it at every chance, what of the plan to farm it? Would this, like the Priddis cabin, prove to be an elusive dream?

*   *   *

When it was said earlier in the chapter that Grant MacEwan "would continue writing," it was understated.

The lieutenant-governorship appeared to be made for a man who persisted in carrying along several lives at the same time. As early as 1943 he had resolved to devote his writings to the delineation of "the color and romance in the history of Western Canadian agriculture" and the many old-time characters "who played a dominant role in its development." The stories would serve to revitalize factual drabness with interesting narrative, providing thereby equally as much information "with the added spice of enjoyment for the reader." When he took office in the Alberta legislative buildings and as he became accustomed to the duties, shaping them to the needs of his avocations, he soon beat a pathway along the marble halls between the vice-regal suite and the legislative library, for it was there he did much of his research and it was there His Honor could usually be found if he was in town but not in his office. As a writer MacEwan entered his most creative period when he became Queen's representative for Alberta.

He had been preparing for it all his life as he traveled about the countryside with his notebook, avid for the stories of the country and its pioneers. His formal duties were not demanding but in fulfilling the number of engagements throughout the province that he did, in continuing his newspaper columns and his radio programs and in producing a continuing stream of book-length manuscripts, his effort constituted a staggering achievement. What is more, his comprehension of the West, its land, people, and beasts was to prove indispensable to a country coming to an understanding of itself.

His method of writing is simple. He claims he is a slow writer but by efficient use of his time he manages to spend long hours at it, writing early in the morning and far into the night. "I don't play golf, poker or bridge, so I use my poker and bridge time for writing." He writes anywhere: on buses, trains, in aircraft, but prefers buses. The first draft of a book is written out in longhand as his thoughts flow better "when I have a pen in my hand." He then transcribes the rough draft, using a thirty-year-old Royal portable typewriter — "I've changed the ribbon a few times and it has been serviced about once." As he transcribes, he revises the text and polishes the language and that, with possibly a few hand-written corrections, is the draft that is sent to the editor.

When he claims to be a slow writer one must remember that he speaks in relative terms. What might be slow to Grant MacEwan might well be lightning fast to another. An illuminating instance of book production occurred shortly after the 1950 New Year's celebrations. On January 16, 1950, at a meeting of the Western Association of Exhibitions, following a discussion which pointed up a need for some sort of a history of fairs and exhibitions, MacEwan undertook to write a book on the subject. He returned to Winnipeg and went to work immediately, fitting it in with other engagements and his regular duties as dean of agriculture.

That was the year of one of nature's disastrous aberrations — the Winnipeg Flood. As mentioned previously, the flood and its aftermath added greatly to the dean's responsibilities. Nevertheless, the book, *Agriculture on Parade*, promised in January, was handed over to William McCulley at the Toronto publishers on August 6 of the same year.

* * *

Grant MacEwan is an ideal author for any publisher to deal with. He is honest about delivery dates and his manuscripts arrive either on time or a few days early. He is open to suggestion and goes to any lengths to expedite the transition of manuscript into book form. To send him galley proofs is to get them back within four or five days with few major changes. Page proofs are returned almost as quickly, accompanied by an index which never fails to enhance the value of the work despite the fact that he produces it in record time. In short, Grant MacEwan is the kind of author editors dream about but rarely find.

"I'm constantly amazed at the number of ideas you have for new books," one editor told him. MacEwan retorted that there was no great mystery to it. "I learned early," he said, "that if you are a writer the first thing you must do is open a file on your subject, collect information through reading, research and interviews, and when the file is thick enough, write a book." The ideas come from his filing cabinet and the relatively thick files contained therein. Neither does he wait for the publisher to present the finished book before starting on another. Writing is a continuous process with him; he is addicted to it. "It's just a bad habit, once you start, you can't stop. Asking me if I'm going to write another book is like asking an alcoholic if he's going to have another drink," he told one interviewer.

* * *

His works altered the climate of western writing, his examples opening the eyes of readers and other writers. His readers discovered that his works were revolutionary: here was an academic writing about heroes in

Western Canada's most prolific writer of popular western history at work in the Alberta Legislative Library, Edmonton   *(R. H. Macdonald photo)*

a country heretofore thought to be bereft of such things, at a time when it was not fashionable to do so, and in language the ordinary man could understand. Those who heard his lectures or read his books shared one common reaction: Grant MacEwan made the history of the West come alive.

Some of his early colleagues were not so charitable. Academe, if it acknowledged his work, tended to look the other way. When his books made a direct contribution to his field of study, they were accepted. However, when the professor of animal husbandry's works dealt with local and regional history, if they admired his originality they were confused by the lack of the customary connection between the author's primary vocation and the subject matter of his writings. His books were treated as an aberration to be tolerated or grudgingly accepted. As the number of MacEwan books mounted, one professor imbued with intellectual snobbery, if not envy, quipped, "they say that Grant MacEwan has written another book — too bad he hasn't read any," thus making the least of a colleague's accomplishments, with words that would be widely quoted.

Much later, MacEwan was to cast his mind back over the years and acknowledge the fact that the initial criticism which greeted his books was a worry to him, but one soon dismissed, for, as has been said about another, he was too busy "to play academic games or even to recognize that they were being played." Rather, he would range the land, in search of those with an individual western outlook on life. More often than not he found them among the simple folk in the rural areas, the farmers, ranchers, horsemen, and herdsmen. When confronted with important personages, he thrust aside the facade of success to reveal their common humanity.

He set down his findings in unaffected prose, fast-paced, lucid, and popular. In short staccato sentences — written almost as he spoke — his books were remarkably individual, his very own, and they did the job he set out to do, for, from first to last, MacEwan aspired to be, above all, a good teller of stories. In this he achieved success, measured by the acceptance of his books by his growing public (not formerly noted for the number of books they purchased) who bought them by the thousands, placing a number on the all-time western best-seller lists. For example, *Fifty Mighty Men* has sold close to 20,000 copies and is still in print and moving well.

His objective was not to elicit praise for great literature but to be a successful teller of stories about his country and its people — the basic aspiration of writers throughout the ages. Dr. Kenneth Glazier, chief librarian at the University of Calgary, said: "He writes about Western Canada out of his own experience, what he has learned through the soles of his shoes."

Speaking for her customers, Carmen Moore said: "The readers like Grant MacEwan because he never talks down to people." His writings were designed more to get a message across to the reader than to reflect glory on the writer. "Grant MacEwan never bothers with style but his figures are exquisite," she said.

Some of those who came into her shop, perhaps the more scholarly, were critical of MacEwan books as history books pure and simple. Mrs. Moore allowed them a point, saying that perhaps they weren't as thorough as a history textbook ought to be:

> . . . perhaps you wouldn't go to them as reference books to find a specific date for a specific event but his growing following of readers turn to him because he's a good story teller and he makes history come alive before their eyes. There are hundreds of people who have read about western history because of Grant's writings who would never crack a book otherwise.
>
> You wouldn't go to, say, his book *Calgary Cavalcade* to find the exact date the CPR first arrived in the city — but Grant would know. He doesn't write reference textbooks, he writes anecdotal material that people will read.

The motivation behind the lengthening list of books written by MacEwan is not hard to find. In his introduction to *Between the Red and the Rockies,* he says: "The conversion of half a nation from wilderness to an enterprising agricultural community in a single generation is without parallel" in world history. It was his object to reveal "entertaining, academic and cultural values" in a story that should be told in school and college classrooms.

He adds to his philosophy of writing in his introduction to *Fifty Mighty Men:*

> It is a striking record, but for many of us, the most inspiring part of the story concerns the distinctive people in the vanguard. Their performance, characterized by vigor, courage and resourcefulness, holds priceless messages for today. It would be a tragic misfortune if the records became lost or if the trials, triumphs and humor of those early years of our section of Canada were ignored.

A reader of the *Western Producer,* Stanley Harrison of Fort Qu'Appelle, who is a writer of some stature himself, wrote to the editor in 1960 when the newspaper was publishing the series of articles that eventually became *Blazing the Old Cattle Trails,* commenting upon it and upon MacEwan's position as an original instigator, a popularizer of western history:

> No man has interpreted the robust western spirit better than Grant MacEwan; his love and pride in the West is alive in everything he writes. He has served this land well in whatever sphere of action he has entered, but perhaps "whatever gods may be" will honor him most for his desire — and ability — to bring breathing to his page the vision and courage of the living past when men lived strongly — and knew that they lived!

Grant MacEwan has taken as his task the responsibility to see that the story of western Canada is not ignored. While honoring all his duties, he made use of his time as Queen's representative right up to the end to fulfill this responsibility.

*   *   *

In June 1974 when the time had come to end his term of office, Albertans by the thousands turned out to say farewell. It took two large public receptions to do the job; one in the Edmonton Gardens sponsored by the city of Edmonton, and one on the legislative grounds sponsored by the province of Alberta.

There were pipe bands, military bands, songs and dances by groups of native and other ethnic backgrounds, young and old — all of whom at one time or another had been helped, encouraged, guided, or inspired by Grant MacEwan. Praise showered on both Grant and Phyllis MacEwan from the platform, and from individuals, as the couple mingled with the throngs on the legislative lawns.

Mayor Ivor Dent of Edmonton expressed for his citizens their debt to Dr. MacEwan; for his contributions to western history, the example he set by his love of nature, promotion of conservation, physical fitness and the easy humor and informality he had brought to the vice-regal office, capturing even the admiration of the most skeptical. The city presented the couple with an antique Canadian washstand, a captain's chair, and two rockers, all dating in the 1820s. It also presented them with a foot-thick volume containing an estimated half a million names of Albertans who joined in wishing them well.

On the sun-splashed lawns of the legislature, Grant, in white shirt open at the neck, and Phyllis, looking charming in summer attire topped by one of her broadbrimmed picture hats for which she had become famous, strolled among the hundreds of people for an hour, shaking hands, exchanging stories, listening to complaints, and accepting well wishes. There were tears in many eyes, not least those of the MacEwans from time to time.

Premier Peter Lougheed spoke for the people of the province when he described him as the most versatile man to call Alberta "home." "He writes history . . . but he has made history in this province. Grant MacEwan has been known not just in the capital but in the whole province. The more humble the group that asked him to take part, the quicker the acceptance."

Later on at this retirement reception, the province presented him with what to most men would be a dream car — a big, shining vehicle loaded with auxiliary services.

The smile didn't change on Grant MacEwan's face but as he eyed the luxurious automobile he said in a low-voiced aside to Phyllis, "whoever suggested that gift doesn't know me."

The party went off without a hitch and as many hands were shaken in the allotted time as only Grant MacEwan could manage. The province had said farewell to their singular lieutenant-governor.

The next day Grant MacEwan went down to the dealer who had supplied the gift car. He inspected the showroom and picked a much smaller model that would consume less gas and fit into any community in the province without attracting attention. He negotiated a trade and directed that the balance of the money left over from the deal be returned to the treasury of the people of Alberta.

*   *   *

He had come a long way since the days on the North Brandon farm, the destitute days in a converted granary on the Melfort farm, but from the beginning he had been marked, set apart somewhat from his contemporaries. MacEwan had been born with a strong enterprising strain to which was soon added an equally strong agricultural/conservation motive. When refused land by his father, it was then that he altered course in the direction of public service which would become a dominant factor in his life at the expense of normal pleasures. However, the other strains and motives persisted. While he ceased the active pursuit of profit which characterized his boyish years, he never lost his respect for the dollar — although he would never become preoccupied with what it could buy. Through honest, honorable, and canny investments, he became independent earlier in his career than most contemporaries in similar positions and ended with holdings that would place him well within the millionaire category — although he bridles at the suggestion.

It is not for the foregoing that he will be chiefly remembered, however. In the years to come the MacEwan tree will continue to flourish, nurtured as it is by reverence for God and all His creatures, love of the land and all that it produces, and an abiding respect for humanity, especially as it is embodied in the many courageous, hard-working and determined founders of western Canada whose stories he has captured and conserved for posterity. The fruit of that tree in the form of MacEwan books will continue to nourish a land up to now desperately short of such food for the spirit. The seed from the fruit, falling on fertile ground will, no doubt, germinate, take root and multiply greatly the profound effect of the original MacEwan seed stock on the history of the West. Whenever MacEwan the writer puts down his pen — if that day ever comes — his place among the immortals of western Canadian literature will be assured.

About the man himself, the secret of his singular career is that Grant MacEwan never studied to be anything other than what he is. He is no poseur and, while he usually ended up occupying center stage wherever he was, he never sought deliberately to do so. It was not his objective to create myths, they came naturally — and copiously. He is always himself and will always be himself without affectation of any sort. That he enjoys immense contemporary popularity and has become a legend in his own time is simply due to the fact that Grant MacEwan is no ordinary man.

Epilogue

On one occasion before he left office, Grant MacEwan met a friend who had been both student and assistant under him.

"I've retired," "Willie" Wilson announced.

"You've retired!" exclaimed Grant, ". . . for how long?"

The exchange reflects the attitude that has governed MacEwan in his own retirement.

The question of where the MacEwans were to live arose and Phyllis made the choice. Heather and Max were in Calgary (Priddis) with their two daughters and that is where they would live. Grant had been toying with the idea of settling in one of the towns along the Edmonton-Calgary axis — Red Deer, Olds, Innisfail, High River, Carstairs, Didsbury — but he knew that if he were to continue writing he would have to be much closer to adequate library service and so the small centers were out of the question. While he would possibly have chosen Edmonton, he deferred to Phyllis in her choice of Calgary.

The decision was made. Max, Heather and their two daughters, Fiona and Lynwyn, would live at Priddis and Grant and Phyllis would take over their home at 132 Hallbrook Drive in southwest Calgary.

* * *

There was scarcely a pause in MacEwan's stride from regal office to civilian life. Calls for public service continued, people asked him to speak and to judge livestock. He continued writing and bringing out at least one book a year, including . . . *and Mighty Women Too* during International Women's Year as a companion to his *Fifty Mighty Men*.

Three months after "retirement," he became a professor of history at University of Calgary, giving a credit course in the exploration and settlement of the Canadian Prairies. He also undertook to give two lectures a week at Olds Agricultural College on the history of western Canadian agriculture. The following year, he began a western history course for the elderly, meeting with such response that it was necessary to repeat the lectures to handle the overflow.

Still there was room for more. In time he was to be chairman of a royal commission on a proposed grassland national park and served on a commission studying the education of Indians. The provincial government named him chairman of the Historical Resources Foundation of Alberta, also chairman of the Advisory Committee of Alberta Heritage Learning Resources Project, the objects of which were ideally suited to MacEwan interests and philosophy — the conservation of the province's history.

In October 1977, Premier Lougheed chose Dr. MacEwan as the first recipient of a newly instituted "Premier's Award for Excellence" in recognition of singular achievement which had brought distinction to the province.

Noting that he was an "ardent naturalist, conservationist, anthropologist, educationist, writer, historian, statesman, monarchist, politician and physical fitness advocate," the premier could be excused for not mentioning that he was also a broadcaster and an accomplished agrologist. However, the citation was unerring in summing up his nature and career, especially in one sentence which applies not just to Alberta but to western Canada:

With down-to-earth humanity and with an astounding stamina which allowed him to fulfil a staggering number of engagements in every corner . . . Dr. MacEwan reached out and touched thousands . . . endearing himself to all.

Index

(Boldface page numbers indicate illustrations)

Abbey, Moses, 7
Agricultural Institute of Canada, 163
Aikenhead, J. R., 108
Alberta, first impressions, 116
Alexander, Mrs Joyce (Hodson), 104
Ames, Iowa, 89, 90
Anderson, of Iowa State College, 91
Anderson, Premier J. T. M., 152
Animal Husbandry Society, 66
Argall, Mamie, 59
Auction sale, 23
Auld, F. Hedley, 93
Auld, Gordon, farm of, 67
Aunts, Annie and Aggie, 75

Baker, Frank, 86,100
Baker, Professor, 68
Baldwin, Colonel D'Arcy, 175
Baltzan, Dr. David, 129
Bank director, 160
Beatty, Ike, 101
Beef Producers' Council, 192
    eases out of, 195
Bell, Charlie, 107
Bell, Dick, 152
Belle Plaine, 99
Benam, Mr. and Mrs., 67

Bethune, 99
Better Farming Train, 86, **87**
Blackwood, Professor W. C., 75, 76
Boom ends, 31
Booster era, 13
Bowman, James, farm, 67
Bracken, John, 152
Bradley, W. J., 186
Brandon, 7
    Grant's impressions of, 22
    Grant visits relatives, 68
    home, **25**
    move to, 24
    North Brandon, 7
    street scene, early 1900s, **29**
    view from MacEwan farm, 14
Brickley, J. J. (Joe), 72, **78**, 108, 109
Bringham, Harriet, 93
Broadcasting, 110, 142-144, 205
Brockelbank, E. E., 101, 111
Brooklin Young People, 67
Brothers, relationship between Grant
    and George, 52
Bruce, Dorothy, 68
Bryden, Tom, 130
Buchan visit, **139**, 141
Burnett, Jim, 101

Burns' Society, 112
Business with George, Melfort, 52-53
Byers, Beatrice, 67
Byng, Lord, 83

Calbert, Ab., 109
Calgary Exhibition and Stampede,
    185
Calgary, 1952, 191
Campbellford, Ontario, 74
Campus, 1930s, 132
Canadian Arabian Breeders, 140
Canadian Northern Railway, 21
Canadian Pacific Railway, 4, 7
Canora Fair, 83
Carter, Irene, 67
Cavanaugh, Len, 71
Chalmer's Church, Guelph, 67
    Young People's Society, 67, 68
Charyk, John, 1
Chater, Man., town of, 14
Chicago stockyards, 72
Churchbridge, Sask., 124, 127
Civic politics
    aldermanic candidate, 192
    Calgary and CPR debate, 209, 214,
        215
    Calgary citizens, 212
    campaign, 1963: Nickle, Carl, 209;
        Taylor, Nick, 209; Watson,
        Bruce, 209
    CPR plan rejected, 213
    Dawson, Peter, 205
    elected, 193, 199, **211**
    end of Mayor's career and
        comment, 215
    Hays, Mayor Harry W., 206
    Heather with Mayor, **212**
    impressions of civic politics, *Poking
        into Politics*, 193-194
    Mayor as judge, **214**
    MacEwan-for-Mayor Committee,
        210-211: Ayer, John C.; Nickle,
        Carl; Salter, Hardy; Shannon,
        Mel; Taylor, Nick; Watson,
        Bruce
    MacEwan policies, principles, 213
    MacEwan, Smith compete for
        mayorality, 209

MacEwan wins election, 210
    named mayor, 206
    re-elected alderman, 199
    severs party connections, 207
    tops polls, 205
    victory smiles, Grant and Phyllis,
        211
Clark, H. R., 102 passim
Cline, Phyllis Winnifred, **109**, 110,
    112
Cline background, 128
Cline, Mrs. Vernon, **126**
Clinkskill, James, 109, 111, 126
Clydesdale horses, 21, 50
Colborne, Fred, 196
Coldwell, M. J., 152
Coles, Hooper, 125
Colleagues J. G. Rayner, R. Ramsay,
    MacEwan, **153**
Collins, M. A., 101
Commonwealth Games, 1
Congregational church, 67
Cook, B. A., 100
Cooke, O. A., 86
Coppock, Kenneth, 156, 187, 191
Council of Canadian Beef Producers,
    187
Cowan, Agnes, 5
Cowan, Audrey, 216
Cowan, James, 30
Creelman, President George C., 65
Crerar, Hon. T. A., 50
Cross, A. E., Calgary, 116
Cruickshank, George, 79, 80
Culliton, E. M., 156
Cumming, Martha, 4
Cypress Hills, 115

Daily journal, sample entry with
    names, 67, 68
Davin, Nicholas Flood, 142
Day, Professor George, 68
Demock Brothers Ranch, 116
Des Moines, Iowa, 90
Devlin, Tom, 81, 86, 101
Dixon, Arthur J., 196
Downham, Howard, of Strathroy, 71
Durnin, James, 39
Durnin, Olive, 41, 43, 44
Dyer, Bill, 67

East Lansing, Michigan, 80
Eaton, Gladys, 74, 75, **76**, 108
Ede, Cyril, assesses Grant as
    schoolboy, 42
Education, 61
Elliott, J. J., farm of, 67
Ellis, Miriam Green, quoted in *Family
    Herald*, 167
Emery Filbey, Institute of Meat
    Packing, University of Chicago,
    93
Entertainment, 16, 131
Estey, J. W., 152
Evans, Mrs. (J. H.) Muriel, 112
Ewen, A. J., 103, 110, 111, 121, **122**,
    124
Examinations, 43
Extending the Boundaries by Carlyle
    King, quoted, 123

Fairy Glen, 83
Farm and Ranch Review, 192
Farm Boy's Camp, Regina, 54
First House, 130, **133**
Follet, Harry, 86
Four generations, **15**
4-H buy land, 254
Foran
    Max, 216, 217
    Max with Fiona and Lynwyn, **254**
    move to Priddis, 262
Forestry Farm, 126
Forrester, Mayor W. R., Emerson,
    175

Galbraith, Mrs., 68
Gammie, Jack, buys Melfort farm,
    149
Gardiner, Hon. James G., 136, 152
Gearry Brothers, farm of, 68
Gilchrist ranch, 116
Glenbush, 100
Graham, Dr. V. E., 165
Grant, Aunt Marion, **20**
    dies, 160
Grant, Bertha, 4, **9**
Grant relatives, **155**
Grant family, **3**
Grant, 4
Grant, James Alexander, 4 passim, 68

Grants, John, James, Aunt Marion,
    108
Grant, John Gray, 4
Grant, John Walter, 3, 108
Grant, Maria Corlette, 19, **108**
Grant origin, 5
Grants of Pictou, 3
Gravelbourg, 101
"Greater Production Fleet," 51

Haggerty, Swanton, 101
Hamilton, Hon. C. M., 94
Hamilton, Z. M., 142
Hannam, Herb, **79**
Happy Farmer Tractor Co., 50
Harms, of Oregon, 91
Hartnett, Maurice, 101, 185
Haultain, Premier, 97
Harvest
    quotation from *Between the Red and
        the Rockies*, 47
    stem rust, Melfort, 1916, 44
    1917 a good year, 48
    1918 a good year, 56
    1919 a bad year, 56-57
    1920 a good year, 58, 61
Harvey, J. G., 88
Hawke, Doctor, 58
Hays, Harry, 206, 209
Hays, Ken, 100
Heather, 146, 160
Heather marries, 217
Helser, M. D., 91
Hill, O. D., 83
Hood, Doctor Grace Gordon, 169
Horsemeat, experiment, 147
Horses, six horse hitch at Melfort, **51**
Hudson Bay Route, 119
Hughes, J. R., 107
Humane killer, 124
Humesville Church, **18**, 68

Illinois State College, 80
Influenza epidemic, 57
International Harvester Co., 43
Iowa State College, 88, 90
Iowa University, offer from, 106

Jacobs, F. M., 191
Jameson, D. N., 69, 87

Johns, Sid, 151
Jones, Nathan, 91
Joslyn, C. E., 175
Judging livestock, 68, 74
  Calgary Exhibition and Stampede,
    140
  Chilliwack, **198**
  Climax, **101**
  Chicago International Exposition,
    77, 78, 80
  dangers, 141
  debut as official judge, 83
  first public judging, 69
  in B.C., 145
  in Saskatchewan, 99
  OAC International team, **79**
  OAC wins Canadian meet, 79
  position of judge, 100
  The Farmers Advocate reports results,
    80
  Toronto Royal Winter Fair, 77, 79,
    140
  University of Alberta team, 79
  University of Manitoba team, 79

Kaufman, Larry 91
Kay, Robert, 91
Kearns Hereford Ranch, 116
Kennedy, Arnold, 79
Keown, Herb, 83
Kildee, Dean, 91, 109
King, Carlyle, 123
King, Prime Minister Mackenzie, 83
King George Hotel, 110
Kirk, Dr. L. E., 134, 162
Kirby, W. C., 203
Kiwanis, 112, 163
Knox, Bill, 78, 80
Knox, H. A., 79, 80
Knox United Church, 112

Lacombe Farm, 88
Land
  buys ranch at Priddis and
    Longview, 148
  first purchase, 107
  Resource purchase, 108
  sold White Fox land and Resource
    farm, 148
Lamont, Ronald 21
Leslie, Allan C., 100

Lincoln Zoo, Chicago, 80
Lieutenant-Governor of Alberta
  accommodation, modest, 226
  appointment, 217
  cabins
    Battle Lake cabin, 225
    Priddis ranch, 225
    Westward Ho cabin, Sundre, 225
  eccentricities, 224 passim
  engagement policy, 237
  Edmonton house, 220
  Happy Birthday, 253
  Honorary Blood Chief, **236**
  honors, **235**, 248
  Hyde, Mrs. Marion, 228
  Israel, 225
  Kathy of Mayfair, 232
  Lieut.-Gov. rides, **252**
  Manning, Premier, 219, **221**
  more MacEwan parties, 231 passim
    party invitations, **232**
  MacEwan and chauffeur, 221, **223**
  MacEwan and cleaning woman,
    239-240
  MacEwan and First Lady dance,
    222
  MacEwan and the Moores, **228**
  MacEwan and Nature, **226**
  MacEwan and Premier Manning,
    221
  MacEwan gets new boots, **243**
  MacEwan in kilts, **239**
  MacEwan at walkathon, **240**
  MacEwan on travel, 225
  MacEwan speaks mind, 233, 234,
    235, 236
  MacEwan with Hutterites, **244**
  Miller, "Chic" and "Billie", **227**
  Moore, Arthur, Carmen, **228**
  New Government House, 246-**247**
  porridge party, recipe, 233
  Page, Dr. J. Percy, 219
  Queen Elizabeth, 240-241
  rafting on Red Deer River, **230**
  relationship with chauffeur,
    method of operation, 244-245
  secretarial impressions of Patricia
    Halligan, 236-239
  Snaddon, Andrew, quoted on
    MacEwan, 221

Smith, Chief Justice S. B., 219
  sworn in, 219, **220**
  term ends, 260
    Mayor Ivor Dent, 260
    Premier Peter Lougheed, 261
  Walkathon, first, described by
    Linda Curtis of the *Calgary
    Albertan*, 241-2
  Weber, Henry, chauffeur, **223**
  White Fox secret revealed, 248
Little Theatre, **151**
Lots traded, 33

MacDonald, Hugh John, 196
Macdonald Hall
  freshettes, 69
  student hijinks, 74
MacEwan, Alexander Hedley, 5
  Bertha Grant, 5
    marriage, 12
    death, 159
  buys land, 7
  dies, 160
  first child, 14
  first farm home, 14
  goes West, 6
  thresher, **8**
  to White Rock, 149
  sells farm, 148
MacEwan, George Alexander,
    brother, **32**
  birth, 21
  death, 75
MacEwan, George, of Guelph,
    grandfather, 5, **6**
MacEwan, John Walter Grant
  accepted at Iowa State College, 89
  acting Dean, 133
  admitted to degree course, 72
  Agricultural Editor, 186
  as professor, 102 passim
  as tourist, 118 passim
  in Scotland, 118, 119
  at Churchill, 119
  at 40 years, 150
  awards, 253
  Beef Producers offer job, 155
  beliefs, 249-251
  born, 14
  builds cabin, **255**-256
  buys Model T, 71
  Calgary home, 190
  Calgary, public service, 192
  Canadian Club officer, 199
  church, 249
  church union, 112
  class photo, **26**
  club secretary, 69
  Cockshutt director, 199
  commission chairman, 263
  conservationist, 251-253
  consultant, 195-196
  contribution, 262
  courtship, 124, 125
  credo, 250, 251
  Dean of Men, 124
  Deanship accepted, 164
  Deanship escapes, 134
  debut as writer, 88
  emergency at Tompkins, 117
  escapades, ventures, 27 passim
  Exhibition director, 141
  Farm manager, 134
  Fitton's Grocery, 30
  freshman parade, 167
  George and Grant, **32**
  government advisor, 136
  graduation, 81, **82**
  Gunns Limited, offer, 81
  history professor, 263
  history speech, 142
  honeymoon, 126, 127
  honors at Iowa State College, 95-6
  investment policy, 108
  Job offers, Iowa State, 93 passim
  leaves for east, 63
  lecture debut, 102
  manages Exhibition, 151
  marriage, 125, 126
  memorabilia, 244
  millionaire, 262
  move to Calgary, 188, 189
  "Mc" becomes MacEwan, 89
  North Brandon, farm, **18**
  observations, 115 passim
  Olds Agricultural College, 263
  on OAC campus, **66**
  on OAC judging team, **79**, 80
  on Palomino "Laddy", **103**

on Student's Council, **77**
offered Deanship, 164
Premier's Award, 263
President J. S. Thomson's tribute, 165
promotion, 121
reaction to new Dean, 166 passim
refused land, 60
resigns editorship, 188
resources chairman, 263
river voyage, **123**
Santa Claus, 19
school, Brandon, 25
School Director, 134
showing cattle, **83**
sleepwalking, 19, 49, 140
spike pitching, **72**
textbook, 127
Toronto Royal Winter Fair director, 199
tractor course, 43
United Kingdom, 117
U.S. speeches, 93
vegetarianism, 250
visits grandparents, 23
western history, 141, 263
with school children, **218**
with Heather, **146**
work habits, 113
World War II, 147
MacKay, Ian, 71
Mackenzie, Rev. James, 112
Rev. James and Mrs. Mackenzie, 108
MacLean, J. S., 161
MacLean, Malcolm, 83
MacPhail, Malcolm, 53, 62, 63
MacPherson, Willa, 62, 66, 92
and Grant, **55**
arrival at Melfort, 59
Maguire, Judge Percy, 105
Manitoba Boom, 21, 24
Manning, Premier, 197
Margo, Sask., venture, 33, 36
Martin Brothers Ranch, 116
Martin, Curtis, 54
Matador Ranch, 114
Matador results, 118
Mayo Clinic, 92
McGugan, Archie, 79, 80

McIntyre, of Chilliwack, 67
McKenzie, Jim, 116
McKinnon, D. J., 187
McLean, James, 126
McLean, James and Mrs., 126
McLeay's Rocking P Ranch, 116
McPhail, Jean, 67, 68
McPhail, Olive and Roy, 154
McPherson, Aimee Semple, 91, 92
McSpadden, Maurice, 91
Meat Demonstration, 111
Melfort, Sask.
Agricultural Society, 54
Fair, 83
farm, 37
farmhouse, **49**
Grant milks cow, **39**
in early 1900s, **62**
Melfort Moon, 88
shack, 40
test plots, 69
Theatre, 88
Millay, rancher, 116
Miller, W. F. "Chic" and "Billie", **227**, 228, 229, 230
Minor Brothers, 116
Mississippi River, 72
Mills Hall, 72
Moore, Arthur, Carmen, **228**, 229, 230
Moose Jaw — Regina route, 102
Moosomin Fair, 99
Mortlach, 99
Morton, Dr. A. S., 109, 141, 142
on Better Farm Trains, 86
with MacEwan, **139**
Morton dies, 160
Morton, Professor W. L., quoted on war, 147
Murray, Dr. W. C., 98, 99, **100**, 106, 109, 110
and Kiwanis Club, 112
portrait, **133**
dies, 160
Music, Edison Victrola, 58
B-flat flute, 30
bagpipes, 30

Nanson, rancher, 116
National Research Council, 114

Nelson, Wesley Gordon, 188
Nelson, Mrs. Wesley G. (Maria
    Corlette Grant), **109**
Newspapers, periodicals, direct
    quotes
    Calgary Albertan, 178, 182, 183, 209,
        210 (Peter Thurling), 211, 214
        (Inger Voitk), 218, 241-2 (Linda
        Curtis)
    Calgary Herald, 193, 196, 197, 206
        (Johnny Hopkins) 210 (Hopkins),
        215 (Hopkins), 217 (Walter
        Nagel), 235, 248 (Eric Erickson),
        253
    Canadian Press, 256
    Country Life, 166
    Edmonton Journal, 200, 204, 220, 221
        (Andrew Snaddon), 253
    Edmonton Report, 222
    Family Herald, 167
    Regina Leader Post, 157
    Saskatoon Star-Phoenix, 126, 135
        ("W. J. M.")
    The Edmontonian, 219 (John Stanley),
        223 (Lynne Cove)
    The *Farmers' Advocate,* 80
    The Financial Post, 209-10
    The Manitoban, 167
    Western Producer, 166, 186, 260
    Winnipeg Free Press, 126, 135, (R. M.
        Scott), 177, 178, (Hugh Boyd),
        182
    Winnipeg Tribune, 167, 181
Nicol, Dr. John L., 126, 146
Nipawin, 107

Ontario Agricultural College, 61, 64

Palliser Hotel, 189
Parents and son, 1941, **149**
Parker, W. J., 164
Pathlow, 88
Patterson, W. J., 152
Peace River, 71
Perdue University, 80
.Pet skunks, 131
Picnic, **17**
Pictou County, 3
Pleasant Valley, 83
Pleasant Valley Church play, 88

Politics (See also Provincial Politics,
    Alberta)
    campaigning, 181-183
    characteristics, 210
    comment on by-election, 178-9
        Albertan
        Winnipeg Free Press
    defeat, 183
    Dinsdale, Walter, 182
    election, 1926, 83
    first rally, 83
    Gardiner persists, 155
    invitations to run 1933, 1943, 1944,
        152-3
        another invitation, 154
        in Brandon, 177, 178
    Matthews, L. MP Brandon, 178
    Maybank, Ralph, 178
    nomination committee, 178
    nominated in Brandon, 180
    offered leadership, 156
    pile operation, 157-58
    Regina-Leader Post report, 157
    Spinks, Doctor J. W. T., 184
Power, horses vs machine, 50, 51
Presbyterian
    Knox Church, Brandon, 29
    St. James Church, Melfort, 46
    The *Presbyterian Record,* 73
    upbringing, 16
    Zion Church, 4
Priddis cabin, Uncle John's, 154, **190**
Provincial politics, Alberta
    Anton, Gordon A., 202
    as Opposition Leader, **201**
    Calgary-North results, 204
    elected, 196
    election disaster, 203
    first opposition speech, 202
    impressions of, in *Poking into
        Politics,* 197-9
    Johnson, Floyd A., 203
    Liberal leader, victory, 200
    maiden speech, 197
    MacDonald, H. J., 201
    proportional representation, 204
    provincial election, 1959, 202
    Prowse, Harper, 197, 200
    resigns leadership, 204
    women candidates, 203

Publications
  Agriculture on Parade, 257
  . . . and Mighty Women Too, 263
  Blazing the Old Cattle Trails, 205
  book reviews, 135
  Breeds of Livestock, 148
  Calgary Cavalcade, 205
  Calgary Herald column, 205
  collaborates with Foran on *A Short
    History of Western Canada*, 254
  "Cominco Commentary", 205
  Entrusted to My Care, 216
  Eyeopener Bob, 199, 205
  Family Herald, 111
  Fifty Mighty Men, 199, 205, 263
  Free Press Prairie Farmer, 111
  General Agriculture, 145
  Institute of Applied Arts, 216
  John Ware's Cow Country, 205
  Poking into Politics, 216
  Saskatchewan Farmer, 111
  Scientific Agriculture, 106
  signs contract, first book, 135
  Sodbusters, first popular history
    book, 144, 199
  The Canadian Cattlemen, 191
  The Feeding of Farm Animals, 161
  Western Producer, 111, 199
  Western Producer Prairie Books, 216
  "The Western Farm Scene"
    column *Western Weekly
    Supplement*, 206

Radville Fair, 102
Raithby, George, 78
Ramsay, Rupert, 153
Rayner, John, 54, 83, **153**
Reaves, Bill, 67
Recruiting, 43
Regina, 86
Reid, Rod, steam outfit, 47
Renner, Mr. and Mrs. Tom, Bob, 190
Reynolds, President Joseph B., 65, 92
Richard, 99
Ridley, Ed, 89, 107
Robertson, Colonel J. G., 81
Rockne, Knute, 92
Rogers, Will, 91
Ross, Hugh, 86
Russian thistle, 137-9

Rutherford, Dean W. J., **55**, 62, 88,
  95, 99, **100**, 109, 160

Saskatoon, 97
  Archaeological Society, 124
  Exhibition, 112
  Light Infantry, 147
  Riding Club, 112
Shannon, Mel, 193, 196
Shaw, Professor A. M., 99
Shaw, Dean, **100**, 114, 133
Short, John, 107
Simpson, Jim, **78**, 80
Skinner, Pilot, 102
Sloan, Miss, 68
Smith, Arthur, 193, 196, 209, 210
Smith, Bella, 10
Steam threshing, *Sodbusters* quotation,
  10
Speers, Fred, 116
Sporting spirit, 17
Sports
  as university professor, 104 passim
  basketball, 69, 74, **105**
  football (rugby), 74
  OAC basketball team, **70**
  OAC football team **75**
  track and field, 69
  Varsity Grads, 105
  volleyball, 67
Spry School, 41, 68
SS *Silksworth*, 119
St. Andrew's College, 99
St. Andrew's Society, 112
Staples, Milton, 91
Star City, 61, 77
Stayner, Ontario, 71
Steckley, Jack, 78
Stevenson, Lorna and Enid, 190, 225
Stevenson, Professor, 91
Stewart, Doctor W. O., 67
Stewart, Dunc., 86
St. James Church, 159
Stoughton, 99
Student Christian Movement, 65
Student parade, **168**

Telephone, 58
Theatre trophy, 152
The Canadian Cattlemen, 191

Thompson, J. A., 142
Thomson, J. S., 165
Tinney, Thomas, 116
Tolton, Tubby, 72
Toole, Wade, 78, 79, 80, 109
"Town and Gown," 112
Tractor
  arrival of, 50
  Grant on Fordson, **51**
Trueman, Doctor A. W., 164
Tucker, Walter, MP for Rosthern,
  156 passim
Turtleford, 99

University of Manitoba
  Board of Governors, 169
  Crawford, F. W., 169
  Curriculum Committee, 168
  Dean at work, **171**
  Dean on Red River Valley Board,
    175
  Evans, H. H., deputy minister, 171
  first year's record, 170
  Fry, H. S., 169
  Gillson, President A. H. S., 173
  Governors accept resignation, 180
  research in north, 172
  James, Dr. Norman, 168
  McKay, Norman, Extension
    Department, 171
  Morton, W. L., comments, 173
  problems facing MacEwan, 168
    passim
  reaction of Governors, 179
  research, 172
  Savage, Doctor Alfred, 181
  Shank, Professor Lawson, 173
  social life, 169
  testimonial dinner, 181
  Winnipeg Flood, May 1950, **174**
University of Saskatchewan
  aerial view, 1928, **98**
  in depression, 120
  MacEwan arrives, 97
  University Farm, **138**
Usher, Miss Janet, 168

Victoria School, 110

Waldron, A. P., 186
Walker, Hank, 91
Walking Buffalo, 250
Waskesiu Lake, 109
Watts, J. A., farm of, 68
Weber, Wilf, 65
Weir, Hon. Robert, 126
Western Canadian Exhibition Assn.,
  151
Western Canada Fairs Assn., 177
Western Producer, 186
Western settlement, 2 passim
White Fox district, 107
Wilkinson, Mrs. Rose, 197
Williams Lake, 145
Willow Bunch, 102
Wilson, William M., 139
Winnipeg house, 168
Wilson Shady ZL Ranch, 116
Wilson, W. A., of Canada House,
  119
Wiseton, 111
Woodville, Ontario, 71
Wood whittling, 255
Wright, Doctor Norman, 112
Wright, Esther, 110, **126**, 225
Wright, H. O., 153
Writing, assessments,
    Glazier, Dr. Kenneth, 259
    Moore, Carmen, 259
    Harrison, Stanley, 260
  criticism in Academe, 258-9
  early resolve on writing, 256
  effect on readers, 257
  method of writing, 256-7
  motivation, 259-60
  philosophy, 260
  relations with publisher, editor,
    257
  source of ideas, 257
  style, purpose, 259
  writer at work, **258**

Yorkton, 101
YMCA, OAC, 68
Yule, H. Charles, 185

Better known as "Rusty", the writer has been a prairie journalist for thirty-five years, with the exception of a three-year stint as an RCAF pilot during World War Two. A reporter with the Leader-Post in Regina, he joined The Western Producer as a feature writer in 1949, advanced to magazine editor, and was appointed Executive Editor in 1953. He held that position until 1977, when he left to become a consulting journalist.

His years with The Western Producer took Mr. Macdonald into every corner of Manitoba, Saskatchewan and Alberta. Seldom without a camera, it was during such trips that he captured his photographic essay of the prairies which was published in 1975 as FOUR SEASONS WEST.

An Arts graduate of the University of Saskatchewan, Rusty Macdonald has been actively involved in the development of public library service in rural as well as urban centers in Western Canada. His future plans include researching subjects which first drew his interest in the early 1950's.

He is married with two grown children.